# Brendan Behan
# Interviews and Recollections

## Volume 2

*Also by E. H. Mikhail*

The Social and Cultural Setting of the 1890s
John Galsworthy the Dramatist
Comedy and Tragedy
Sean O'Casey: A Bibliography of Criticism
A Bibliography of Modern Irish Drama 1899–1970
Dissertations on Anglo-Irish Drama
The Sting and the Twinkle: Conversations with
Sean O'Casey (*co-editor with John O'Riordan*)
J. M. Synge: A Bibliography of Criticism
Contemporary British Drama 1950–1976
J. M. Synge: Interviews and Recollections (*editor*)
W. B. Yeats: Interviews and Recollections (two volumes) (*editor*)
English Drama 1900–1950
Lady Gregory: Interviews and Recollections (*editor*)
Oscar Wilde: An Annotated Bibliography of Criticism
Oscar Wilde: Interviews and Recollections (two volumes) (*editor*)
A Research Guide to Modern Irish Dramatists
The Art of Brendan Behan
Brendan Behan: An Annotated Bibliography of Criticism
An Annotated Bibliography of Modern Anglo-Irish Drama
Lady Gregory: An Annotated Bibliography of Criticism

# BRENDAN BEHAN

## Interviews and Recollections

## Volume 2

*Edited by*

# E. H. Mikhail

**BARNES & NOBLE BOOKS**
**TOTOWA, NEW JERSEY**

*First published in the USA 1982 by*
BARNES & NOBLE BOOKS
*81, Adams Drive*
*Totowa, New Jersey 07512*

ISBN 0-389-20222-3

*Printed in Hong Kong*

## Library of Congress Cataloging in Publication Data

Main entry under title:

Brendan Behan, interviews and recollections.

    Bibliography: p.
    Includes index.
    1. Behan, Brendan—Interviews.  2. Authors, Irish—20th century—
Biography—Addresses, essays, lectures.
I. Behan, Brendan.  II. Mikhail, E. H.
PR6003. E417Z63  1981      822′.914  [B]   81-8042
ISBN 0-389-20222-3                    AACR2

# Contents

# Acknowledgements

I wish to express my gratitude to Dr Brian Tyson and Dr Colbert Kearney, who read this work in typescript and made many valuable suggestions. At various stages I also received useful comments, information, support or assistance from Mrs Beatrice Behan; Mrs Kathleen Behan; Mr Rory Furlong; Mrs Paula Furlong; Mr Seamus de Burca; Ms Marianne Levander; Dr Olof Lagerlöf; Mr Louis Burke; Mr Desmond Mac Namara; Mr Paddy O'Brien; Mrs Teresa Monaghan; Mr Brian McCoy; the Canadian Broadcasting Corporation; Mr Manus Canning; Mr Tony Aspler; Mr John O'Riordan; Mr Cathal Goulding; Mr Michael Cormican; Miss Alice E. Einhorn of Doubleday Publishers; Miss Kate Mackay of Eyre Methuen Ltd; Research Assistance Routledge Associates, London; Microfilming Executors and Methods Organisation Ltd, Dublin; and Radio Telefis Éireann.

I am grateful to Miss Bea Ramtej for her usual skill in preparing the final typescript.

Thanks are due to the University of Lethbridge for granting me a sabbatical leave, during which this work was completed.

It is also a pleasant duty to record my appreciation to the staff of the University of Lethbridge Library; the British Library, London; the Newspaper Library, Colindale; the National Library of Ireland, Dublin; Trinity College Library, Dublin; the Bibliothèque Nationale, Paris; and the New York Public Library.

The editor and publishers wish to thank the following, who have kindly given permission for the use of copyright material:

Granada Publishing Ltd, for the extracts from *Brendan Behan* by Ulick O'Connor.

The *Daily News*, for 'Behan Back on Booze Binge'; © 1960 New York News Inc.; reprinted by permission.

Mr Iain Hamilton, for 'Among the Irish' in *Encounter*.

Gill and Macmillan Ltd, for the extracts from *Remembering How We Stood* by John Ryan.

The *North American Review*, for 'Brendan Behan: Vital Human Being'; reprinted with permission; © 1964 by the University of Northern Iowa.

Mr Seamus de Burca, for the extracts from his book *Brendan Behan: A Memoir*.

The *Irish Press*, for 'In Jail with Brendan Behan' by Sean O'Briain; and 'Brendan Behan' by Francis MacManus.

The *Sunday Press*, for 'The Behan I Knew Was So Gentle' by C. A. Joyce; and 'Rich in Talent and a Great Personality' by Benedict Kiely.

The *Evening Press*, for 'The Man Brendan Behan' by Tim Pat Coogan; 'He Ran Too Quickly' by Sean O'Casey; 'Great Man' by Sean Kenny; and 'Behan's Mother Wasn't There' by Clare Boylan.

The *Manchester Evening News*, for 'Behan Takes Swallow' by John Alldridge.

The *Observer*, for 'Deckhand on Collier' by Maurice Richardson; and the untitled obituary of Brendan Behan by Joan Littlewood.

The New English Library, for the extracts from *The World of Brendan Behan*, edited by Sean McCann.

Mr Brian Behan, for the extracts from his book *With Breast Expanded*.

Mrs Peter A. Sebley, for the extracts from her book *Brendan Behan: Man and Showman*; for her Preface to *Confessions of an Irish Rebel*; and for her Afterword to *The Scarperer*.

The *Daily Telegraph*, for 'Brendan Behan: Uproarious Tragedy' by Alan Brien.

A. D. Peters and Co. Ltd, for 'Behan: a Giant of a Man, Yet Gentle' by Kenneth Allsop in the *Daily Mail*.

Mrs Beatrice Behan, for the extracts from her book *My Life with Brendan*; for 'The Only Thing I Blamed Paris for' by Brendan Behan in *L'Express*; and for 'The Woman on the Corner of the Next Block to Us' by Brendan Behan in *Vogue*.

The *Guardian*, for 'But Not in the Pejorative Sense' by W. J. Weatherby.

The *Irish Times*, for 'Dublin Boy Goes to Borstal'; 'Behanism'; 'Book and Author'; 'Brendan Behan Insists on Use of Irish in Bray Court'; 'Brendan Behan Fined £30 on Assault Charges'; 'Talking to Mrs Stephen Behan' by Marion Fitzgerald; and 'Tribute'.

The *New Statesman*, for 'Brendan Behan at Lime Grove' by Malcolm Muggeridge.

The *Sunday Independent*, for 'Was Poet, Comedian, Rebel and Lover of People' by Proinsias MacAonghusa; and 'He Was So Much Larger Than Life' by Frank O'Connor.

The *Washington Post*, for 'The Behan' by Walter Hackett.

The editor has made every effort to trace all the copyright-holders; but if he has inadvertently overlooked any he will be pleased to make the necessary arrangements at the first opportunity.

# Behan Comments on the Theatre*

## LOUIS CALTA

Brendan Behan, the uninhibited, fun-loving Irish playwright with the awesome reputation for quaffing the 'sauce', arrived in New York yesterday as sober as the proverbial judge and as amiable as a vote-getting politician.

Dressed in a two-tone ensemble of brown, freshly shaved and barbered, slimmed-down by 'two stone' (twenty-eight pounds), Mr Behan appeared in sharp contrast to depictions of him as a roisterous, unbridled personality given to heckling actors and brawling with officers of the law.

The thirty-seven-year-old playwright, who stands five feet nine inches, flew here from Dublin with his wife, Beatrice, to be on hand for the Broadway opening of his play *The Hostage* on 20 September at the Cort Theatre. Although he brought five bottles of Irish whiskey with him, he said he did not plan to drink them. They were for some American friends.

Several hours after he had landed at Idlewild Airport, Mr Behan was interviewed at the Algonquin Hotel. The voluble and jovial writer, speaking with a not-too-thick Irish brogue, commented on critics, Sean O'Casey, Eugene O'Neill, newspaper men ('I was one myself') and politics.

Mr Behan, whose dislike for maintainers of public law and order is fabled, was asked if he placed drama critics in the same category. 'No,' he said, 'I'm all for them. They keep the show on the road.'

Noted for his public displays, the author was asked if he were going to 'break out in New York'. Mr Behan said that he would not. He said he hoped to be able to continue his abstinence during his stay here. He has not had any liquor since last March on doctor's orders. Nor, he went on, would he take part in the performance of his play. During the London run of *The Hostage* last season he harassed the performers from the audience because he felt they were not doing justice to his lines.

Mr Behan said that he would have loved to have lived in America

---

* 'Behan Comments on the Theatre; Irish Dramatist Arrives for Opening of Play – Backs Critics and Kennedy', *New York Times*, 3 Sep 1960, p. 8.

during the 1870s. 'I would have been a carpetbagger or a scallywag, whichever was the most obnoxious.' He also expressed regret that he had not essayed 'drugs in my flaming youth', but that it was too late now. He said he found 'the atmosphere' in New York suitable. 'Newspaper men here are not so aggressive as in London. There they are always catching an edition. They give me the impression of always being very busy.'

The author said he planned to remain in New York until Christmas. But if his play failed to receive the support of the public and critics he planned to join 'the Fire Department'. Mr Behan paused a moment to speak in a strange language to his wife. 'Is that Gaelic?' a reporter asked. 'Yes,' he replied, 'we use it if we think you don't understand it.'

Mr Behan said that he was writing a book called *the catacombs*, which might eventually be done as a play. 'It's about a lot of no-gooders or harmless people', he said. Then, veering to the subject of 'beatniks', he observed, 'The thing I have against them is that they're always looking for a job – my job.'

Dwelling on the themes of his plays, Mr Behan admitted that it was 'the custom of people like myself to attack the middle class, but essentially they're the people who support the theatre. The upper classes expect to get in for free, while the lower classes look at television.'

What did he think of O'Casey? Mr Behan's mien grew serious. 'He is a great man, and it is a credit to the United States that he's appreciated here. I think praising O'Casey is like praising the lakes of Killarney. And, praising the plays of O'Neill is like praising Niagara Falls.'

While in New York, he said he intended to 'sneak down to the Empire State Building in honour of King Kong'.

The Irish playwright also came out for Senator John F. Kennedy for President. He recalled that the forebears of the Democratic Senator came from a part of Ireland where 'the apples grew alongside the road' and where – alluding to the uprighteousness of the people of that community – 'no one touched them'.

Although declaring that he was 'no politician', Mr Behan freely discussed politics. 'Eisenhower is a very great man and he's for peace. I'm for Kennedy because he's of the Roosevelt party and Roosevelt was a great man.'

Emphasising that he was a writer and had interviewed people, some of whom 'you couldn't get to shut up', Mr Behan concluded the talk with a warning that he was studying his American interrogators and that they would be the subject of a future article.

# Brendan Behan's Sober Side*

## ARTHUR GELB

New York has been violently aware, since 2 September, of the arrival of a bawdy, iconoclastic, ex-Irish revolutionary, ballad-singing, jig-dancing, stocky, rumpled, wild-haired, thirty-seven-year-old Dublin playwright named Brendan Behan. Though Mr Behan has been represented in this country only by a not very successful off-Broadway production of *The Quare Fellow* and by his autobiography, *Borstal Boy*, he is already as much of a public pet here as he is in Europe.

Met by reporters when he arrived at the airport, converged upon at his Algonquin Hotel suite, pursued in Third Avenue bars and followed on his rambles along the streets of New York, Mr Behan hasn't stopped talking (in English, French and Gaelic) since he stepped off the plane – and most of what he has said has found its way into newspaper and magazine columns.

Mr Behan, who is in town for the opening at the Cort on Tuesday of his recent London hit, *The Hostage* – an event he plans to attend in a borrowed tuxedo – is a victim of his own ebullience. It is his pleasure and his passion to hold court – anywhere, anytime and for anyone. This has had a snowballing effect that has prevented him from getting much sleep. Saloon-keepers, head waiters, freshly arrived young members of Ireland's Revolutionary party, chance passers-by, all have equal claim, with the inevitable interviewers, on Mr Behan's time. For most of them he plays the clown. But Mr Behan has another side.

The playwriting Behan (as opposed to the performing Behan) has depths of seriousness, sensitivity, tenderness and erudition. These depths are not easy to dredge up from the self-created legend. For Mr Behan finds it difficult to avoid the temptation of saying what he knows will make good copy. (Having once been a reporter himself, he has affection, but little reverence, for the breed.)

At times he sounds like an Irish William Saroyan (as when he states, 'I wrote *The Hostage* because I like people. I like all people'). At other times he sounds like the precocious revolutionary he was when he was sent to reform school for trying to blow up the British Empire. ('Politicians who call upon the people for sacrifice and duty to their country are dangerous. They are entitled to six ounces of lead between the eyes – not in the brain, because they have no brain.')

* *New York Times*, 18 Sep 1960, Section 2, pp. 1, 3.

But he believes in a great deal of what he says, even though it is often contradictory and deliberately shocking: even his outrageous buffoonery springs from an earnest desire to make people laugh in a world that he believes takes itself too seriously.

'Brendan has a gutsy, humorous viewpoint about everything – even death', was the way Joan Littlewood, director of *The Hostage* and a close personal friend, explained it recently. 'He has his serious side, but he's a great clown. He's not publicly searching his soul, like some playwrights, but trying to find some fun out of life. It's the key to his popularity.'

The private, or playwriting, Behan is seriously concerned with the subjects of religion and politics, though he often expresses this concern with rowdy irreverence and in Anglo-Saxon terms that cannot be reproduced in a family newspaper.

'I suppose I am inclined to believe in all that the Catholic Church teaches', he said last week in his pleasant brogue. 'I am accused of being blasphemous. But blasphemy is the comic verse of belief.' He smiled with unaffected pleasure at his aphorism, revealing that several upper teeth were missing. His smile is at once cocky and shy.

'My sins aren't any more interesting than anyone else's. Sins are only horrifying to God. If a man is horrified by another man's sins, it is because he is uneducated, inexperienced or a hypocrite. Certain things must be restrained in the world for our convenience – but for our convenience only. Why can't we let it go at that? The nearest thing to a horrifying act in a reasonable society is a crime against a child. One thing I respect about Catholic teaching is that one mortal sin is as bad as another.'

Mr Behan, seated at a table in the Algonquin's restaurant, puffed on a cigar and cast an anticipatory glance about the room. He was rewarded by the arrival of a smiling waiter, with whom he immediately fell into animated conversation in French. The waiter having departed, Mr Behan exchanged a few words in Gaelic with his wife, Beatrice, an attractive, dark-haired, soft-spoken woman who was keeping a watchful but unobtrusive eye on her husband.

In *The Hostage*, which concerns a young Irish country girl in love with a Cockney who is being held prisoner by the Irish Republican Army, Mr Behan attacks the snobbish and pretentious aspects of religion, politics and nationalism.

'Why do I ridicule my country?' he asked rhetorically. 'The first duty of a writer is to let his country down. He knows his own people the best. He has a special responsibility to let them down.'

Mr Behan was born into the theatre – on 9 February 1923. His mother acted with the Abbey, his father performed in vaudeville and an uncle owned a theatre in Dublin. Between the ages of four and sixteen (when he was sent to reform school) he went to the theatre every week. At the age of ten, he made his stage debut.

'There were three theatres on the north side of the river Liffey – the Rotunda, the Star and the Torch', he said. 'The Rotunda put on an act featuring a singing newsboy. This was in an area where everyone was either the father, mother, brother or sister of a newsboy, if not a newsboy himself, and the act was a winner. The Star went the Rotunda one better, and put on an act with a *crippled*, singing newsboy. The manager of the Torch decided to outdo the Star by putting on an act with a *blind*, crippled, singing newsboy. He gave me the job, and I went on and got lots of cheers.'

Mr Behan rose to his feet and tore into the pathetic lyrics of the poor, crippled, blind newsboy, whose heart was full of joy and who could hear sweet voices calling. He did a jaunty jig step and flung himself back into his chair. His greenish eyes glinted with candid self-approbation.

In and out of reform school, Mr Behan continued his education by reading voraciously, and was particularly struck by the works of Sean O'Casey, James Joyce and, of all people, Dion Boucicault.

'I wrote my first play in jail', he said. 'It was called *The Landlady* and was about a boy who was going to marry a girl who lived in the kitchen and tried to commit suicide. Anything written in jail is rubbish, and that includes *Pilgrim's Progress*.'

Out of jail, he wrote newspaper stories, and then tried another play, which he submitted to the Abbey Theatre and which was rejected. He later retitled it *The Quare Fellow*, and as such it was eventually produced by Joan Littlewood in London.

*The Hostage* was written in two weeks on the island of Ibiza, off Barcelona, where Mr Behan, plagued by rheumatism, had gone to escape the Irish winter.

'When he starts working,' Mrs Behan interposed with a smile, 'he works very fast. And there were lots of interruptions in Ibiza. Drink was very cheap there. He drank everything available.'

Mr Behan sipped his ice water and commented that his grandmother started him drinking whiskey and stout when he was six but that he hadn't had a drop in the last six months. The central character in *The Hostage*, Mr Behan said, is based on two persons – a British soldier who had been held by friends of Mr Behan's in the IRA, and an Englishman Mr Behan read about, who was caught by the Egyptians during the Suez crisis and locked in a cupboard, where he smothered.

'At the end of the play', he went on, 'the hostage is killed – but he comes alive again. Why? Send the audience home happy. Death is vulgarised when looked upon as an end. It may be the end in this world as far as the bloke is concerned, but life goes on. I don't know what life is – whether there is a life force. I'm a very confused man. But I'm all for resurrection. There should be resurrection every week for the dead.'

# 'There's No Place on Earth Like the World!'*

## CAROLINE SWANN

The gratification of sharing in the presentation of *The Hostage* in New York has made me feel with Brendan Behan, 'There's no place on earth like the world!' In London, the play appeared first at the Theatre Royal, Stratford (October 1958), the off-Broadway of London's East End, moving later to the West End's Wyndham's Theatre, where it ran successfully for over a year. I had read the published version, and to my delight found it a revelation and a revolution in the theatre. Despite the topical British references and the Irish slang, my co-producer[1] and I wanted to bring it to America just as we saw it, complete with cast, director and author.

Then began the problems of importing *The Hostage*. First we had to get permission from Actors' Equity to bring over the entire cast, which we felt was a necessity because the members had been working together for so many months that they could improvise, ad lib, talk to the audience during the performance and receive impromptu visits from the author on both sides of the footlights with great ease. The second problem, obtaining visas for cast, author and director, is entitled 'Spending the summer with the Immigration Department'. Next we had the problem of costumes and set. The English ones were like fine wines, too old to travel, so we had new costumes made in England to fit the actors, and new scenery built in America to fit the theatre. Our scenic designer went to London to confer with Joan Littlewood, the director, and the English designers. Miss Littlewood approved the plans for the scenery. But when she arrived and saw the model she turned green. It had a pervading Celtic gloom. And when she learned that the set was built, she fainted. Between interminable casting calls for understudies, the scenery was mounted in the theatre. Then came the requests and demands for changes. New colours to eliminate the gloom; flats repainted; a brighter bed substituted; gayer curtains hung at the top of the stairs; gaslight lamps mounted and wired; and posters and pictures put up. We searched for an appropriate sampler

* *Theatre Arts* (New York), XLVI (Nov 1962) 26–7.

to hang on the wall but could not find one, and so we decided to paint our own. It read 'God Bless our Home'. I thought it should be more Irish and Brendan suggested translating it into the Irish 'Pog Mo Hoin'. I ordered it and our prop man got it up for us speedily. It broke up all who had even a smattering of Gaelic, and put me ever after on my guard with Brendan, who had given me a universal and censorable obscenity.

The cast and author had been scheduled to land *en masse* at Idlewild Airport. Brendan appeared in bright green Harris tweeds, carrying a carton of – surprise? – Irish whiskey. On his lapel was a big campaign button with a slogan 'Up Down'. He sweltered in our warm September weather but was gracious and expansive for almost an hour to reporters and photographers who questioned him about politics, critics, the Irish, the Americans, and particularly about drinking. Brendan felt sure he would stay on the wagon during his three months in America. He drank four glasses of milk at the airport, then refused more, saying, 'I am not a cow.'

New York suited Brendan's generous temperament. His talkativeness was his way of entertaining as many people as possible. His flamboyance covered his shyness. He wanted people to like and admire him. One day, walking with his publisher, he came on a blind Negro, begging with a cup, and his Seeing Eye dog. When Brendan put fifty cents in the cup, the publisher commented on his generosity. 'It's not that,' replied Brendan, 'I'm afraid of his big dog.' Brendan loved traipsing around New York, dropping into bars and talking to his fellow drinkers. As a writer, he was entitled to call his pleasure business. The pubs he frequented were his clubs and research centres.

Little rehearsal time had been scheduled for *The Hostage* and no out-of-town tryout. Had the company not just completed two years preceding their Broadway debut? However, a few conversations in New York showed the actors, all of whom were here for the first time, that the play needed translation into American English. So the changes started, harder to relearn than lines in a new play. Some changes seemed impossible to make; for some words there were no synonyms. Others were too 'blue'. In the United States we have no official censor such as the English Lord Chamberlain. But we had to consider the 'old lady from Dubuque' who is very set in her ideas or our beautiful play would not have survived long enough to spread its message of unstuffiness, good will, youth in revolt, and love. *The Hostage* had been written originally in Gaelic.[2] Brendan himself had put it into his second language, English. We worked on the script speech by speech, sometimes coming on phrases even more pungent and pertinent than the original. At other times we were stumped and had to wait for something to come out in the performance or Brendan's peripatetics. One day he came back with the story of the Irish immigrant's letter home and gave it to Pat [in the play] to read to Monsewer: 'This is a great country over here. They let me sleep until five in the morning and then I get ten dollars for pulling down a Protestant church!' The phrases we needed came from everywhere, even from our preview audiences. Brendan always said that he 'incited' *The Hostage*. Miss Littlewood abetted the incitement by stirring a talented cast into performances that had the spontaneity of *commedia dell'arte*. She never allowed interpolations to become stale. Brendan could always freshen them up by telling about the original house and characters in Dublin that inspired *The Hostage*, and by recounting stories of the many colourful people he knew and loved in Dublin. A great principle of Miss Littlewood's direction was inviting audiences to participate. They laughed, cheered, sometimes booed, and occasionally called out to Pat, Meg, Leslie, or to Brendan whenever he appeared.

The daily newspapers were required reading by the actors who would insert references about current events virtually every night. They warmed up before each performance by reading aloud choice bits from the newspapers and then going into some rousing singing and dancing, that was in progress as the curtain rose. On one of these nights Patience Collier (Miss Gilchrist) brought in an item which she wanted to use. It described Queen Elizabeth's and the Duke of Edinburgh's tiger hunt in India, emphasising the Queen's costume and the Duke's bagging of a tiger . It was immediately included, plus Brendan's ad-libbed verse:

> Tiger, tiger, burning bright,
> In the forest of the night,
> Tell me, was it just a fluke
> You got potted by the Duke?

The freedom from the restraints of the Lord Chamberlain gave rise to broader gestures and more emphasis on erotic bodily contacts which created shock and hilarity, and often brought down the house. But Joan [Littlewood] kept all in good taste, telling the company how Chaplin and Fernandel had made actions charming that could have been revolting in clumsy artists. 'If the contacts in the play become heavy or lecherous for the sake of lechery, they will be repulsive to the audience', she said. 'There is no lechery in Behan; all his lavatory doors have little hearts cut in them.'

Brendan had never intended the sampler joke on me to be seen by the public, nor did he want 'blue' lines that would offend. He loved to go onstage and joke with the audience. Although a few asked for their money back, most were delighted when he appeared. He always gave a lift to the company, making every member feel more alive and more determined to cut through the artificiality and hypocrisy of our times and share with the audience, as Brendan shared with 'the world', the truth and warmth and vigour of *The Hostage*.

NOTES

Caroline Swann, co-producer of the Broadway production of Behan's *The Hostage*.
1. Leonard S. Field.
2. It was called *An Giall*.

# Behan Back on Booze Binge*

ARTHUR NOBLE, HOWARD WANTUCH AND SIDNEY KLINE

Brendan Behan, Ireland's gifted, irrepressible playwright, ended his dry run yesterday. He resumed his favourite true life role last night in the Cort Theatre, where his play *The Hostage* is running. He was beautifully biffed and the audience loved it. The stage manager didn't. Repeating a performance which knocked them dead in London in July 1959, Behan invaded the Cort and took the play away from the actors.

Behan's fall from grace settled many bets along the Third Avenue saloon circuit and elsewhere.

Arriving sober on 2 September and vowing he would stay that way, Behan exchanged wit amid sips of milk with newsmen who were on hand for the arrival.

The wise ones said it was only a matter of time until Brendan left the wagon. They were right.

Yesterday was the day.

The first scene opened at about 3 p.m. in the Monte Rosa restaurant at 128 W. 48th Street, just down the block from the Cort.

Brendan, his wife and two companions entered during the matinee. Brendan ordered champagne. Mrs Behan said no, Brendan said yes. As head of the household, Brendan won his point.

Before he and his remonstrative companions left in late afternoon, Behan had consumed – according to a witness – seven bottles of champagne.

He gulped his wine from a water glass.

Behan interspersed swallows with bits of soft shoe and frequent ballads. Songs of the Irish Republican Army predominated. Brendan is an expert, having entertained as a broth of a boy in a British Borstal – reform school – during World War II.

* 'Behan Back on Booze Binge; Goes into Orbit in Theatre', *Daily News* (New York), 27 Oct 1960, pp. 3, 80.

By early evening Brendan had had his fill of the grape and felt an overwhelming urge to perform in the theatre. Came Scene II.

*The Hostage* had a 7.30 curtain. The house was packed.The curtain had already risen when Behan showed up. The ticket-takers kept him out. Brendan went backstage.

A *News* reporter saw two burly stagehands restrain Behan from going onstage. Soon after, Brendan staggered down the stage-door alleyway toward the sidewalk for a second foray at the front entrance.

News cameraman Frank Castoral tried to snap his picture. Perry Bruskin, the stage manager, smashed the camera and struck the photographer. On complaint of the photographer, Bruskin was arrested on a simple assault charge.

The curtain fell on Act One.

In Night Court, later, Magistrate Morton R. Tollers paroled Bruskin, forty-four, of 221-07 Manor Road, Queens Village, Queens, for hearing 4 November.

Act Two, in one scene, was a hilarious success.

Behan successfully brushed past the unwary ticket-takers at 8.45 p.m., during the second act of *The Hostage*.

From the right aisle front, Behan interrupted the action to address the audience in words they unfortunately were unable to hear, since the monologue was incoherent.

Bypassing the audience, Brendan turned his attention to the actors. They did their best, which is very good indeed.

They got laughs from the audience and laughs from the author. There came the time when a dozen of the cast were front stage in a row. Brendan indicated he wanted to join them. An actor gave him a hand onstage.

The Line moved off-stage right, taking Behan with it.

In the next episode, actor Glynn Edwards, portraying the owner of a castle,[1] appeared in cloak and white wig. Behan moved in from the wings and joined him. Edwards wrapped his cloak around the author and bundled him offstage.

Behan permitted himself to be assisted to a dressing-room – from which his words and song could be heard by those in the front of the house.

Act Three came with the curtain call. Brendan joined the cast to receive the audience's applause and made a brief speech.

'I hope you will tell your friends we have a clean show here', said Behan. (Bawdy, was the critics' consensus.) 'Tell your friends we have decent people in the play. Tell your friends to come see them.'

Amid much handclapping, Behan bowed.

Behan's wife, Beatrice, got him back to the Hotel Algonquin, where they are staying. In the dining-room, Brendan gulped down a few more drinks and entertained astonished and delighted fellow patrons with more song.

Epilogue? Presumably a monumental hangover.

NOTE

1. Monsewer.

# Meeting Brendan Behan in New York*

## MANUS CANNING

I came to New York in November 1960 and a day or so after I came I had a telephone call from Brendan Behan. He said, 'You may have heard about me from Cathal Goulding[1] and he mentioned that you were here and I would like to know if you would like to go to the races with me.' And I said, 'Sure'. So we met that day and we went to Aqueduct Racetrack[2] and we spent the day together and had dinner together that evening with the party. We went to Jim Downey's Steak House[3] in Manhattan. That was a place where Brendan used to stay, used to visit almost every night. At that time, while *The Hostage* was running here, Brendan took me to see the show and for several evenings we met together, usually around Jim Downey's. I think that was perhaps the high point of Brendan's life for pleasure here. At that time he wasn't yet drinking too heavily; he was witty and germane and pleasant and he was unexcitable. It was a very warm and pleasant thing to walk around New York with him at that time. He made it feel like a small town. This was perhaps one kind of greatness that his humanity came out. He knew the cops in the street; he knew their names, they knew him. The doorman, the waiters, everybody knew Brendan and he could quite often come up with their names and slap their back, shake their hands and, as I say, it gave one a pleasant feeling of being in a small town. He made New York feel like a small town at that time. Of course, later on he drank more heavily and his life and his writing degenerated because of this. Now I am not sure if it was the drinking *per se* that killed him. The fact that he had diabetes, this combined with the alcohol is what really killed Brendan Behan, I believe. A man without diabetes could perhaps have taken the same amount of alcohol without ill effects.

When I first met Brendan he was staying at the Algonquin.[4] Afterwards he came back a couple of times and he would sometimes call me, usually from a bar and often he had been drinking and asked if I'd go to meet him.

* Extracted from taped recollections. This is their first appearance in print.

I went there and got a ride for him and steered him home to the Hotel Chelsea.[5] This was not quite so pleasant any more because I felt that he was destroying himself and I was sorry to see it. At that time, while he was in the Chelsea, there was a young actor who stayed with him or who acted as a kind of bodyguard, I feel, to try to cut down on his drinking or take care of him when he was.

The last time that I remember meeting Brendan was when he and his wife were staying in the Hotel Chelsea and I asked if I could bring a girlfriend of mine at that time, a young Greek girl, who was very enthusiastic about Brendan's writing and wished to meet him. And we went to the Chelsea. Unfortunately, when we went there Brendan was drunk. When he met me he had this idiosyncrasy that perhaps he associated me with his early days, with his early republicanism and nationalism and he would only talk to me in Irish, which was fine by me when we were alone together. But it was little of a down evening, you might say, for this girl that I brought because Brendan would insist on speaking to me only in Irish and spoke hardly any English to the girl. At that time he was reminiscing about people we had known or he had known in the IRA who were now dead, and it was rather a depressing evening, and, as I say, not the way I'd hoped when I introduced this girl to him. I don't remember that I met him afterwards until he died.

## NOTES

Manus Canning, a friend of Cathal Goulding, Brendan's close friend with whom Canning was imprisoned in Wormwood Scrubs Prison, London, between 1953 and 1959.

1. For a note on Cathal Goulding and his recollections of Behan see p. 282.

2. 'I went racing many times . . . at the Aqueduct Race Track, or the "Big A" as it is generally called. It is a beautiful course and the only way I can describe it is by calling it a luxury racecourse compared to anything we have in Ireland' – Brendan Behan, *Brendan Behan's New York* (London: Hutchinson, 1964) p. 45.

3. Jim Downey's Steak House on Eighth Avenue. 'There are many very famous restaurants on Broadway and I have chewed many excellent theatrical steaks at Jim Downey's Steak House which, like Vincent Sardi's, is packed with actors some of them doing very well, otherwise neither Mr Sardi nor Mr Downey would be able to use the kind of automobiles they do, while other actors, as the saying has it, are resting' – *Brendan Behan's New York*, pp. 44–5.

4. Algonquin Hotel, 'Another excellent institution' – *Brendan Behan's New York*, p. 82. See references to this hotel in Edmund Wilson, *The Twenties: From Notebooks and Diaries of the Period*, ed. Leon Edel (New York: Farrar, Straus and Giroux, 1975), pp. 44–5.

5. Hotel Chelsea, an *aficionada* of late-Victorian architecture on 23rd Street. Many famous people have either lived or stayed there. See Behan's references to it in *Brendan Behan's New York*.

# Behan Boxes the Conversational Compass*

## BROOKS ATKINSON

According to a strict notation on the schedule, Brendan Behan, the Borstal boy, was due at the Players at 1 p.m. to account to the *New York Times* for his rowdy play, *The Hostage*, and his considered view of life.

At a quarter after one, an excited staff officer called to say that Brendan had gone to Staten Island to see a cousin, but was headed back as fast as the ferry could sail him. A half hour later a frantic bulletin said, 'There has been no contact with Behan for a long time. He's probably lost.'

But there was a flurry of excitement in the lobby at about 2.20. Stocky, articulate, good-humoured, unpredictable, Brendan was cascading conversation over a group of Players who felt that they had always known him and were delighted with what he said. Mrs Behan, who had him in charge, stood slightly to one side, looking crushed, as if she expected Howard Lindsay, president of the Players and chief of protocol, to drive her from the door. Since women are contraband at the Players, it was necessary to expel her before the members became implicated.

Four of us started wheeling down Irving Place to Pete's Tavern, Brendan continuing his galloping chronicle of the voyage to Staten Island. Bursting into the tavern, we swept through the bar in formation, like three henchmen attending a gangster chief.

Everyone in the bar came to attention. The Irish presence galvanised them. Although none of them had met the Borstal boy, they cried 'Hey, Brendan', and rushed up to shake his hand. Pete's head man, Ozzie Schaefer, took charge like the referee in a prize ring.

Accustomed to pandemonium, Brenden shook hands here and there and said 'hello' without interrupting the foray to a booth in the restaurant. Mrs Behan ordered veal tenderloin, the specialty of the day; Brendan ordered a rare steak and a pot of hot water with at least six of those flow-through teabags. A guy named Joe ambled up to the table: 'I want to shake your hand, Brendan. I'm Irish on my mother's side.'

* 'Behan Boxes the Conversational Compass: From People to Plays to Bar Mitzvahs', *New York Times*, 9 Dec 1960, p. 28.

The volcano kept on erupting anecdotes, comment, obscenities and gibes – about central heating; the Toronto waiters who make you go straight through the meal 'or else' (apparently the waiters cowed him); the Polish motorcycle cop in Boston who asked whether Brendan rated police escort in Dublin ('Yes, but usually I'm handcuffed to them'); J. P. Donleavy's[1] *The Ginger Man*, based on a disorderly American notorious in Dublin; the Roman Catholic Church, to which Brendan adheres as a hedge against a hot future, and the new Behan play, which will be called for ribald reasons *Richard's Cork Leg*.

Joe turned up again to ask for an autograph for a cousin in the hospital: 'It will give him a great bang.'

Since Mrs Behan had heard most of the conversation, she suffered in silence, though occasionally she smiled at new phrasing.

When the steak arrived, Brendan gnawed at it in the one corner of his mouth where teeth remain, while the small restaurant reverberated with his tight-jawed Irish discursions: don't give pens for Bar Mitzvah presents; there are only two nationalities in the world today – the French and the New Yorkers; Samuel Beckett; Sean O'Casey; James Joyce; Jack Kennedy; the nuisance of drunkenness: 'It was no fun for anybody when I was drinking.'

Joe came over again and drew up a chair. He settled down to high-level conversation about the night when he met Jack Kennedy in Brunswick, NJ, and the marvellous film about F. D. Roosevelt called *Sunrise at Acapulco* (*sic*).[2]

Not a man to be put off by bores, Brendan set Joe right about the English political record before World War II (ignoble), and who won the war: 'The Red Army and the US Army, or the US Army and the Red Army, if you prefer it that way.' Under the barrage of talk, Joe began to wilt: 'You're probably right', he would say weakly, or 'Who am I to dispute Brendan Behan?'

Toward four o'clock Brendan asked for change for a $100 bill and proceeded to pay the check. 'What check?' asked Ozzie Schaefer. 'What food?' Everyone in the bar looked proud and pleased. Bundling into a cab, the four of us started uptown. Brendan imitated an Irish tenor singing Joyce Kilmer's 'Trees'.

And so back to work.

NOTES

Brooks Atkinson, American drama critic.
    1. J. P. Donleavy, Irish-American novelist and dramatist.
    2. *Sunrise at Campobello.*

# Large, Rumpled and Belligerent*

In the lobby of the Algonquin Hotel, an old theatrical inn and water hole in midtown Manhattan, a resident actor who resembled the late Frank Morgan in a mild state of petulance was speaking on the telephone to his agent.

'The part doesn't interest me, old sport', he said querulously. 'It's hardly more than a walk-on. I'm highly offended at this. I'll take it, of course.'

Meanwhile, surrounded by acolytes at a table in the middle of the room, Brendan Behan, the distinguished Irish playwright, raconteur and television star, was eating an apple.

'Glory be to God,' he said in a voice that rattled teacups all over the lobby, 'I wisht I was out of this [deleted] hotel and sitting someplace heltz – in a quiet shebeen with a glass of the gargle there on the table and me shmoking a handsome dudeen. The customers here in this hotel, they're liberal enough, mind you, but the staff is all Tories, particularly that waiter over there. He says he's a [deleted] Parisian, now mind you, him that was a pig boy from the bogs of the Vosche. That's spelled V-o-s-c-h-e, my illiterate friend.'

Behan's illiterate friend snapped his notebook shut and gave his host a baleful look. 'Listen,' he said, 'I'll have you know I can spell V-o-s-c-h-e as well as the next man.'

'Well, you [deleted]', Behan responded with a great roar of laughter that festooned the floor of the lobby with small pieces of apple. 'And we'll have a little tay on that.'

He turned to a waiter. 'Now, look here, August, or whatever they call you, we'll all have a little tay if you playse. And some of the jar for this man here, the internationally recognised speller of V-o-s-c-h-e. And it is terrible service they give me here now but you really can't blame them, I guess, because look at me now, there's no tie on me, nor no teeth in my head and a shifty-eyed [deleted] I am. They'd shoot me, the [deleted], before they'd sarve me some tay.'

Indeed, the famed poet was an unusual sight. Sitting there, large, rumpled

---

* *TV Guide* (Philadelphia), 28 Jan 1961, pp. 22–3, where the complete title is 'Large, Rumpled and Belligerent: Playwright Brendan Behan Lets Go with a Few Considered Words and Some Not So Well-Considered'.

and belligerent, he looked like the low man in a pyramid of Hungarian acrobats. One would hardly guess that at that moment Brendan Behan was as much in demand for appearances as any TV performer in New York. (He has since gone back to Dublin, promising to return.)

As the author of *The Hostage*, a highly charged play, and *Borstal Boy*, Behan had become the most talked-about Irishman to visit this land since the arrival of Danno O'Mahoney, a suety wrestler, some twenty-five years ago. Billed in advance as a roistering fellow with an affection for a glass, Behan had, like a real trouper, lived up to his reputation.

When he appeared on *Small World* a year ago from Dublin, he sang a bawdy song and cracked a bawdy joke about a bicycle, causing fellow guest Jackie Gleason to observe that he was 'coming through 100 proof'. In this country, on the David Susskind show *Open End*, Behan talked five other windbags, including Susskind himself, into the ground without half trying, and on two visits to Jack Paar's show, he observed that 'I have met only one intelligent man in America: a very knowledgeable chap I encountered at Belmont Park.'

Behan's next outing on American TV will be as an interviewee on a two-part (29 Jan and 5 Feb) CBS *Twentieth Century* visit to Ireland, filmed last summer. 'It is a daisy', he has reported with high confidence.

With this background, would Mr Behan care to unburden himself of some observations regarding TV?

Of course he would.

'Occasionally,' he said, 'there's a day-cent ray-mark made on the telly. But this is only occasionally. Now most of the time they're doing this, they're doing that, they don't know what the [*deleted*] they *are* doing.

'Now here I was on the Jackie Paar show twice and I said to myself here is not a sad fellow at all, but a nervous kind of fellow and I like the lad because he looks like he likes the people out in the audience.

'But they put me on this *Open End* and there the [*deleted*] paid me a dollar for signing my name. Now for the love of heaven I get seventy-five cents a word for every word I write out, so [*deleted*] I was losing twenty-five cents for every word that I spoke.

'Now this is the richest country in the world, and now why can't you afford at least one free television show where they don't overburthen a man with all those [*deleted*] commercials?'

He paused reflectively.

'Now as I look about this hotel I see before me a good cross-section of all the boneheaded [*deleted*] in the whole [*deleted*] world. And please don't excuse me, you girls over there, right now you are having your tay and your're not some of those women shmoking their cigarettes, puff, puff, and arfther you light it for them they puff it right into your face, the likes of them. Can you explain that to me, you [*deleted*] speller of V-o-s-c-h-e?'

Well, it was getting late, Mr Behan – and perhaps –

'Late? Now hold it a minute and don't give me that business about being late. I don't say I'm an aisy man to interview but you don't have to give me heroin to make me talk. We'll have a little more tay, if you playse. Now, bless your soul, August, and may your son be a bishop.'

Behan sighed and produced another apple from his pocket. He bit into it briskly.

Here, gasping, a bellhop appeared as though he had run from Thermopylae, to announce that the poet was wanted on the telephone.

'Ah,' said Behan, 'it's a rough time I'm having to be sure. They're interviewing me all the time and then I have to answer the telephone every five [*deleted*] minutes. But, I'll tell you, it's better than carrying a hod.'

On the way to the phone, Behan passed the Frank Morgan type who was still arguing with his agent.

'Pipe down, old sport', suggested the actor to Behan. 'I can't hear this bloody chap on the other end of the pipe.'

'I beg your pardon', said Behan graciously. 'Are you speaking English?'

# Brendan Behan's Last Wake in Montreal*

### TONY ASPLER

'I love THE United States, but I'm a friend not a client. Understand me? The Big Apple, now that's the place...' The Big Apple: New York. Brendan Behan toyed with his eggs and gazed out wanly over the frozen streets of Montreal. 8 December 1960. Brendan had just arrived in *la belle province*, unheralded, tired after a nine-hour drive from the Big Apple.

After the adulation of Broadway, the spectacular success of *The Hostage* and the instant recognition in the streets, Brendan found himself in French Canada where neither the myth nor the man was known. To add to his discomfort it seemed his own personal furies had laid on a cold spell; temperatures dropped to fifteen below, and this raw cold which makes every Montrealer his own Scott of the Antarctic sapped Brendan's energy.

If he could not saunter around a new city, talking to doormen, paper boys, buying magazines, he was unhappy. Now, caged in his hotel room,

* *The Montrealer*, XL (Sep 1966) 19–20, 35–7.

the prospects for the week were dismal indeed. Oh God, oh Montreal.

'I want to see the real Montreal, *le vrai Canadien*', he said to me. So we toured the city – Brendan, his wife Beatrice, and an ex-IRA friend who drove him up – Eamonn Martin – and we only got out of the car at the look-out on the top of Mount Royal to see the snowscape of Montreal sliding gently down into the grey St Lawrence like a ski slope. Brendan made the sign of the cross over the sullen city and then urinated in the snow.

He had six days before his appearance at the Comédie Canadienne and four before his scheduled performance at McGill University ('An Evening with Brendan Behan'). Four days to soak up the atmosphere, to capture the city as he had done in the Big Apple.

Whenever Brendan said the word 'Canadian' he gave it a French intonation. As far as he was concerned Canada was French, or at least the most sympathetic part was. He insisted that first night on visiting the French quarter, so we all went down to a steakhouse on St Lawrence Boulevard.

As we drove along the Main, Brendan said, '*Alouette, gentil Alouette*. There's nothing goddammed *gentil* about it. This is a city of hatreds, I can smell it.' During the meal Brendan was in fine form; he regaled us with stories of Ireland – how he tried to seduce an American girl in a graveyard, how he fed a carthorse a bottle of Irish whiskey in Sligo (the animal died and Brendan performed the burial rites over its carcass and had it interred on the beach). Halfway through the meal he disappeared and Beatrice looked glum.

'He's gone to have a sup', she said sadly. Brendan had been on the wagon for about six months, apart from a champagne lapse in New York – though this had been written off cynically as a publicity stunt. He had drunk nothing stronger than soda water and had thrived on it.

But a combination of Montreal's savage cold and his own sense of let-down forced him back on his old friend in the bottle. He came back to the table some twenty minutes later, ordered champagne and Guinness, and began to sing, 'I'm Lady Chatterley's lover, a game gamekeeper am I . . . .'

He came to the line, 'Evelyn Waugh's a push-over', and suddenly leaped up throwing a fistful of dollar bills on the table and said: 'I want to see the French'. Seeing the French meant zig-zagging our way down the Main from beer parlour to bar to sleazy night-club. The French atmosphere struck an mnemonic chord in Brendan and his Paris experiences flooded back to him.

Wherever we went he introduced himself, 'Je suis ancien maquereau de Paris', and as if to prove it he produced fistfuls of crumpled bills which he called his 'ammunition'. In each bar he sang the *Marseillaise*, the first French song to come to mind. The *habitués* of those seamy bars did not see the sensitive Irish poet; they saw only a happy, drunken man with his shirt unbuttoned to the navel, hair awry, lashing money out on drink for anyone who entered his charmed circle.

At some stage in the evening Brendan had acquired a short, twitching French man with a pencil-thin moustache whose name was La Flame, and he used him as a crutch to negotiate the icy pavements. Brendan later described him as 'small but exquisite'.

With Brendan supported by La Flame our party began to swell on the march; miscellaneous people attached themselves to us like disciples and they followed us farther east, applauding Brendan's recitals of the *Marseillaise*, encouraging him to speak French ('*Mon char est gratiné*, my car is scratched') and lapping up his liquor.

About midnight we arrived at a cement-floored night-club on Amhurst Street. The room, half-heartedly furnished in local *habitant* style, was thick with smoke and the smell of drying clothes. A band played desultorily in one corner and the clientele sat hunched over shot glasses at zinc-topped tables. When Brendan entered the whole place seemed to galvanise into action.

He marched up to the band and demanded, 'D'you know the *Marseillaise*? Well, play it and I'll sing.' And we all sang. Then Brendan began his Irish ballads, in a voice that ranged from fruity baritone to nasal, reedy tenor. He stood on the bandstand, his hands clasped in front of him, eyes closed, swaying slightly. He was home again. And they listened – they did not know what he was singing, but they listened. He had created a little Dublin about him right there in that tawdry French Canadian *boîte*.

The next morning the Montreal press carried stories of Brendan Behan rolling down St Lawrence brandishing a gin bottle, shouting 'I'm the king of the castle.' I had never seen Brendan touch gin, even in Dublin, and such a statement would have been contrary to his republican instincts. Brendan dismissed the reports lightly and tucked into a breakfast of steak tartare with a raw egg on the top.

Two journalists arrived with a tape-recorder and Brendan consented reluctantly to be interviewed. Believing he was speaking coast to coast live to 18 million Canadians he snatched the microphone and for twenty minutes proceeded to vilify Canada and Canadians with a stream of invective remarkable for its sustained invention and elegance of phrase. He ended on the note that all he wanted to do was to get back to the Big Apple, to civilisation, 'not like this dung heap'. He handed the microphone back and asked 'How was that?'

Scenting blood, journalists were calling his suite and congregating down in the lobby. I did my best to protect him from them, but Brendan was not the man to back away from a fight; in fact, with his highly developed sense of self-dramatisation he walked into the very jaws of it by presenting himself that evening at the Montreal Men's Press Club. He held court

there, accepting the proffered drinks while reporters stood in a semi-circle around him scribbling his every word.

That night Brendan swore off alcohol because the following day he was to appear at McGill University. He put on evening dress for dinner as a token of his change of heart and he seemed happy. He even joined the hotel band to sing a song or two after removing his jacket and placing his thumbs firmly in his braces. A middle-aged woman had been hovering about our table during the meal and when Brendan sat down again she insinuated herself into a chair beside him.

She said she was from Belfast and Brendan replied that it wasn't her fault and he wouldn't hold it against her. She wanted Brendan to come out to visit her: she lived at the other end of the island, half an hour away by car. Brendan thanked her courteously and we thought no more about it.

The following day was the Feast of the Immaculate Conception, which meant that every bar in the province was closed. Brendan rose early that morning. At 8.30 I had a frantic phone call from Beatrice to say that he had disappeared. After trying all his haunts I remembered the woman from Belfast. I phoned her and in the background I could hear music and Brendan's voice roaring above it, 'Glory-o, Glory-o to the bold Fenian men . . . .' Beatrice, Eamonn and I drove out to collect him.

When we arrived we found him celebrating the Feast of the Immaculate Conception with Irish folk song and Scotch whisky. His fellow celebrants – relations of the Belfast woman – accompanied him on the fiddle, drums and accordion. Brendan was singing a fascist song as we entered, but when the band took it up he flew into a rage and knocked the accordionist's head against the wall.

He was about to set on the drummer and the fiddler when we bundled him out into the snow. The Belfast woman's cries of 'murderer, murderer', rang out across the fields as we made our getaway towards Montreal. It was as much as we could do to restrain Brendan from jumping out of the car to finish the job, but since it was the Feast of the Immaculate Conception peace and goodwill prevailed. Again Brendan forswore alcohol.

We had lunch at a fish restaurant downtown and he seemed to recover from his morning's exercise. In fact, he would have been all set for the evening's university appearance had it not been for a gesture on the part of the proprietor. Delighted at having Brendan Behan under his roof, he sent over his compliments and four Gaelic coffees. Brendan drank three of them and ordered wine... I telephoned McGill at five o'clock to say that Brendan could not appear that night and I advised them to refund the tickets.

When I told Brendan of this decision – as diplomatically as I could – he would not hear of it. He insisted that I drive him to the university, and to keep the peace I did. McGill, like Trinity College, Dublin, is an oasis of instant erudition beleaguered on all sides by the city. It stands there stately and permanent and you can almost hear an organ playing 'Gaudeamus Igitur' as you walk up the tree-lined drive to the main buildings.

That evening the steps of the Arts Building were thronging with disgruntled students, demanding to know why 'An Evening with Brendan Behan' had been cancelled. When they saw his rotund figure cantering up the campus they rushed back into Moyse Hall and roared with approval as Brendan dashed down the aisle, threw his coat on one side and clambered up onto the stage.

He spoke for seventeen minutes in French, thinking he was in a French-speaking university. His theme – De Gaulle and the Algerian crisis. He sang a song. 'The praties they are small over here, over here', and threw in the phrase *de mon père* occasionally for his audience; and he left the hall to the ringing cheers of the students – a tired, spent man, drained of all energy.

We put him to bed at the hotel and called a doctor who gave him a shot of Vitamin B Complex and shook his head sadly. 'He's a sick man', he told us, but we only had to look at him to see it for ourselves. As Brendan lay there high above the city, feverish and exhausted, listening to the intermittent jangling of the phone and the hushed whispers of his wife and his friends, he turned to us and said hoarsely, 'Have a bit of respect, please, that's all I ask.'

I cancelled the appearance at the Comédie Canadienne and two days later I saw Brendan and Beatrice off at Windsor Station; they were catching the train to Halifax from where they would take the boat to Dublin and home for Christmas.

I watched Brendan standing at the window, the last time I was to see him; ashen-faced, dishevelled, his collar turned up against the biting wind. The man was going home, leaving his myth behind him. In seven days his name was a household word in Montreal; idolised by the students, badgered by the press, lionised and fawned over, criticised and neglected, Brendan Behan had left a mark on the city. Glory-o, Glory-o to the bold Fenian man.

## NOTE

Tony Aspler, Canadian novelist and broadcaster.

# Christmas at Luggala*

## BEATRICE BEHAN

Luggala,[1] as Brendan used to say, was a house where you could say anything you liked provided you didn't take too long and were witty. On Christmas Eve he had been at his best and was still in high spirits when everyone else had gone to bed. He had a habit of wandering through the maze of winding corridors, singing 'Adeste Fideles' to the tune of 'The Coolin'. He was in the middle of his song when he tumbled head over heels down a flight of narrow, curving stairs leading to the servants' quarters. He lay at the bottom with his feet wedged against a door.

Sis, the housekeeper, heard his cries for help. She tried to open the door from the servants' rooms. But as she pushed mightily from her side, Brendan's feet kept jamming the door from his side. He was inextricably wedged in the cramped space between the bottom steps and the door.

Cummins[2] had a theory that if Brendan wasn't put to bed he would fall down the stairs, and it had happened. There were times when Cummins had helped him climb the stairs and placed a bath-towel under his head on the pillow lest he should throw up during the night; there was even a time when Lucien Freud had hoisted him on his shoulders and carried him to bed. But now he lay at the foot of the stairs while I slept in one of the Blue Room's two single beds, unaware of the commotion.

'For Jaysus' sake, get me out of here!' Brendan called to Sis.

'Are you all right, Mr Behan?'

'How in Jaysus' name could I be all right when I've fallen down the fucking stairs? If I was all right I wouldn't be here. Why don't you get me out?'

'I'm afraid I can't, sir. I can't open the door.'

'Well, get someone who can.'

Sis roused May, one of the housemaids, and May went running through the labyrinth of corridors, up and down stairs, until she reached the foot of the staircase where Brendan lay.

'How in God's name did you get there, Mr Behan?' she wanted to know.

Brendan kept his patience.

'I missed the light', he said. 'I put my hand up for the switch at the top of the stairs and I missed it.'

* *My Life with Brendan* (London: Leslie Frewin, 1973) pp. 37–9.

May gripped him under both arms and heaved him into a sitting position.

'You may be a big man, Mr Behan,' she told him, 'but you're not heavy.'

Blood was oozing from a gash on his head, and when Sis was able to open the door from the other side she brought a basin of water and bathed the gash and then placed a damp towel around his head.

'It's Christmas morning isn't it?' Brendan enquired.

'That's right, Mr Behan.'

'Well, I only hope the holy Mother of God will look after you for what you've done for me.'

As the dawn broke they made him tea. May brought a cup to me in the Blue Room and I noticed the other bed had not been slept in.

'Where's my husband?' I asked.

'He's had a little fall, Mrs Behan', said May. 'But don't worry, he's not hurt bad.'

Later we helped Brendan into the Rolls, and Sam, who was the farm manager, drove us back to Dublin. Brendan lay inert in the back seat. I told him that as soon as we reached the town of Bray I intended to go to Christmas Mass.

'You can go where you bloody well like.'

Then as an afterthought he added, 'I suppose I might as well go too.'

His white shirt was grubby and open to his navel and his chest and face were spattered with blood. People turned to stare at us in the church. But I pretended not to notice them.

When Mass was over we bundled him back into the Rolls. I decided to visit friends of mine who might provide us with Christmas lunch, for there was no food in our house, not even a loaf of bread.

Brendan disagreed. 'We're going to my friends', he said. 'Sam, take us to Bill Finnegan's.'

Bill Finnegan was a taxi-driver who had been a barber. If he and his wife were surprised to see a Rolls draw up outside their small house in Inchicore, they did not show it.

'This is my friend, Sam', Brendan told them. 'He'll have a drink.'

I could see Sam was impatient to return to Luggala, so I asked Brendan where he intended to spend the evening.

'Crumlin', he said, which was where his parents lived.

Sam drove through gloomy streets lined with Corporation houses until he found Kildare Road.

'Sam,' invited Brendan, 'come and have some Christmas dinner.'

Someone produced two slices of bread with a piece of chicken between them and a large mug of tea. Sam ate the food dutifully and then said, 'I must be getting back now, Mr Behan.'

'You're not going yet', Brendan protested. 'We have more calls to make.'

'Sam must get back to Luggala', I told my husband. And with that Sam and the Rolls were gone.

I sat in the Behan living room in the bosom of my in-laws. This was the family I had chosen to join when I married Brendan Behan in what had been described as the most unlikely union in Ireland. And of that family Brendan was the most remarkable member.

## NOTES

1. The eighteenth-century country house of Lady Oonagh, of the Guinness family.
2. The butler.

# Brendan Behan Fined Thirty Pounds on Assault Charges*

Brendan Behan, the Dublin playwright, was fined thirty pounds and ordered to pay nineteen pounds five shillings compensation by District Justice O'Hagan in the Dublin District Court yesterday when he was found guilty of a number of charges of assault and malicious damage. Medical evidence was given that Behan is a diabetic and that alcohol makes him more easily unbalanced than the average person.

One of the biggest crowds ever seen at the district courts jammed Court No. 2 long before the hearing began. Behan was dressed in a white shirt and blue, three-piece suit. He wore dark sun-glasses into the court, but put them in his pocket in the dock, revealing marks of injury to both eyes.

Behan, whose address was given as 5 Anglesea Road, Ballsbridge, was charged with having, between 4.30 and 5.30 p.m. on 8 February at 6–7 St Stephen's Green North, assaulted Kenneth Fox-Mills, Bushy Park, Rathgar; with having on the same occasion used threatening, abusive, insulting words and behaviour whereby a breach of the peace might have been occasioned. He was also charged with having at the same time committed malicious damage to a telephone receiver, the property of Messrs Robert Smyth and Co.; with causing malicious damage to a watch, the property of Thomas Byrne, Beechfield Road, Walkinstown; and with assaulting Station Sergeant Patrick McCarthy and Guards Michael Harlow and Henry R. L. Sherlock in the execution of their duty, with intent to resist lawful apprehension.

* *Irish Times* (Dublin), 18 Feb 1961, p. 5.

There was a further charge of being guilty of violent behaviour at College Street police station.

The hearing lasted for over three hours, and the witnesses for the defence included Miss Joan Littlewood, who was with Mr Behan when some of the incidents which gave rise to the charges took place.

Thomas Byrne, salesman in Messrs Smyth's of St Stephen's Green, said that Behan entered the shop accompanied by a woman, and he inquired the price of four bottles of champagne. When told that the cost was thirty-five shillings a bottle, he called the witness 'a thief, a robber, an "eejit" and a lot of other words'. Byrne went to the wine department to get a cheaper champagne, and Behan followed him there, swearing violently. He then approached another assistant, Mr Smyth, and struck him on the head. With the help of Mr Kenneth Fox-Mills, secretary and director of the firm, they brought Behan to a small office, where he knocked over a table and struck Mr Fox-Mills.

In answer to Mr Con Lehane, solicitor, who defended, Mr Byrne said that when he took Behan away from Mr Fox-Mills and knocked him down into a chair to quieten him, Behan had an injury to the left eye. 'I would like it to be known that we did not use force. We did not hit this man.' The first eye injury was caused when he fell in the office and hit his eye on the corner of a chair, and he could have damaged his other eye when he hit the wall with his head. He had tried to strike Byrne, who ducked and Behan struck the wall.

Mr Byrne denied that he called Behan a blackguard, or that he heard Miss Littlewood say, 'For God's sake, stop beating him. I will take him home.'

Kenneth Fox-Mills, in evidence, said that he was quite agreeable to allowing Miss Littlewood to take Mr Behan home in a taxi, and he went across the road to a taxi-rank. On his return he was about to say that there was a taxi ready when Behan attempted to strike him, 'and then he went for me'. A table was knocked over and a telephone was smashed on the floor. He took Behan to the office to save the customers in the shop from the embarrassment of the filthy language which Behan was using.

Mr Lehane: I have to put it to you that he was badly beaten when he was in that office? – That is untrue.

Station Sergeant Patrick J. McCarthy said that he went in a patrol car to Messrs Smyth's. They had to use force to get him into the car after he had been arrested. 'He was very violent and called us —— rats and —— Black-and-Tans.[1] Immediately we released his arms he struck at me, but the blow hit the peak of my cap. I would say that he had quite a lot of drink taken but he was quite capable of using his hands, his feet, and his tongue.'

The Sergeant said that he had known Behan previously and would respect him as a citizen if he would conduct himself. 'We met under happier circumstances before. He was in Donnybrook handing in a sum of money to the benevolent fund, because of some kindness the guards had done to him', he said.

Mr Lehane: That sort of kindness is typical of him? – Yes, he is impulsive, but he should never drink.

Guard Sherlock said that in the office of Messrs Smyth he asked Behan what had happened to his face and he replied, 'Get out, you sewer rats.' In the station when the charges were being read, Behan used filthy language and demanded that the charges be read in Irish. He refused to listen to them and had to be returned to the cell.

In evidence, Behan said that he was a playwright and author, and also a house-painter. On 8 February, Miss Littlewood had come from London and they were working on a play. Gael Linn[2] rang to say that some of the language in his play *Lá Breá san Roilg*[3] was not suitable, and they asked for a great number of last-minute cuts. This upset him.

Up to this time he had not been drinking – not since last March, with the exception of a couple of occasions in New York, and once in Montreal. He was so annoyed by the Gael Linn request that he started to drink locally, and then went to the centre of the city.

He did not remember very much except that he was drinking around Grafton Street. He met Miss Littlewood, and he thought that she was trying to bring him home. He knew that he had been in Messrs Smyth's but could not remember any of the incidents there. He did not remember being brought to the barracks, but he remembered being there and of having asked the Station Sergeant to read the charges in Irish.

'I am genuinely sorry if I interfered with people in the course of their work. I am sorry about that, but I think they employ fairly efficient chuckers-out there', said Behan. He did not think that he had been assaulted by the police. 'I think they were given a great deal of trouble. If I did assault them I apologise. I think they treated me all right and that I was nuisance.'

Cross-examined by Mr Thomas McDonagh, assistant State Solicitor, who prosecuted, Behan said that he was more upset than in a temper. Afterwards he did not know what had happened. He had given the guards a great deal of abuse that they did not deserve, and he was very sorry for what had happened.

George Morrison, a film-director, said that on that morning he called on Behan, who seemed emotionally upset and agitated. He offered the witness a drink but said he was not drinking himself.

Miss Joan Littlewood, theatrical producer, said that she had produced two of Mr Behan's plays and was staying with him while working on a new production. Behan was 'on the dry' and was working hard. He was a happy man.

About ten o' clock on 8 February he had a phone call about his play in Irish which hurt him very much. He left the house, and Miss Littlewood found him drinking in a local public-house. The following day was his birthday and he said he would bring home some champagne.

Behan went into Smyth's about 5 p.m. when he was drunk. He asked for champagne but refused what was brought. A young man whom she had not seen in court passed Behan by and seemed to mutter something to him. He made some theatrical gesture and immediately two men pounced on him. One of them put a 'half-nelson' on him, and he was dragged to an office. In the office she saw him struck five times in the face and given several body blows while being held down. When she pleaded to the men to let him go one of them said that he was a blackguard. Behan heard that and started to fight.

Miss Littlewood said, 'I am one of the many artists who are deeply concerned that he should carry on with his creative work. If he drinks that cannot be.'

To Mr McDonagh, Miss Littlewood said that she saw Behan raise his fist to a man. It was after that that he was dragged to the office. She did not see Behan take the watch off Byrne but she saw Byrne hold him and hit him.

Dr Rory Childers[4] said that the defendant had been a patient of his for four years. He was a diabetic and his system had an intolerance for alcohol. He was less well able to assimilate it than an ordinary person and had been advised that it would be in his own best interests to leave it alone.

One of the defendant's black eyes could have been caused by falling on a chair, but not the second one unless he fell a second time.

Dr John Dunne, St Brendan's Hospital, Grangegorman, Dublin, said that Behan's system had an intolerance for alcohol which would make him more easily unbalanced by the consumption of alcohol than the average person. Otherwise he was perfectly normal and his conduct as described was contrary to himself. He must have taken sufficient alcohol to make him suffer from a temporary aberration of his reason. There had been very high hope that Behan would overcome his addiction to drink. An emotional upset to an artist could be catastrophic.

Mr Lehane said that he was instructed by his client to say that he was primarily responsible for the disturbance at Messrs Smyth's premises. He had received enough punishment for that on the premises. All the incidents stemmed from the fact that Behan had been emotionally upset that morning. He was a man who could not safely take alcohol. He was at present committed to going outside the country next month on a contract and if he could not go it would mean catastrophic financial loss.

District Justice O'Hagan found each charge proved. He said that the excuse had been given of emotional upset, but that was little consolation to Mr Fox-Mills, who had been physically assaulted. The defendant had admitted making a complete nuisance of himself, and an emotional upset was no excuse.

Owing to the medical evidence, however, he would not send him to jail. He fined him a total of thirty pounds and ordered him to pay nineteen pounds five shillings compensation.

The district justice said that Behan should take the advice of Sergeant McCarthy, who had said, 'I would respect him as a citizen if he would conduct himself. He is a man who should never drink.'

## NOTES

1. Auxiliaries supplied by the British in 1920 during the Anglo-Irish conflict.
2. For a note on Gael Linn see p. 113.
3. *Lá Breá san Roilg* ('A Fine Day in the Graveyard'), a one-act Irish version of *Richard's Cork Leg*. For the origins of this play see Ulick O'Connor, *Brendan Behan* (London: Hamish Hamilton, 1970) p. 270; and Rae Jeffs, *Brendan Behan: Man and Showman* (London: Hutchinson, 1966) p. 148.
4. See Dr Roderick Childers's recollections of Behan, p. 96.

# Behan in Jersey City*

A jovial, beaming Brendan Behan was the St Patrick's Day guest of this city today.

Banned from the New York parade by Special Seasons Justice James J. Comerford, a parade official, who called Mr Behan a 'common drunk' and 'disorderly person', the Irish playwright cheerfully accepted the invitation of this city's Irish-American Committee of 100 to the celebration.

At City Hall Mayor Charles S. Witkowski was waiting on the steps with the key to the city to greet Mr Behan and his wife Beatrice. The playwright, resplendent in a deep blue shirt and bright green tie, accepted the key and presented to the Major a hundred-year-old Blackthorn shillelagh.

At a luncheon in the Casino-in-the-Park, Mr Behan sang Irish folksongs and then he and his wife returned to New York.

'This is the best St Patrick's Day ever for me', Mr Behan said as he left. 'Maybe I should send a note of thanks to those in New York for not letting me wear myself out marching so I could be over here enjoying myself.'

* *New York Times*, 18 Mar 1961, p. 46.

# 'We Don't Have Leprechauns, Paddys and Magic Mists'*

Among the millions who celebrated St Patrick's Day last week was raffish playwright Brendan Behan, the sweet singer of Dublin, who was in the US to star in the new revue *Impulse!* Barred as 'disorderly' from the New York parade by the committee chairman (a judge), Behan spent the day in Jersey City exile. Strolling about the streets like a Gaelic Pied Piper, the 'leader of the banned' let fly on many subjects. Some samples:

*Ireland's Irish*: 'I'll tell you what I miss about Ireland, and it's this: it's the scurrility – the things they say to, and about, one another.'

*New York's Irish*: 'They're always giving you advice. And they're always asking you how the people are back in Ireland, like they were struck with the bloody plague or famine or in the Congo, or something.'

*St Patrick's Day*: 'In Ireland, the day is treated as a religious observance. If you get drunk, which I confess I have done in the past, they don't exactly regard it as funny.'

*Judges*: 'The way to win friends and influence people in the US is to have a judge say nasty things about you... I now have a new theory on what happened to the snakes when St Patrick drove them out of Ireland. They all came to New York and became judges.'

*New York dislikes*: 'The buses and professional Irish – all terribly anxious to pass as middle-class Englishmen.'

*Drinking*: 'I like the stuff and one excuse is as good as another. If it wasn't for my wife I'd be dead long ago. I have tremendous powers of recuperation, thanks be to God, but I don't want to push me bloody luck. My interest in the next world is purely academic.'

*Cigars*: 'I enjoy smoking expensive cigars made in Cuba by Castro. You can feel radical and bourgeois at the same time. That's what I'd like to be most of all – a rich radical.'

*Fire Engines*: 'I think they all must be driven by Micks from the mountains who were fed up with all that silence and like to make a lot of noise.'

*Swimming*: 'A great cure for a hangover. I'm not of course a good swimmer. More like an Irish cop, you might say – stupid but willing.'

* *Newsweek*, 27 Mar 1961, p. 28.

*Religion*: 'I'm a daylight atheist. After dark, and when I'm sick you should hear me squawk. My normal attitude is one of infirm cowardice.'

*Ireland*: 'We don't have leprechauns, paddys in top hats, and magic mists. We're proud of our hydroelectric plants, our transport, and our housing, none of which are run by leprechauns. We are now wiping out tuberculosis, and we're prouder of that than all the blather about Glocca Morra.'

# Notes by Sage of Nonsense*

Speaking of the part he will play as conferencier of an evening of improvisation, *Impulse!*, which will open for one week on Monday night at the O'Keefe Centre,[1] Brendan Behan declared he will 'get up and talk a lot of nonsense'. Asked what he knew about jazz, since *Impulse!* is advertised as a jazz revue, he stated, 'I can't read a note of music but I can certainly read a cheque.'

Not averse to coming out with startling statements or the unvarnished truth, as he sees it, here are some of Mr Behan's ripest dicta:

'Your O'Keefe Centre looks to me like a sanctified garage. Yet it's a wonderfully big theatre and the acoustics are good.'

'In Hamilton, I tried to pay for a drink with a US dollar and the man wouldn't have it. I told him I'd met some strange people in my time, but he was unique. The city fathers ought to make him their main tourist attraction. "Roll up, roll up," says I, "and see the only man in the world who refused an American dollar"!'

'Your Toronto liquor laws are good enough for you because you're used to them. For me, they're a puzzlement.'

'I like Toronto. It's not Dublin, of course. The difference is that there's not the scurrilous talk here that there is in Dublin. I dread to think what they're saying about me in Dublin now that I'm not there.'

'It's not that the Irish are cynical. It's rather that they have a wonderful lack of respect for everything and everybody.'

'A Torontonian is a fellow who leaves the arts to his wife. He does this because he thinks it's sort of feminine for a real he-man Torontonian to be interested in the theatre or art or poetry.'

'My father first saw me from his cell window during the civil war. I was born after he was captured, and when I was six weeks old, my mother

* *Globe and Mail* (Toronto), 18 Mar 1961, p. 13.

brought me to the jail and held me up, on the road outside, for him to see.'

'I wrote my first play in jail. It was called *The Landlady* and it was rubbish.'

'Montrealers love France, but now France is led by madmen, gangsters and collaborators.'

'The New York tourist bureau should spend a free weekend in Toronto obtaining a few pointers on how not to attract tourists.'

'At one particularly low point in my life, I thought of coming to the New World to be a house-painter. I must have been out of my mind, or drinking poor stuff, indeed, at the time.'

'On the wagon is an amateur phrase. You'd never hear it from a professional alcoholic. It's a tribute to the sheltered life of the person who uses the expression.'

'Drama critics are like eunuchs in a harem: they see the tricks done every night, they know how it's done, but they can't do it themselves.'

'The Irish are so chauvinistic they'll even accept me.'

'I like nuns better than priests.'

NOTE

1. For a review of this show see Hugh Thomson, 'Improvisation Taken Too Far in New Revue', *Globe and Mail*, 21 Mar 1961, p. 9.

# Behan Brings Back New Hate – Publishers*

## ARTHUR BRYDON

Brendan Behan was not drinking yesterday when he arrived in Toronto. He was talking, cursing, guffawing, snorting and spouting sparks and ashes all over the rugs of the Royal York Hotel.

Waving a cigar which kept frustrating him by going out, he added a new target to his long list of hates, the invasion of London's Fleet Street by Canadian newspaper proprietors. He expounded upon the subject at considerable length but with little depth.

(Mr Behan's condition *vis-à-vis* the consumption of alcohol was

* *Globe and Mail* (Toronto), 20 Mar 1961, p. 17, where the complete title is 'Sparks, Ashes, Insults. Behan Brings Back New Hate – Publishers'.

somewhat in doubt but it was reported that considerable drinking had been going on. A man who had been his companion since Mr Behan arrived by train in the early morning hours reinforced this report by leaning forward to light a cigarette and falling on his face.)

'I have always found that reporters are kind people,' Mr Behan said, 'but newspaper proprietors are swine...in fact, they are hypocritical swine.'

He went on to explain that he is still a member of the National Union of Journalists in Great Britain and charges very high prices for the stories he writes.

'Fleet Street was a very pure place until it was infiltrated by the Canadians', he said. 'The more I see of the Canadians on Fleet Street the more I like the Limeys.'

He said Canadians are apt to see London as a place where the rules of the game are suspended and described their contribution to Fleet Street as disastrous.

'*The Star* is gone,' he said; 'finished by the Canadian blight brought in by one of those educated fellows from Goose Bay.'

Mr Behan attempted, to the anguish of his companions, to try to explain his role as conferencier of the new jazz revue *Impulse!* The show, which includes Nina Simone, Olatunji and Maynard Ferguson, opens tonight at the O'Keefe Centre and proceeds to New York to open 1 April on Broadway.

'In spite of the signals I'm getting from the sidelines, we're not sure how this thing is going to go', he said. 'I am supposed to interrupt and explain the universality and catholic quality of jazz.

'There are some Africans in the show and at one point I talk to the drum. I make some snide remarks and I may knock Canada a few times. I think it is not a bad place for other people. The performers have a lot of fun and Ferguson will send the people who know jazz.

'What I am supposed to do is explain to the ordinary people that every time Louis Armstrong blows down a trumpet, God does not appear at the other end.'

Mr Behan's pronouncements were not all negative. He thinks that Toronto Transit Commissioner William Russell is a fine Irishman, second only to Gene Tunney. He also favours *Pogo* cartoonist Walt Kelly and most of the columnists on US papers.

'Editorial writers are another matter,' he said, 'they do not have enough application to be reporters and not enough talent to do what I'm doing.'

The final thing of which he was in favour was the National Film Board. He described it as Canada's cultural representative abroad and said it was known everywhere for the beauty of its documentary films.

'At least it's known in all the nut-houses I visit on the continent of Europe', he said.

# Brendan Behan Sips Seltzer at Fishermen's Wharf*

## MIKE THOMAS

Brendan Behan, the writer with the wild Irish prose, paid a quiet visit to the Peninsula Friday.

It was quiet by Behan standards, anyway (he was drinking mineral water), although he didn't go completely unnoticed.

Most of the people who were having lunch at Neptune's Table probably didn't know who he was, but they noticed him, just as they would have noticed a polka-dot elephant playing a clarinet.

Preceded by several moments by the sound of some tuneless ditty, the words of which were (perhaps fortunately) indistinguishable, Behan made his entrance to the restaurant doing a little jig, stopped to direct a few friendly remarks to a passing dog, who listened attentively, then addressed himself to any who might be listening: 'Where', he said, 'is the john?'

Given directions, he strolled into a telephone booth, then corrected his heading and exited, stage right through the door marked 'lounges'.

Behan's wife and a friend, C. Louis Davis of San Francisco, exchanged a few quiet words while they waited. Then Behan was back and it wasn't quiet any more.

Convoyed by a reporter and photographer, he talked and sang his way to the corner table with the best view in the house.

He pulled and shoved two or three chairs, then settled on the one which took the greatest advantage of the view.

'I'll take this one and you go over there', he said to newsmen. 'After all, if it wasn't for me, you wouldn't be here.' Davis and Mrs Behan took the chairs that were left. The interview began, more or less.

You don't interview Behan. You attend him – as you attend a performance of *The Hostage*, the Behan play which has been running in San Francisco amid headlines about the playwright's unscheduled appearances on stage, his offstage champagne sprees and his most recent drying-out period in a hospital. The latter accounted for the fact that Behan ordered mineral water, although he insisted that everybody else have a cocktail.

* *Monterey Peninsula Herald*, 15 May 1961, p. 5.

While he was looking over the menu, Behan sang a song about a town in England 'where people wash their faces three times a day'. He left an impression that, for some unaccountable reason, he had cleaned up the words a bit.

ⁱ By the time his blurry brogue tumbles out through the emptiness where his upper front teeth used to be, a California-attuned ear has to strain considerably to understand more than half of what Behan is saying – and maybe that's just as well, considering that some Peninsulans with tender ears may have been having lunch at Neptune's Table Friday.

A good many heads turned to stare at the tousle-haired, rather lumpy, blue-eyed man with the loud, garbled voice which seemed to be saying somewhat shocking but nevertheless entertaining things.

Behan's language may be described most delicately as uninhibited, and his decibel count is exceeded only by the astonishing frequency with which certain colourful little Anglo-Saxon words recur in his conversation.

He'd come down to the Peninsula just for the afternoon, he said, because 'I wanted to go to Carmel (he pronounced it CARE-ml) and post some cards.' He has, he explained, a sister named 'CARE-ml'. Both the village and his sister, he recalled, were named for Mount Carmel in the Holy Land.

'They make a particularly vicious kind of arak¹ there – Mount Carmel arak. They ought to give it to – Eichmann.'

Behan said he was working on another play, called *Richard's Cork Leg*. 'I'll finish it within the next fortnight, I think.'

He said he's also working on a novel, called *the catacombs*, for publisher Bernard Geis, who 'gave me $4000 for one sentence... I'll tell you the sentence, but your paper can't print it.'

He did. It can't.

*Richard's Cork Leg*, Behan revealed, is about 'sex, politics and religion, in that order'.

The novel? 'It isn't about –' Behan moved to another subject at that point, and never got around to saying what *the catacombs* wasn't about.

Behan talks mostly in wandering monologues. He starts to answer questions, but leaps to other topics before he finishes the answers. His wife, who sits solemnly by most of the time, breaks in quietly on rare occasions to register mild disagreement with something he's saying, which nobody else understands well enough to disagree with.

Some intelligible bits of his monologues went something like this:

'I've got so many —— prejudices that one kinda cancels out the other.'

'San Francisco is, as they say, a good place to visit, but I wouldn't want to live there.'

'It's like paradise down here.'

Word arrived that a seaman who'd been injured aboard a ship was being brought ashore.

'Isn't it funny', said Behan. 'We're sitting here, and there's that poor ——out there.'

He went on about places. London seemed to be his favourite: 'The conversation of the British upper classes is rather shocking to anybody who's not used to it. I like it.'

'I like the little places in England outside of London, where celebrities or notorieties or whatever I'm supposed to be can get drunk without being bothered.'

'New York is real...You've got the freedom of the streets all night... For a moocher or an intellectual or a writer or whatever you're supposed to be, New York is the best —— place.'

'I'm a barbarian. I'm open for an offer, though. I could become a —— south California phony, live on —— blackstrap molasses and wind up in —— Forest Lawn.'

'I used to go to Brooks Brothers, but I bowed out. They were trying to charge me seven dollars more for a suit than they charge the President... A typical Behan costume is a Brooks Brothers suit with two buttons off and a big —— booze stain on the front.'

On newspaperman: 'The biggest creative writers I ever saw are the guys that write the political intelligence.'

About his success: 'You never know about these things. Every writer ought to be allowed to be famous for a month, then given a pension... Alcoholism tends to thin them out....'

'I'd rather be famous than a —— house-painter.'

## NOTES

Behan was in San Francisco to attend the production of *The Hostage*, which opened there on 2 May 1961.

1. A kind of liquor.

# In Defence of Brendan Behan *

### TIM PAT COOGAN

Is Brendan Behan as outrageous in private life as he often appears to be in public? No, he is not.

I had invited Brendan and his wife, Beatrice, to our home for the evening. At that time we lived practically on top of a mountain. So, to

* *Irish Digest*, LXXII, no. 1 (July 1961) 15–18.

prevent our guests getting lost, I left my wife, Cherry, dropping eggs into a pan with one hand and our children into their beds with the other, and descended into the village two miles below to meet them and guide them back.

By the time we returned Cherry had completed the two operations and we sat down to our meal straight away. Beatrice, Cherry, and I sat down, that is. Brendan took one look at his food and said, 'Ah, no, Cherry – I never eat anything like that.'

Cherry looked at him and said faintly, 'What would you eat, Brendan?'

'Well, I'd eat a steak.'

Steak! At seven o'clock on a Sunday evening with all the butchers' shops shut. It says much for Brendan's charm that when he left Cherry turned to me and said, 'He's one of the nicest men I ever met.' He had won her over completely by the fondness he displayed for our children (he insisted on getting them up!) and by his obvious devotion to Beatrice.

Beatrice is tall, slim, with dark hair, which she wears short, and a quiet, shy manner. The daughter of a distinguished painter, she is herself a talented artist. She is devoted to Brendan as he is to her. When he is speaking at a public function she sits tensed in her seat, following every move, every gesture, her own lips moving as he speaks.

At parties Brendan has a habit of suddenly extending an arm in the middle of a song or a conversation, and while he continues to sing or talk Beatrice will stand up unobtrusively and quietly walk over to touch his outstretched hand for a moment. It's a nice way of saying 'Yes, darling, I'm here.'

Feelings about Behan run very deep in Dublin. There is continuous controversy about him, and, because he is such a public figure, every wayward thing he does or unthinking thing he says is seized upon and commented on, often harshly.

A Chinese proverb says, 'When you lift your head over a crowd, people throw muck at you.' Certainly, as part of his fame, Brendan Behan has to face criticism from many of his countrymen.

He is accused of letting the country down by the way he portrays it in his plays; of letting himself down by his drinking and of letting his wife and family down by his behaviour. And I suppose that if one attempted to judge him by ordinary standards it might be possible to substantiate these charges. But ordinary standards don't apply in Behan's case.

To begin with, his impressionable teenage years were spent in a Borstal institution. On top of this one must consider the fact that he had very little formal education. Yet he has written successful plays, a best-selling book, speaks three languages and is generally acknowledged to be the best conversationalist in Dublin.

Genius is traditionally accompanied by temperamental instability, yet Behan's occasional follies committed while under the influence of drink never fail to make the headlines.

His critics say he drinks for the publicity. This is not true. When he was in New York recently a newspaper correspondent wrote about the often shameful length to which some journalists went to encourage his drinking in order to get a story. If he was nothing but a publicity hound there would have been no need for these efforts.

The truth is that Brendan Behan suffers from diabetes and has what doctors call an 'intolerance' for alcohol, which means simply that drink affects him more powerfully than it does other men.

A disastrous appearance on television was caused by his drinking to steady his nerves before facing the cameras. He wasn't trying to show how little he thought of either television or the British people.

In fact, he thinks the British are a wonderful race. 'First they put me in jail, then they make me rich!' Of Princess Margaret he says, 'She's a good sport. She came to see my play *The Hostage*.'

Brendan Behan is not the sort of man to invite to your house to spend a cosy evening watching telly. He would probably become so bored in the first hour at having to sit quietly while someone else did all the talking that he would be liable to tear the knobs off the set. Nor is he the sort of man one would expect to do odd jobs around the house, even though were he to attempt this last he would probably be able to do very well, because he once earned his living as a house-painter.

Highly unorthodox, he regards owning a home as relatively unimportant. I remember himself and Beatrice having an argument over a diamond ring. He wanted to buy her a £650 'rock' (as he called it). Beatrice thought that the money should go towards buying a house. Brendan settled the dispute in characteristic fashion by getting both!

I remember meeting the two of them coming along a beach near Dublin one fine day. They were walking in Indian fashion, the brave (Brendan) out in front and the squaw (Beatrice) meekly bringing up the rear, bent under the weight of the knapsack.

His mother and father, often to be seen with him at theatres, debates and press conferences, are a typical, cheerful Dublin couple. She has a kindly, downright sense of humour. He is a gay old boy. Both are very proud of Brendan. But Brendan's irreverent attitude to life also extends to them.

'The President of Ireland in 1922 must have been a collector of curios – he locked me father up in that year', he says. He was born soon after and his father, a political prisoner, first saw him through the bars of a prison.

Brendan's own period of detention led to his famous novel *Borstal Boy*. He was found to be in possession of gelignite and spent three years in a Borstal institution. *Borstal Boy* was a run-away best-seller – Behan couldn't say how many languages it was translated into. At the moment it is selling like hot cakes in Japanese.

*The Quare Fellow* also came to flower from seeds sown in his prison days, and *The Hostage* was based on his experiences in the IRA. Today Brendan is possibly the best-known Irishman, with the possible exception of UN

President Boland, who thinks very highly of him,[1] and at the beginning of the year US President John Kennedy invited him to his inauguration. He didn't go because Beatrice advised against the trip. He had just arrived home from a North American tour and was recovering from it.

Beatrice's concern was based on the fact that Brendan had twice gone off the wagon while they were on that tour. The first time this happened was during a performance of *The Hostage* in New York, when he listened at last to the urgings of those who wanted him to 'have a jar'. He drank too much, interrupted the play several times from his seat in the stalls and wound up by climbing onto the stage to sing a song that brought the house down.

The second incident occurred in Montreal. He gave a lecture which the organiser, hearing he was on the bottle, had vainly tried to cancel. The audience were completely won over by Behan's personality and wit – in spite of the fact that he said the only things he liked about Canada were the pubs – and they wouldn't let Beatrice in.

Behan has undoubtedly been a very heavy drinker. He told me that he used to drink a quart of whiskey a day at one stage. However that was over ten years ago, and nowadays he drinks only occasionally with an interval of several months between.

His most recent appearance in court stemmed from the fact of his being informed by the organisation which originally staged *The Hostage* (it was written in Irish, which Behan speaks fluently) that heavy cuts would be required in his new one-act play, *A Fine Day in the Graveyard*.[2]

He is more sensitive than most people give him credit for, and the thought of these cuts upset him. When he went down to the local to have a drink, his 'intolerance' got the better of him.

Most of his critics have never met him. His friends are willing to forgive him practically anything. He has an alive fresh quality and the gift of being able to get on friendly terms with anyone.

The one thing his critics don't accuse him of is dishonesty. People trust him on sight. On the island of Ibiza off the coast of Spain he and Beatrice ran out of money shortly after arriving. They had brought enough with them to keep another couple well supplied during the entire holiday, but Brendan is a lavish spender.

Because of currency difficulties and postal delays they waited for nearly two months for more cash to arrive. This could have been serious. No one knew them and they didn't speak Spanish. But Brendan became so popular that credit was freely extended.

With his talents he has it in him to produce work that will become the literature of our age *if* he doesn't destroy himself by drinking.

## NOTES

Tim Pat Coogan (1935– ), Irish journalist and author of *Ireland Since the Rising* (1966).

1. Behan was in New York shortly after F. H. Boland was elected President of the UN General Assembly. Mr Boland was going in to see the first American performance of *The Hostage* when he met Behan in the foyer. Their conversation went this way:

BEHAN. I opened a show tonight.
BOLAND. I also opened a show tonight.
BEHAN. How did your show go?
BOLAND. Quite well. How did yours go?
BEHAN. I'll ring you tomorrow morning and tell you.

– see Sean McCann, *The Wit of Brendan Behan* (London: Leslie Frewin, 1958) pp. 87–8.

2. For a note on this play see. p. 184.


# Behan Takes Swallow – But Won't Touch the Bait*

## JOHN ALLDRIDGE

It was past twelve o'clock of a soft Dublin afternoon and we were looking for Brendan Behan.

There are some 11,000 licensed drinking places in Dublin and its environs. At that advanced hour Mr Behan might have been in any one of them.

The film-publicist, whose tricky job it is to keep track of the elusive Brendan, had drawn up a short list for just such an emergency.

He suggested we start at the top and drink our way steadily through.

Fortunately, we found him at the first attempt. He was presiding over a quiet little family party in a very respectable pub in Duke Street, where they have been serving cockles and mussels for a hundred years and the stout comes to the table with a neat little shamrock of froth on top.

There was Brendan, and Brendan's mother, and Brendan's Aunt Maggie; and an actor chum from his Theatre Workshop days. And it was all as decorous as a Quaker meeting.

We ordered the first round of stouts and waited for the fun to start. Nothing happened. Mr Behan continued to sip his beer quietly. He looked sick and sad at heart.

* *Manchester Evening News*, 21 Dec 1961, p. 3.

Suddenly, I felt ashamed of myself. I had come to a bear-baiting, and the bear did not want to perform.

He must have read my thoughts. For he looked up at me out of great liquid brown eyes that seem as out of place in that round, red, Irish-potato face as a kilt on a bishop.

He pushed his glass away as if he never wanted to see it again.

'I used to enjoy my drink. Even as a wee lad I was a great one for the drink. There used to be fun in drinking. But there isn't any more.'

He went on, 'The trouble is, I look like anyone else when I'm sober. It's only when I've a few inside that I look interesting. For it's then they get out their cameras to take their pictures of the Wild Boyo.

'And it's then they start scratching down in their notebooks all the idiocies that any man is capable of in his cups.

'It's Brendan the drunk they've come to see. Not Behan the writer. Yet every word I've ever written has been set down when I am sober.'

To thousands of tourists who pour into Ireland every year Behan is now the most interesting phenomenon in Dublin. He is a tourist 'must', like the Blarney Stone and Killarney. In a city as narrowly parochial as Dublin this has made him wildly unpopular.

Dublin, as a whole, thoroughly detests Behan. Brendan, as warmly, returns the compliment.

I have always thought Dublin the most friendly city in the world. Behan, who was born and bred here, takes another view of it.

'It's a city where there's familiarity without friendship, loneliness without solitude.'

London he dislikes too.

'London's detestable. A great place for freak-shows. I never want to go back.'

If he could have his way, and his wife would let him, he would live in New York.

'A warmhearted place where they take you as you are, not as they would like you to be.'

The trouble is, I think, that Brendan Behan would find it difficult now to live anywhere. Fame has caught him up and turned him into a one-man, three-ring circus, in which he must clown and clown until he drops.

A pleasant, convivial, rather gentle fellow at heart, he has been given a part to play that secretly scares him. Always a lusty liver, at thirty-seven he is sick at heart and sick in body. For Behan, the fun is going out of life.

To Behan being famous means being prodded on the bus to see if you are sober.

Some time soon his next play will be having its London premiere.

He calls it *Richard's Cork Leg*.[1] According to Brendan, it's a 'dramedy'.

'It's a play of losers. I've always been interested in losers. The hero loses everything worth losing. He's a shy, quiet sort of chap who just wants to be liked. But nobody takes him seriously.'

He might have been describing himself.

Fifteen miles away, at Ardmore, among the green hills of County Wicklow, they are filming *The Quare Fellow*[2] – the play he wrote while serving a term in prison.

The dramatic impact of the play came out of its claustrophobic setting – an Irish jail just before and just after an execution. The condemned man – the 'Quare Fella' – is never seen, but his disturbing presence is always there.

The film version has taken certain liberties with the original.

They have 'opened it up', as they say. For one thing, the 'Quare Fella' is seen – briefly but harrowingly on his way to the scaffold. And he has been given a wife, played by one of the film's stars, Sylvia Sims.

The play was essentially a play without stars. But a film must have a star; so they have built up the part of Crimmon, the young apprentice warder from the West Coast, to the 'star' measurements of Patrick McGoohan.

Producer Joseph Dreifuss has loaded his film with 'atmosphere'. For his locations he has 'borrowed' Kilmainham Jail where so many distinguished Irishmen from de Valera down have done 'time' under the British Crown; where young Brendan Behan got his first glimpse of his father.

He was six weeks old at the time and his father was serving a sentence for political reasons.

'Me mother held me up in a basket so me father could see me through the bars. I don't think he was too happy about it.'

Apart from acting as technical adviser on the prison sequences, Mr Behan is taking no part in the film. But he hopes they will let him be heard singing that strange melancholy prison dirge which adds so much to the macabre mood of the play:

> A chilly feeling
> Came o'er me stealing
> And the mice were squealing
> In my prison cell.
> And that old triangle
> Went jingle-jangle
> Along the banks of
> The Royal Canal.

## NOTES

1. *Richard's Cork Leg* was first produced at the Peacock Theatre on 14 March 1972 during the Dublin International Theatre Festival.

2. The world premiere of the film version of *The Quare Fellow* took place at the Cork Film Festival in September 1962. The film was not successful. See 'This Wasn't "The Quare Fella"!' *Sunday Independent* (Dublin), 23 Sep 1962, p. 5.

# Irish Author, Playwright – and Talker*

## THOMAS QUINN CURTISS

The state theatres of France rarely produce living foreign dramatists. As a gesture to Great Britain the Comédie Française staged James Barrie's *The Twelve-Pound Look* during the 1914–18 war and Jean Vilar's Théâtre National Populaire, a theatrical enterprise supported by municipal funds, has done T. S. Eliot, O'Casey and Brecht.

Now Jean-Louis Barrault is about to defy tradition with another exception, his production of Brendan Behan's *The Hostage*. It will have its premiere at the Théâtre de France (formerly the Odéon) in a few days in an adaptation by Jean Paris,[1] and Madeleine Renaud, Arletty, Pierre Blanchard and Georges Wilson, all stars, are in its cast.

*The Hostage* was seen in Paris in English when the Stratford East troupe of Joan Littlewood visited the annual Théâtre des Nations festival three years ago and it deeply impressed Parisian theatregoers and Parisian directors, actors and critics. Behan's other play, *The Quare Fellow*, has already been seen in French and a distinguished French critic has proclaimed that the theatre of Behan is the theatre of Brecht humanised by the warming glow of Irish humour and imagination.

As Behan's alcoholic exploits have occupied much space on front pages he is better known to Americans for his drinking than he is for his thinking or his theatrical accomplishments. That he is now on the wagon – drinking only orange juice, soda water and tea – is probably surprising and disappointing news to those who have revelled in accounts of his stage-Irishman antics. His scenes in public, alas, have attracted a wider audience than the excellent scenes in his plays. But perhaps the tide has turned. *The Hostage* is enjoying success off-Broadway and he has put the bottle away and gone back to the typewriter.

'I telephoned O'Casey before coming over', he told me over countless cups of tea in a Chinese restaurant in the West Forties the other evening. 'He told me to stop drinking. "Why?" I asked. "Because you have work to do", he replied. I think he's right.'

The burly giant of Falstaffian girth has not only sobered but mellowed.

---

* *New York Herald Tribune Book Review*, 25 Feb 1962, p. 8.

His innocent moon face and friendly smile, his soft voice and gentle manner, give no inkling of his turbulent past.

At thirteen he joined the IRA in its terrorist campaign. At sixteen he was apprehended in Liverpool and sentenced to reform school in England and during the following ten years he was in and out of jails in England and Ireland. A final sentence of fourteen years was commuted by the general amnesty in 1946. It was these experiences about which he wrote in his autobiographical memoir *Borstal Boy*. A moving and memorable book, it aroused great interest when it was published in the United States in 1959.

'My new play is called *Richard's Cork Leg* and you probably wonder why', he went on. 'In 1914 James Joyce sent his play *Exiles* to Lugné-Poë, director of the Théâtre de l'Oeuvre. Lugné-Poë sent it back, saying that France had bought herself a war and the theatre would only do war plays. Joyce remarked that he should have given his hero, Richard, a cork leg.

'My play is about a young Dubliner who becomes the victim of political strife, though he has no political sympathies. The scene is a cemetery where memorial services for some members of General O'Duffy's[2] Blue Shirts are taking place.

'The Blue Shirts were Irish Fascists in the 1930s. In 1937 General O'Duffy took his troops to fight for Franco in Spain. Oliver Gogarty[3] used to say that O'Duffy achieved the greatest military victory in history. He left Ireland with 500 men and returned with 1000.

'The hero of my play has come to the cemetery to meet a girl, but he is mistaken for an anti-Blue Shirt and is killed in the turmoil that arises.'

'Like my Richard, I don't know where I stand politically today', said Behan. 'I'm against more things than I'm for. I'm opposed to the John Birch Society[4] and I'm opposed to the Soviet Government's treatment of Pasternak.[5] I'm opposed to all movements that curtail freedom.'

'Philosophically, I'm a daylight atheist. However, whenever I'm ill I try to find a priest. You might say I live by calculated cowardice. The most important thing in life, as I see it, is to remain in a state of good humour.'

Though his residence is Dublin, Behan prefers living in France and the United States. He has tramped the South of France as a hobo and was a guest of the French Government when *The Hostage* was played in Paris in English. He would like to tour America, but *Richard's Cork Leg* is keeping him at his writing desk in a Broadway hotel.

'I spend the mornings writing', said Behan. 'In the afternoons I see my friends and in the evening I go to the theatre. Thornton Wilder, Tennessee Williams and Arthur Miller are my favourite American playwrights. O'Neill was so great that it would be an impertinence for me to praise him.

'I was a columnist in Dublin for a while. I did sort of a humorous column, but it was packed with information. I tipped the winner of the Grand National twice by listening to talk about the pubs. I was censored once when I wrote that the private park in Marion [sic][6] Square should be opened to the children of the tenements who live in the neighbourhood.

Lennox Robinson was drama critic of the same paper. He was given half a page to write about my first play, *The Quare Fellow*.[7] He praised it, but after the lead about the play he filled the rest of the space writing about his own plays.

'Joyce and O'Casey were the writers that influenced me most. I admire Brecht and probably he has influenced my stage technique, but I imagine he's a different playwright in German than he is in English. I wonder if I'll be another playwright in French.'

## NOTES

Thomas Quinn Curtiss, theatre and film critic for the Paris *Herald Tribune*. He was on a visit to New York when he met Behan. A revival of *The Hostage* was playing at One Sheridan Square.

1. For more details on this French adaptation see Jean Paris, '*Un Otage*', *Cahiers Renaud-Barrault*, no. 37: *Le Théâtre Irlandais* (Feb 1962) pp. 54–65.

2. For a note on O'Duffy see p. 96.

3. Oliver St John Gogarty (1878–1957), Irish physician, writer and Senator.

4. The most important far-right group of the early 1960s was the John Birch Society, named in memory of the 'first victim of World War III', an American pilot shot down over China while fighting Mao Tse-tung's Communists. Sweet-manufacturer Robert Welch founded the society in 1958. See John Allen Broyles, *The John Birch Society: Anatomy of a Protest* (Boston Mass.: Beacon Press, 1964).

5. Boris Pasternak (1890–1960), Russian poet and novelist who was not able readily to accept the Bolshevik regime and who was looked upon with suspicion by the authorities. An offer of the Nobel Prize was made in 1958, but this the Soviet Government refused to allow him to take up.

6. Merrion Square, Dublin.

7. L[ennox] R[obinson], 'Acting Was Superb in Behan Play', *Irish Press* (Dublin), 20 Nov 1954, p. 9.

# Brendan Behan's Quare World*

## EAMONN MARTIN

Brendan Behan and I were only fifteen when I felt my first and deepest disappointment in him. I had been sent to boarding school, while he was ordered by the Irish Republican Army to blow up the battleship *King*

* *Globe Magazine* (Toronto), 15 Sep 1962, pp. 4–6.

*George V*. Caught in a Liverpool lodging house while he was attempting to dispose of his explosives, Brendan was convicted of treason. He delivered a fine fighting speech from the dock, but he failed to get himself hanged. On that day, Ireland lost a great martyr.

We had both been born into IRA families, and we met at thirteen because of this. The circumstances were dramatic enough to stir the blood of any two youngsters like us and bind us together as fast friends forever.

On that memorable day in the fall of 1936, a group of IRA sympathisers had gathered at St Stephen's Green in Dublin to hear my father, Ambrose Victor Martin, denounce Fascist intervention in the Spanish Civil War. (He was later to fight in the International Brigade with Frank Ryan's IRA contingent.) Then, through the drizzling rain, appeared a large and ugly mob organised by the Irish Christian Front, otherwise known as the Blue Shirts, or Animal Gang, which supported Generalissimo Francisco Franco. (This group sent Eoin O'Duffy's Blue Shirts to fight on the Fascist side.) The Fronters were armed with an array of wicked weapons – razor blades, broken bottles, iron bars and bicycle chains – and I feared for my father's life.

As the IRA men prepared to defend themselves with their bare fists, a small boy with a wild shock of hair ran from their ranks waving a pistol nearly as big as himself and yelling a wonderful string of obscenities. He stopped only a few feet from the Fronters and fired two shots close over their heads. They stopped in their tracks and the boy screamed, 'Get back, you filth, or I'll kill every bloody one of you!' The attackers didn't wait to count the bullets in his gun, and I watched with delight as they retreated in hasty disorder.

Brendan Behan, at thirteen, had saved my father and the others and set the pattern of impetuous behaviour that was to cause him so much trouble later on.

After this, Brendan was considered a man in IRA circles. He was given suitable assignments to fit his new stature. He made several trips to England, performing more and more important acts of sabotage, until finally he was caught trying to blow up the battleship. Once his age was discovered, Brendan was sentenced to serve a term in a Borstal reform school. There, he received most of the education, academic and otherwise, which enabled him to write his first novel, *Borstal Boy*.

When Brendan was released from Borstal late in 1941 and deported to Ireland, he found himself a national hero. And this was the excuse for some of the happiest rip-roaring parties I have ever attended – they seemed destined to go on forever. In fact, Brendan was well on his way to becoming the most famous ballad-singer in all of Ireland when the police interfered again.

On the bright Easter Sunday morning of 1943, during an IRA parade to the graves of the Irish martyrs, Brendan found cause for argument with two policemen and pulled a revolver. The resultant fierce gun battle caused a Dublin military tribunal to sentence Brendan to fourteen years in prison.

It seemed a shame to me that anyone who could sing as well as he could should remain rotting in prison. But this is facetious in the light of political strife that was tearing Ireland apart at the time. Scores of young men were imprisoned, suffering inhuman indignities, for what we thought was no other crime than a love of their country.

Those of us who were still free, breaking with the traditions of the IRA, decided to carry on the fight with political weapons. We formed a political party, the Clann na Poblacta (Family of the Republic), with the immediate aim of releasing our boys from jail, and I found myself working twenty hours daily directing election campaigns.

Our first victory came in 1947 with the success of our leader Sean MacBride in a County Dublin by-election. This was followed in 1948 by a general election after which we sent eleven members to Parliament. Joining with four other parties, we were able to topple the sixteen-year-old Fianna Fail (Soldiers of Destiny) government of Eamon de Valera. And we released all of the IRA prisoners, including Brendan Behan.

The welcome-home parties this time were even happier, and lasted longer, and I think Brendan decided to adopt them as a way of life. He has been on a party ever since.

Since I was then studying law, and working in the office of a Dublin barrister, Brendan would seek my advice and help in his continual scrapes with the police. Many were the early mornings I had to bail him out and arrange to have him defended in court. Sometimes, he would arrive at our house, battered and blood-smeared after a fight that had ended in his arrest. My mother and I would clean him as best as we could so that he would look well before the judge, but making Brendan presentable after one of his drunken riots was indeed a task to test the faithful.

Well I remember one beautiful May morning walking with Brendan down the Dublin Quays toward the Four Courts where he was to face the familiar charge of assaulting the police. I was dressed in my best suit and Brendan in my second-best.

As we walked beside the River Liffey, Brendan stopped and said, 'Look Eamonn, you know, that I'm a fine swimmer. So you jump into the Liffey and pretend to drown and I'll jump in after you and save you. When we get to court, they'll ask us why we're wet and you can tell them I'm a hero. Perhaps they'll let me off.'

One imaginative look at the scummy, oil-slicked water convinced me that my two good suits were worth more than three months of Brendan's time. I refused his generous offer. As it was, Brendan stood in the dock wearing the halo he affected in those days as if he was the injured party. He got off with one month.

This proved to be one of the most significant months of Brendan's life. He was a painter by trade (his father is still president of the Irish painters' union), and it was easy for him to charm his way into the job of painting the death cells in Mountjoy Jail. The condemned prisoners were allowed cigarettes and even stout. They were a generous bunch, and Brendan got along well with them all. But during his month behind bars, one of the prisoners was hanged, and this had a profound effect upon him.

When he was released, he talked incessantly against what he called the barbarous custom of legalised murder. The seed had been sown that was to grow into his first great stage success, his own loud outcry against capital punishment – *The Quare Fellow*.

This first success of Brendan's was begun at my Dublin house, continued at my country cottage, and completed at a monstrous, dreary old castle I received from my father.

*The Quare Fellow* was started as a result of my impatience with Brendan when he dropped into my office one day and asked for some money for a drink. He seldom did this. The man's pride is too great, and I knew that he must be in dire straits. But I also knew that he had this play inside him and it would stay there forever unless someone coaxed it out.

'You'll get no money from me today, Brendan', I told him. 'You're coming home with me and I'll sit you in front of a typewriter. While you write, I'll supply the stout. When you stop, so does the drink.'

He accepted this verbal contract, and began his great play. He finished *The Quare Fellow* at Gibbstown Castle, County Meath, which was turned over to me by my father, along with all the troubles that went with it.

My father, an import–export merchant, had purchased the castle while pursuing his hobby of collecting antique real estate. But it is significant that after I had enough of the place, and gave it back to him, he offered it to the Trappist order, and it has since become a monastery. That castle was beset with troubles.

Brendan shared these with us – in fact, I think he enjoyed them. The castle was cold, damp, enormous and impossible to heat properly unless the tenant was a millionaire, and I was not. Far from it. We lived there for a year until we could stand the misery of the place no longer – there were actually stalactites in the basement – but before we left, Brendan brought his marvellous sense of the commercial to the force.

All the windows in this miserable pile had sash cords with lead weights attached. Brendan suggested we detach the weights and sell the lead in Dublin. I agreed, and we wound up selling one and a half tons of lead. This successful venture could have been just the beginning for Brendan, but I had to put my foot down.

His next plan was to climb to the roof of the castle and strip the copper from its giant dome. The idea to me was outrageous, as well as dangerous, but typical of Brendan. Once he starts on a skylark of this nature, he carries it through to impossible limits, particularly if there is money involved.

Despite the impossibility of the man on many occasions, only once in my life do I remember deliberately trying to avoid Brendan. I had just met Fionnuala (pronounced Fa-noo-la), a gentle girl who is now my wife, and I was desperate to protect her from Brendan's fearful language. When with Fionnuala, I avoided all his known haunts. But it was inevitable that we meet him and sure enough we did, smack in the middle of Grafton Street, one of the most fashionable streets in Dublin.

There stood Brendan, smelling like all the stout in Ireland, unshaven, with his hair all over his face and his shirt open to his belt. He roared a friendly curse. I pretended not to notice him. You might as well try to ignore the wind in a valley. Fionnuala asked to be introduced to him.

For five minutes, I made wrathful faces at Brendan while my future wife coolly fielded his terrible language. Finally, he saw that he was not shocking her, and shut up. He has never cursed in her presence from that day to this, and she, like me, has become a captive of his charm, despite the man's noisy bluster.

Brendan is undoubtedly one of the noisiest men in the world. Becuase of this, or in spite of it, he is beloved by children, especially my own five, who regard him as their favourite uncle. When we lived in Ireland, he sang for my youngsters and clowned for them and generally filled their lives with joy during his many visits to our home. He is particularly fond of my son Maoliosa (Mel), who is now twelve. On Mel's third birthday, when Brendan was in custody and on his way to Dundrum's Magistrate's Court after breaking the plate-glass window of a pub, he sweet-talked his escort into dropping by at my house so that he could give my wife three pounds to buy the boy a present he had promised.

Even an eight-year separation failed to dim Brendan's fondness for Mel. In 1960, when he was in New York for the opening of his play, *The Hostage*, he telephoned me and coaxed me to allow Mel to go to New York so that they could see the city together. I let the boy go and the two of them, kids together, went to the top of the Empire State Building, swam in the Young Men's Hebrew Association pool and ran across the stage of the Cort Theatre during a performance of *The Hostage*.

But the trip ended poorly for Mel. He posed with Brendan while smoking a huge Havana cigar, unaware that a photographer was capturing his devilment for the rest of the world – including his school principal and me – to see. He came home to a hot reception, even if he had smoked his first cigar with the great Brendan Behan.

My children constantly ask me why people criticise Brendan, when to them he is the most wonderful man in the world. I try to explain to them that he often acts in a fashion unacceptable to orderly society, and is ostracised for it by those who feel that his contributions to the world do not balance his single-minded attempts to hold it up to ridicule. I tell them that perhaps he will, like other talented but eccentric persons, be more acceptable when he is dead.

When the English hanged Kevin Barry, a sixteen-year-old medical student caught at the scene of an ambush in 1919, a fine ballad was born that still lives in his name. Brendan was even younger than Kevin Barry when he tried unsuccessfully to get himself executed. He would have made marvellous folksong material.

But perhaps with *The Quare Fellow*, *The Hostage*, *Borstal Boy* and whatever is yet to come, Brendan Behan will yet redeem himself for posterity.

### NOTE

Eamonn Martin, an IRA friend of Behan who used to work in Toronto; he now lives in Dublin.

# True Vintage Behan*

## RAE JEFFS

On 19 October 1953, the *Irish Times* newspaper announced the publication of the first instalment of a serial about Dublin's underworld, *The Scarperer* by Emmet Street. It ran for thirty days and nothing further was heard of the author.

Nothing further indeed might ever have been heard of the author, had it not been for a chance remark I made to Brendan in 1962.

I was being slightly disparaging about a well-known crime writer, when Brendan told me that at one time he would have agreed with me. Since then, however, he had tried his hand at writing a crime story and had not found it quite so easy.

When I asked to see it, he astounded me by telling me that it had already been published. Where? As a serial in the *Irish Times*. He couldn't remember exactly when and he certainly did not have a copy of it (Brendan never kept a copy of anything he wrote).

He did remember, however, that 'I wrote it under the phony name of Emmet Street, which was the name of the street opposite the one I was

---

* 'Afterword', *The Scarperer* (Garden City, NY.: Doubleday, 1964) pp. 157–8. Editor's title.

reared in, in North Dublin. And I wrote it under another name for the following reason:

'I had started writing for Irish republican and Irish left-wing newspapers, and up to this the Dublin intelligentsia were very friendly disposed towards me, because I had published very little. And for a garrulous man, one of the very few things I talk about is my own writing.

'By 1953, I was quite well-known as a poet and a writer, and unfortunately the Dublin intelligentsia had seen pieces of pornography that I'd written for French magazines when I was in France – in English, of course. This didn't exactly endear me to them, so being short of the readies, I decided to write under a phony name.'

Brendan explained that he sent the first draft of the story to the *Irish Times*, who immediately accepted it but would not give him an advance on it. With what little money he had – which was practically nothing – he went to the Aran Islands to write the story in peace and without fear of interruption. Within a few days his money was gone. He wired the *Irish Times* to this effect to enable him to finish it.

A few hours later, he collected ninety pounds from the post office. The *Irish Times* had not failed him and he was never to forget it.

Back in Dublin for the publication, Brendan went round the various pubs in Grafton Street, literally the fashionable centre of Dublin, to hear what the 'intelligentsia' thought of this new Irish writer. Apparently they liked him.

Tracing the serial proved more of an obstacle than I had thought, but eventually with the help of Jack White, the Literary Editor of the *Irish Times* at the time and now with Radio Éireann, I found it.

It is part of the tragedy that Brendan did not live to see the publication of this book for the first time under its rightful author's name. He knew, of course, that it was to appear. It is a story of which he was particularly fond and one which he thoroughly enjoyed writing, with the added kick of knowing it was a hoax. I believe it to be one of the best stories he ever wrote; true vintage Behan. It was certainly born out of the period that produced *The Quare Fellow* and *Borstal Boy*, though Brendan edited and re-edited the latter before the final publication in 1958.

I can think of no higher praise.

NOTE

For a note on Rae Jeffs see p. 109.

# Talking to Mrs Stephen Behan*

## MARION FITZGERALD

*Mrs Behan, tell us something about your sons. How many have you altogether?*

Six. I had seven, but the last one died. I used to rejoice that I had six sons to carry my coffin to the graveyard. Now that's over. Now they bring the coffin in the hearse to the graveyard. I have one daughter. I always say that we are seven, like the poem in the book. Rory is the eldest. He works in Templemore and he's married with four kiddies. Sean is next and he works in London, and he's an electrician, or an electrician's helper would be more like it. Seamus is an electrician in Selfridges. They all have very nice jobs. Brian is a carpenter and he lives in Herne Hill, near Brixton. Dominic is in London working in the BBC. I believe he's just finished a book, *The Laughing Boy*, and he has a play nearly finished, *The Courage of Henry Thomson*. Carmel is married too. But they were all home for the day when the BBC did *This is Your Life*. They brought a brother of mine home from America...a lovely time we had.[1]

Brendan is the eldest of my second family. I was twice married, you know. I was left a very young widow. I was only two years married to Jack Furlong, a '16 man.[2] I was staying with his mother, and Stephen used to visit there, and that's how I met him. Rory and Sean are Furlongs.

*But you have none of your children at home now?*

No, we have none of them at home now. Da and I are here all alone, and it's very lonely. I can't bear to go to the back room where the boys used to sleep. They come home for holidays though – they've just been home. And we spent three weeks in London not long ago. Brendan gave us the money to go. Dominic gives us whatever he can and the others give us what they can. They're all very good boys. Yes, we had a hard time rearing seven of them. Da was fifteen years in a job when I married him, and then he was made a political prisoner, and when he came out the job was gone. He'd get a job for a couple of days, and then be knocked off for a couple of days. But he always worked when he could get it. And we gave all the boys a trade, which was a hard thing to do. Da's mother owned slums in Russell Street, and we didn't have much rent to pay. Da would never have moved out of there. He hates moving anywhere. We only moved out of Russell Street after it was condemned and nearly fell down on us. We're twenty years out in Crumlin now. When all the boys left I'd have gone to a Corporation flat. But you couldn't move Da.

*Were they hard boys to rear?*

Ah well, do you see, all boys are wild, but they were no wilder than any other boys. They always worked when they got it – they had to. The greatest trial was when they left us and went to live in England, and left us here alone. Sean joined the RAF. We didn't like the idea of him joining anything except in his own country. And when the papers used to come for him, I used to burn them. But one day he went and met the postman, and wrote off and joined up. It didn't do him a bit of harm. He's a pension out of it now. The others worked on the unemployment platform here. That's how they had to leave Dublin. Dominic and Sean got a brilliant idea that they'd sell turf, and they managed to get £100 between them. But you'd want to be reared to that, and Sean is a bit of a gentleman in his own way. The poor people were glad to get the turf, and meant to pay for it, but when Dominic went back on a Saturday to collect the money, they wouldn't have it. They lost all the £100 and the horse got killed. Now the people around say – when they want to take me down a peg – 'I remember your sons selling turf.' And I say if they got paid for it, they'd be well away. Do you know when Dominic was four years old, he fell into the Canal near Russell Street! Only his little boots were up and a neighbour plunged in and saved him. It was a basement we had and somebody came to the railing – Carmel had only just been born – and said, 'Dominic is drowned.' But he wasn't, though he spent a week in the Mater after it.

Another day – Da never brought out the children, that wasn't in his line – but one day he came out with us, and we were walking across the Bull Wall with the seven of them behind us, and suddenly we looked round, and he said, 'Where's Brendan?' There was no Brendan. You know the big holes left by the bombs? They were covered with grass, and Brendan was down one of them with grass all over him. But he wasn't to die either.

*Where do you think Dominic and Brendan got their talent for writing from?*

All my children were fond of reading. And my brother, Peadar Kearney, wrote our National Anthem. I suppose it was in them. But they didn't get a lot of schooling once we came over here, because they had to change from one school to another and it upset them terribly. They were all clever children. I never made favourites of any of them. They were all the same to me, although people think Brendan was a pet of mine, but he wasn't. Da's mother – Stephen's mother – petted him a terrible lot, but I didn't. Brendan is very like his father in appearance, but I'd say he takes after my brother, Peadar Kearney, but of course Da's intelligent too. He takes after both sides of the family. I never had any hopes of any of them being writers. And I have always been happy because although they write, they have their trade if anything ever happens. They'll never be poor. It's a great thing to have a trade. Brian and Sean write a little too, but they hide it. I believe they have written a book or two only they didn't let them be seen.

*When did Brendan start writing?*

I think Brendan was writing when he was in the infants' school, because Sister Monica – did you ever hear of Sister Monica? She was fifty years in North William Street.[3] She loved boys and she loved Brendan. I remember going down to her to complain of Brendan being naughty, and she said, 'Mrs Behan, are you aware you are rearing a genius?' And I didn't care whether he was a genius or not if he was good. She was very sad when I cut his curls off; he had lovely brown curls. When she died all Dublin turned out. She had reared hundreds of Dublin boys. She was a wonderful woman, and Brendan never forgets her.

*Do you like what Brendan writes?*

Oh, yes. I love Brendan's plays. I think they are great. I think I like *The Hostage* best. We enjoyed it in London. *The Quare Fellow* was a bit foreign to me, but I liked it all the same.

*How do you feel when Brendan gets into trouble?*

I feel very unhappy. All I can do is pray for him. But Dominic gets into many a scrape too, though not as much as he used to. Although I have a jolly side, I have a very sad side. Brendan is like that too. He can be leaping over the moon, and he can be down in his boots. But Da is always jolly. He doesn't understand moods. I never took to drink. Da likes a drink, and Da's mother used to drink a lot. I like the atmosphere of the pub more than the drink, but when I do drink I like a drop of the 'cratur', because it doesn't make me sick. I can take one bottle of stout but not another. Champagne we get when we go to Brendan. He loves calling for it, and he loves the pop of the cork. He says himself he was drinking since he was nine years old. His grandmother used to give him a glass along with the rest at funerals. My brother drank a lot too. But despite all that, do you know I was ashamed of my life in London when I saw the Irish boys singing 'The Rose of Tralee' outside the doors, and they were stocious.

*What do you think of young people today?*

They are not as national as when I was young. The national feeling seems to be fading away. We went to a ball the other night, and there was not one Irish song sung during the whole evening. There were no high-caul caps, or sixteen-hand-reels or eight-hand-reels. They were doing the twist the whole night. We were cradled in the movement. I could recite every word of 'Who Fears to Speak of '98' when I was seven years old, every word of it. We were reared differently you see. I remember when I was a young girl I used to meet John O'Leary. He was an old, old man, and often in George's place of an evening he'd stop and tell me about the Fenians, about prison. I knew him well. And I knew Madame MacBride. When I was a young widow I used to be receptionist for her on her 'At Home' day. Madame was very kind, a lovely kind soul. But one day she came to me. 'Kitty,' she said to me, 'I have some work for you to do.' So I said, 'Thank you, Madame.' I thought it was to scrub out some offices, and I was delighted because I was a young widow with two small children. 'Yes, Kitty,' said she, 'I want you to sit for an artist.' I was very ignorant at the time, and I said, 'Me, Madame! I couldn't sit for an artist. I'm awful looking.' 'On the contrary, Kitty,' said she, 'You are quite pretty.' So I sat for Sarah Purser for a couple of years. Did I like it? Well I was paid for it, that's the main thing. No, I don't know where the pictures are. Da was often trying to find out.

*Do you like reading?*

My eyes are too bad. They've been bad since I was a child with the measles. Da reads for me. He reads Dickens, Willie Rooney – I knew all his poems of course. And 'Knocknagow'. And of course I read the *Irish Times*.

*Do you go often to the theatre?*

We very seldom go. The last one we went to was *Red Roses for Me*, in London. And I went to *The Rose Tattoo*. I didn't like it. But I liked Shelagh Delany's *A Taste of Honey*.

*Do you like television?*

Oh my eyesight's too bad for it. And then if we had it, Da would say, 'Kathleen can look at the television', and he'd go off. I prefer to go with him. I like knitting. Do you know I have finished a mitten while I was talking to you. I knit all the socks for Brendan and Da. They like them hand-knitted. The others wear nylon. You see I can knit without looking at it, so it doesn't hurt my eyes. I like cooking – beefsteak and kidney pie, apple tart. I like to roast a little chicken for Da. Did you ever meet Da? You'd love him if you met him. He's very jolly. Though he's as quiet as a lamb. I never heard a cross word from him in the forty years I am married to him, excepting I raised it myself.

*Mrs Behan, how do you like to enjoy yourself?*

Well we go out to Neary's on Friday, Saturday and Sunday. Da and myself. We take a little drink, we meet friends, and talk and laugh. So far I have danced through life. We went to a party in London and we enjoyed ourselves so much – I wasn't drunk – that if somebody mentioned China, I'd sing a song about China, and no matter what anybody mentioned I'd sing a song about it. They said they'd send over for us for the next one. Dominic was put in the shade that night. Of course Da sang too. Peadar taught me all the songs, and I taught all the songs to the boys that they are singing now. Do you know we are just after getting twenty-five pounds from the Canadian broadcasting people and all we did was sing a few songs round the fire in Dominic's place in London?[4] I must have been born happy and I must have been born singing. I'll be singing a song when I'm dying, an old 'come-all-ye'. Last night we were down in a pub down here locally, and they were all talking about dogs and cats. They only allow us to sing on Friday, Saturday and Sunday, but when they were talking about the dogs didn't I sing 'My daddy wouldn't buy me a bow-wow-wow'. We had the best of laugh. It's an unheard of thing to sing on a Monday night. But I sang, though I wouldn't have been singing at all. We'd be barred, ruined, only that we were in a little room.

## NOTES

1. For details of this programme see Seamus de Burca, 'In Search of Stephen Behan', *Irish Digest* (Dublin), LXXVII, no. 9 (Mar 1963) 43–6.

2. Kathleen Behan's first husband Jack Furlong, a Belfast man, had fought in the rising of Easter 1916 and had died of influenza the following year.

3. The School of the French Sisters of Charity of St Vincent de Paul, North William Street, Dublin. 'The late Sister Monica . . . taught generations of boys, including Sean Russell, and one of the Editors of the *Irish Digest*, and the present writer, at North William Street School' – Brendan Behan, *Hold Your Hour and Have Another* (London: Hutchinson, 1963) p. 191. Behan also mentioned Sister Monica by name in his short story 'The Confirmation Suit', *The Standard* (Dublin), Easter 1953, p. 5.

4. This interview was broadcast on the Canadian Broadcasting Corporation on 4 November 1962.

# The Ignominy of Success*

### SEAN CALLERY

The bells of hell
Go ting-a-ling-a-ling
For you but not for me.
O death where is thy
Sting-a-ling-a-ling
Or grave thy victory?
If you meet the undertaker
Or the young man from the Pru,
Get a pint with what's left over.
Now I'll say goodbye to you.

(interpolated by Brendan Behan
as the finale of *The Hostage*)

'Traitors, bourgeois bloodsuckers, swine', shouted Brendan Behan.

'Out with that lout and his trollop', cried a toff on the speaker's platform.

'If I was a whore itself, I'd not stop here for long', said Maeve or Nuala, or Mairhe, the girl clinging to Brendan's shabby coat, 'for I know you students. You're all passion and no money.'

We were in an amphitheatre of University College, Dublin in the middle of the winter of great snows, massive floods and shortages of nearly everything that makes life bearable.

Rows of outraged students were shouting behind clouds of steam their fevered breaths poured into the frigid air. They were protesting a slight to conformist, nationalist Catholic Ireland by a rude, indecently passionate intruder.

The occasion of this absurd contretemps was a meeting of the Literary and Historical Society of the university, an organisation whose nomenclature is true to the tradition of Irish hyperbole. Its principal distinction, to my knowledge, is that it claims James Joyce as a former active member. This was a bright evening I recall vividly.

Let me tell you something about the university. It is a government-supported, non-sectarian (in Ireland, for practical purposes, this means

* *The Commonweal* (New York), XCIII (23 Oct 1970) 87–91.

Catholic), nationalist institution. It was gotten together by Irish patriots who protested the British-oriented Protestant monopoly on higher education in their country. In short, a noble attempt to provide for the gifted among the Irish peasantry and merchant and professional classes, a university in their homeland where they would neither be patronised nor proselytised by the tiny Protestant elite, whose influence and wealth were far beyond its numbers. Thus, the National University's affinities and intellectual exchanges were primarily with Louvain, Salamanca, Coimbra and the Italian universities, not Oxford and Harvard. The Latinate institutions are splendid, to be sure, but at that time thoroughly traditionalist and reeling under the pressures of purges and counter-purges due to the political upheavals and wars.

Also, Ireland's neutrality and isolation during the Second World War and the continuing, still-unresolved struggle with England to bring Northern Ireland into the autonomous Irish Republic, broadened the gap between the conventional social thought of Dublin and what advanced political and social theorists were thinking elsewhere.

The purpose of this preamble is to explain how the students of an Irish university in 1945 could seriously debate whether England's celebrated 'Red Dean' of Canterbury should be allowed to speak in Ireland under the auspices of an Anglo-Soviet friendship organisation. (Surely one of the most fatuous tactics the Party ever tried...an Anglican cleric to preach to the Irish masses.) Moreover the consensus among the student debaters was nay, nay to His Grace and now what could they do to provoke Government action or perhaps blow up the lecture hall?

The honoured guests on the dais were in tails and white tie and the students in Sunday-going-to-Mass-and-Communion finery, nicely agreeing among themselves, when suddenly an unkempt but handsome Brendan roared from an elevated tier at the rear of the amphitheatre and demanded to be heard. In accents coarse (calculatedly so, I suspect) by the standards of the average student's ultra-refined Dublin speech, he bellowed a series of egalitarian sentiments familiar enough almost anywhere else, but a novelty to his audience. Freedom to express dissent; freedom to propagandise, no matter what; the Reds are 100 per cent wrong; our country desperately needs radical social reforms...and so forth. He was loudly denounced on all sides and, if memory serves, forced to leave. After all he was not a university student (in fact his formal education was rudimentary).

This was the first time I saw Brendan but we met again soon and often in some of the more outlandish precincts of foggy Dublin. He had begun to circulate among the elite of Dublin's Bohemia. Headquarters was in the basement of a splendid Georgian mansion in Dublin's snootiest street. Our host (something of his character comes out, I think, as Monsewer in *The Hostage*) rented this hovel from a surgeon who was reputed to be the city's most reliable and wealthiest abortionist. His name made more than a respectable splash in the pages of the *Almanach de Gotha* and, indeed, he was surely the only blue blood among us.

Regulars in attendance included many who later went on to fame and fortune. A celebrated novelist, a phenomenally successful film-director, are among the alumni, but somehow their brilliance and future eminence paled by comparison to Brendan's manifest destiny.

Happily, this article is meant to be a species of memoir and though I knew Brendan for rather a long period of time, our relationship was always peripheral, with long periods of not seeing each other. As I am not obliged to create a whole character replete with clinical details, it is enough to say what I know. Many people have asked me why Brendan lived as he did and why he drank himself to death.

This is what I think. This is what I know to be at least part of the truth.

At the time of Brendan's impassioned and ill-received plea to the members of the Literary and Historical Society, University College, Dublin, he had recently been released from an Irish prison. Readers of *Borstal Boy* know of the many years of his precious youth spent in English jails; punishment for adolescent activities in the movement to overthrow British rule in Northern Ireland.

When Brendan returned to Ireland, he joined the struggle against the de Valera government, which in the eyes of orthodox Irish Republicans had made peace with the enemy by accepting partition of the country and external ties to the British Commonwealth. Before long the Irish had him in their own jails.

We learn in *Brendan Behan's Island* that a not unfamiliar sound in his Irish prison cell was the execution of Irish revolutionaries by Irish executioners. Critics who laud *The Quare Fellow* as Brendan's greatest play are usually struck by the simplicity and power of his indictment of the sacrosanct and nearly universal institution of the deprivation of freedom, and even life itself to transgressors of the civil code. Society, jurists and priests are silent or applaud.

Here the first agony. Brendan and people like him risked all, not merely for an independent Ireland (the last thing he could justly have been called would be anti-British) but for an Ireland whose government would be dedicated to promoting social justice. The lads and colleens who confronted him that evening at the University were by and large from privileged classes. Independence from England was an obsession to most of them, even after it had largely been attained. But for the problems of the Irish poor, they cared not at all.

It seems altogether likely to me that Brendan's point of view changed radically at just about this time. Bomb-throwings and wars have a way of destroying the innocent while the wicked flourish. Ideologies kill and their victims die in vain. Isn't that part of what he said in *The Hostage*, to my way of thinking his masterpiece? The singular achievement of this play is the creation of a wildly funny story about politics, sex, religion, bogus piety and jingoism and a most everything else, with no heroes and no villains...only an indictment of the serpent in all of us that devours the world. In short, Brendan had shifted from hidebound partisan politics, to love of all humanity and hated only those things in people that make them less true to their most charitable instincts.

*The Borstal Boy, The Hostage, The Quare Fellow, Brendan Behan's Island,* and the wonderful short essays and stories...a truly distinguished and original body of work in those short years he was at it. Brendan had arrived professionally, and therein, I believe, lay the seeds of his personal destruction. For he had lost the very thing he prized most in life...an authentic connection with the working people of Dublin or wherever else he lived. Brendan was now 'Brendan Behan the Celebrity' in working-class bars and he was never to recapture the feeling of solidarity and identity that was essential to his having a real hold on this earth. In short, Brendan's affluence and success and fame had separated him from the only society he really cherished. And, the other side of the coin, he was subjected on all sides to the adulation of people he loathed. Eventually he would have had enough and one of his well publicised explosions would occur.

Alas, he was also 'Brendan Behan the Celebrity' among the sycophants and imbeciles of Madison Avenue, television alley and café society. People who never read a line he wrote or saw one of his plays surrounded him in posh watering-places and boasted for weeks afterwards about the night they met Brendan Behan, the spectacular drunk and dispenser of vitriol. Most of his barbs went over the heads of this type of audience, but no matter, no matter, they had had a drink with Brendan Behan.

I cannot easily describe Brendan's extraordinary magnetism, drunk or sober. When he first arrived in New York for rehearsals of the Broadway production of *The Hostage* he had been off the sauce for quite a while and was nicely and consistently *compos mentis.*[1] Typically, he agreed to be a drawing card for a backers' party in connection with a disastrous theatrical venture in which I was involved. My living room was full of Maureen Stapleton, Lauren Bacall, the Clancy Brothers, Skitch Henderson, Paul O'Dwyer and people with chequebooks and fountain pens. Yet all sat in rows on the floor and gazed upward at Brendan as he sang hilarious and obscene parodies of the most gauche, commonplace Irish ballads. In short, we were in the presence of an authentic star, whose act was a single and impossible to follow.

The months went by and Brendan went back to the bottle, back to Ireland and England and then showed up suddenly and without warning in New York. I saw nothing of him until a few weeks before he left America forever. He had given up smart bars completely and wandered from saloon to saloon in a fairly regular pattern. Occasionally someone from television would go down to the Chelsea Hotel, where he and Beatrice lived, and drag him off to a panel show or something intended to be a serious discussion: theatricals that were distinguished by some of the frankest remarks ever offered to an audience of millions. At that time I was executive director of the New York Council for a SANE nuclear policy and imposed upon him to be star for one of the cause's fund-raising parties. Brendan was almost comatose that afternoon in Great Neck, I heard. (The effort to get him into the car the committee had provided was too much for me; I stayed behind in Chelsea.)

Yes, Brendan was really and truly lost. Our rounds roughly corresponded at that time, and I observed that Brendan never failed to attempt establishing common ground with people whose childhoods may have resembled his own but who were now light-miles away from his experience in this world. One really dangerous bar was off-limits, at least Beatrice tried to enforce this interdict. (It has since been shuttered by the police.) On one of the few occasions when Brendan had a significant amount of hard cash on his person, a youth who volunteered to see him back to his hotel from this bar (a service he desperately required at that moment) relieved him of his money.

Yet a few days later, not being able to find Brendan in any of his usual haunts, at Beatrice's request I looked into the very cesspool mentioned above. Brendan was there and said he was looking for the thief. I asked him why, since I was certain that nothing on God's good earth could induce him to report the miscreant to the police. Ah, the truth is that pimps and whores, pickpockets and hopheads were a more congenial crowd for Brendan to hang out with and really more honourable in his view than the vulgarly successful people of this world who make money on everyone they meet and imagine they are storing up riches for themselves in Heaven at the same time. Unlike the mob at the Silver Rail, middle-class bandits might not even buy their victims a drink.

Now, I do not mean to convey the impression that Brendan was merely an ordinary proletarian snob; although his class feelings seemed to be among the most ardent I have ever encountered outside of the alumni of the activist Union Square days.

A vivid and, I believe, significant memory of mine is sitting in a bar with him and Beatrice watching a television discussion that had been filmed the day before. Brendan was drunk and eloquent on the telly and drunk and a little self-satisfied at our table. We were watching him discuss (if that is the proper word) something with Cecil Woodham-Smith, authoress of *The Great Hunger*, the definitive account of Ireland's cataclysmic national disaster, the famine of the middle nineteenth century. Miss Smith's book is one of genius, of originality; an absolutely unique explanation of how and why a group of enlightened and middlingly-moral statesmen sent troops to Ireland to seize its produce, shipped it out of the country, and then left the Irish to die of starvation. It is also a book of extraordinary and deeply-felt compassion.

The authoress is unmistakably an aristocrat, a lady and an Englishwoman. Brendan treated her with something like adoration; one might almost say that he was overcome with emotions of gratitude, respect and empathy. The other panellist on this telecast (I forgot what the subject was supposed to be) was an art critic on a New York daily with an excruciatingly affected, tony Irish accent; a sonorous Gaelic name, a sleek, cared-for and burnished appearance, the end-product, I suspect, of a desperate attempt to destroy all evidence of origins discernibily less exalted than lineal descendance from the High Kings of Ireland. It soon became eminently clear that this young philistine had never perceived a connection between the artist's vocation and a ready recognition of, and preoccupation with, all human suffering. Brendan gave him hell! Glory be – even on television, fools are sometimes called down.

Brendan had not fallen from grace according to the credo of his ancestors and his childhood. For it is a tradition among the common people of Ireland that the wealthy are wicked, and poverty, weakness and failure are respected if not always assiduously sought: a pristine Christianity that advanced, industrialised societies have forgotten. Incredible as it may seem, I don't think Brendan ever divined that Americans believe the best Christians are those who go to church incessantly and write the largest cheques for the church building fund.

Bars, bars...they necessarily loom very large in any account of Brendan Behan. For many years, one of my early morning retreats has been the famous spa of the late Timothy Costello (May He Rest in Peace) on Third Avenue near 44th Street. Its chief bartender, Honest John Gallagher, used to preside over the morning ceremonials. Large dinner rolls and butter, coffee and cognac, to get the lousy day started. Now it happens that John has a friend who is a house-painter, who lives in his neighbourhood and frequently drives him to the restaurant in the morning. My most poignant memory of Brendan is seeing him stand outside of Costello's after a bad night waiting for the doors to open. Brendan had also been a house-painter in his youth and was proud of his trade. He and John's house-painter friend repaired to a booth and traded opinions on the techniques of plastering and mixing, and swapped stories of housewives they had dallied with while the first coat was drying on the walls. One had to do something before picking up the brushes again.

It was the closest he got to the not-so-bad old days.

Time passed and then one sunny, menacing morning early in the summer of 1963 I chanced to meet Brendan at the bar of Mr Richard Foran, publican of West 23rd Street, in old Chelsea. Our host, a splendid figure of a man, whose physique serves him well and often in his trade, is rarely given to sentimental display, yet he was mewing earnestly and movingly at a mother cat and her brood and clearly resented our presence, a mere ten minutes after official curtain time.

Foran's is a marred relic of Chelsea's Irish ascendancy. A retreat for elderly regular Democratic precinct workers, to be sure, but also frequented by a rather dangerous looking young crowd and many persons of all ages whose pure Hibernian ancestry is a matter of rather serious doubt. It strongly resembles many working-class bars in marginal areas of the city where Brendan seemed to be relatively less displaced. A great deal of its charm to me, and, I suspect, to Brendan then, is the ease and frankness with which simple people offer their opinions, no matter how outrageous they may be. As when an elderly Irsih lady, trembling mightily and scarcely able to raise her glass to her lips, explained the defeat of the old-line machine Democrats in a primary election. 'All those Communists who moved into the new union co-operative voted for their Red friends.' Not at all a bad analysis of the suicidal war among Democrats, Regular and Reform, if the addled terms are translated properly.

At any rate, there we were at the bar, and Brendan ordered a gin for himself and after a few caustic and obscene remarks agreed that I might shamefully dissipate my patrimony and limit myself to a glass of beer. I had decided to make a mild start that morning.

These were bad days for himself and he looked it. His eyes were clouded and troubled and gazed upon objects surely not of his immediate surroundings and perhaps not of this world. The contours of his tattered shirt were those of an ancient washboard and uncombed, matted curls dangled perilously close to his collar. He weaved in and out of express city traffic with a panache that must have reduced the life span of untold numbers of motorists and he even survived the malevolent advances of hoods in some of New York's worst dives. Not always unscathed, it is true, but at least ambulant and with vital organs intact. But Brendan did not lack purpose and direction. He was a man on the way to the loving arms of Jesus and he wooed death passionately.

That is, more or less, what I would like to talk about in this piece.

Back to Foran's. I tore myself away from the pussycats and the beer and Brendan and a newly-arrived crone who was pounding the juke box with her fists, and later her pocketbook, beside herself with rage and frustration. At a difficult and alcoholic moment in her life, the lady evidently believed the pay phonograph to be a conventional instrument that ought to respond to her assaults as might a piano or possibly a bass drum. A powerful kick in what would have been a most sensitive area had the instrument been animate, and the air was suddenly and piercingly aquiver with 'Sure they scorn us just for bein' what we are'. Like all true artists, she had found a unique method of expression. The proprietor's indifference remains unexplained.

In any case, it was certainly time for me to leave. Brendan's wife, Beatrice, had invited me to join them to a farewell drink on the Queen Mary that afternoon. They were returning to Ireland.

Brendan was a different man by four that afternoon. He held court for the press and the Cunard Line public relations people in a restrained, one might almost say, suave manner. The *Daily News* photographers succeeded in extracting a conventional *bon voyage* pose from him, with a broad smile and one arm around Beatrice and another around his general factotum, Rae Jeffs. A passing priest accepted a drink but good-naturedly declined to bless a tray of cocktails. Brendan allowed as he would do it himself but he was a little shaky on the Latin. His hair was cut and combed and a presentable suit had replaced the morning's outrageous costume. There was even something like a cultivated, cared-for sheen about his complexion. Only the astonishing void where his teeth should have been reminded one that he had not taken the shilling nor slid down the shoot onto the Madison Avenue dung-heap.

This all seemed a bad omen to me and as it turned out, it was the last time I saw Brendan. It was also the last time Brendan saw one of his great loves, New York.

## NOTES

Sean Callery has written for the *Washington Post, Saturday Review*, and various publications in England and Ireland.
  1. Sound of mind; in his right mind.


# Brendan – the Human Behan*

## MICHAEL O'REILLY

The ragged youngster made his way slowly through the narrow back streets of pre-war Dublin, stopping from time to time to pick up a piece of discarded newspaper. He would sit on the steps of the nearest tenement and carefully read every word, sometimes repeating phrases aloud, and then continue on his way – until he saw another piece of reading material.

Errands took a long time and there was often trouble at home, but the young lad had one consoling thought. He says now, 'I always knew that some day I would be a famous writer.' Today he is perhaps the most famous, certainly the most controversial and the most colourful, of living Irish writers.

But for Brendan Behan this has not brought happiness. The once-ragged youngster is now a man in what should be the prime of life but, instead, is a period of disillusionment and sadness. As he gazes moodily across a

* *Irish Digest* (Dublin), LXXVII, no. 3 (May 1963) 15–18.

crowded room, a man alone, he will tell you, 'Success is failure disguised as money. The only thing worth having in life is good friends.' He has made headlines in Europe, America, even Australia, but what really makes him tick is still undiscovered.

His true nature is perhaps best illustrated by a recent incident in the lounge of a fashionable pub near the Dublin Horse Show grounds at Ballsbridge.

In came a young nurse, very nervous but determined to sell flags for needy children. Behan, trying hard to be unobserved, scooped all his change from the counter – quite a sizable amount in silver and coppers – and put it into the flag box, then turned quickly away.

Thinking again, he turned to ask the nurse, 'What is the oldest child you take into your home?' And when she replied, 'About twelve years of age', he sighed loudly and exclaimed, 'That lets me out.'

Behan has had no lack of success. His plays *The Quare Fellow* and *The Hostage* have big box-office takings in London, Paris and New York. The French have voted him the best playwright of the year. His book *Borstal Boy* despite, or because of, its Lady Chatterley-like language, was an instant winner and he can get cheques of $1500 for short articles in the American glossies.

All this, and life in a quiet terraced house in Dublin's highly respectable Ballsbridge district with a wife he dotes on and a pet cat he adores too, might seem adequate ingredients for happiness. But it has proved elusive. Perhaps it is because he has no child of his own[1] or, more basically, an apparent loss of faith.

'My one ambition', he says, 'is to live as long as I can.'

It could be this ambition that has tamed down, to some extent, the desire for wild life and reckless living that threatened to cut his life short a couple of years ago. There are those who say he is finished, that he will never write anything successful again. To that his answer is, 'Why should I finish *Richard's Cork Leg*, the play I have been working on for years now? The income-tax man would take the lot. I write when I am skint, flat broke.

'Television? I've never bothered to write for it because it's too small, not a good stage. The rubbish they have on it now, it's no wonder they call it the "idiot box".'

Behan is a man of many principles, and he will suffer for them if need be. In the days of his youth he carried a suitcase full of explosives through London for the IRA because he thought it the only way to get the British out of Ireland and do away with the Border. He went to Borstal for his trouble but, as things turned out, perhaps that was luck. *Borstal Boy* was the result of that escapade.

When there was a barmen's strike in Dublin and pickets were placed outside all the pubs – 'Nor if I was to die of thirst would I pass a union picket', he declared. This kind of idealism was clearly inherited. His father, Stephen, is still an active trade-union official although nearly eighty.[2]

Mr Stephen Behan likes to refer to himself as 'a breeder of genius', referring not only to Brendan but writer Dominic. 'I write more fiction than either of my sons,' he says, 'and it's good stuff, too. Otherwise, how could my timesheet have fooled the boss every week for years?'

His father's 'no surrender' trade unionism has left its mark on Brendan, who worked on the building sites of Dublin and London as a young man, writing in his spare time. The influence of his uncle, Peadar Kearney, writer of 'The Soldier's Song', the Irish National Anthem, is also evident – for Brendan is still a rebel and a patriot.

On the closing of Dublin's 3400-seat Theatre Royal, the last of Europe's big cine-variety houses, he becomes angry: 'A city without a theatre is like a man without eyes. Soon we will have nothing worthwhile left except new office blocks in the city centre. At least they are at long last building a new Abbey Theatre,[3] but a new building will not make any difference. It's new directors they want. The players are as good as ever, as good as even the famous Abbey Players in the days of Barry Fitzgerald and F. J. McCormick, but the directors will not accept, nor encourage, the right type of plays.

'The critics here must share the blame. They are too provincial and do not learn their trade properly. Perhaps that's why my plays have been more successful abroad than in Dublin, although the people like them here and that's all that matters to me.'

There have been the bad moments, of course. Once he was seriously ill in Canada, away from friends. But a telegram arrived from Tennessee Williams wishing him well, and this did more to restore his spirits than any medical treatment.

Williams and Behan are great admirers of each other's work. Not surprisingly, however, Behan's favourite is Sean O'Casey, who came from, and writes about, much the same Dublin background.

'To praise O'Casey is like praising Niagara Falls. There are no words to describe it', he says. O'Casey captures the humour of tragic times in Ireland, but Behan tries for more depth of human feeling. His plays, like O'Casey's, are based on the times he knows well – times of poverty, rebels in prison: ready wit amid suffering, drinking and sometimes vulgarity.

Success has not spoiled Behan. He is still friendly, talking with a pleasant Dublin accent to those who locate him in a favourite rendezvous. He still has simple tastes, a plate of corned beef, cabbage and potatoes being preferred to the French dishes of the top Dublin hotels.

Behan's winning play *The Hostage* has been bought by film-maker Ray Stark for £10,000. Americans coming to Ireland now want to kiss the Blarney Stone, see Killarney and meet Brendan Behan. But he takes no notice of this notoriety except to have his telephone number removed from the directory. A famous artist[4] did a bust of his head but he cannot locate it.[5] He does not bother keeping photographs or cuttings, although his wife has been writing her own story of *My Life with Brendan Behan*.

## NOTES

1. A girl, Blanaid, was born to the Behans on 24 November 1963, only four months before Behan died.
2. Stephen Behan died in 1967.
3. The new Abbey Theatre was opened in 1966.
4. Desmond MacNamara. See his recollections of Behan, p. 323.
5. See a picture of this bust in Seamus de Burca, *Brendan Behan: A Memoir* (Newark, Del.: Proscenium Press, 1971).

# Brendan Behan*

## OWEN QUINN

Brendan Behan was anything but everybody's darling at that time, about eight, or even less, years ago. Some were against him because he tried to shoot a policeman. Others perhaps did not think much of him because he had missed. In any case nobody was ever short of a public excuse for being down on him. At one end there was his socialism vying in fanaticism with his republicanism, and at the other his occasional admiration for the English, though to judge from what he had to say to me on the subject, it was not the English people he was talking about, but some of their past rulers. Touching Brendan more personally, there was an accusation that he had treated Patrick Kavanagh, the poet, in a manner too boorish to be ever forgiven. It was said Behan told Kavanagh he was a failure – told him to his face in McDaid's pub. 'Poor Kavanagh's spirit will break!' they cried. 'Is Behan trying to dry him up or what?' Brendan was in to see me in *Envoy* office the following morning. He, too, had a conscience, with qualms at that. His point that morning was that, if Kavanagh was as great as his professed admirers claimed, a few words could not diminish his talent, much less demolish it. I gave Brendan no sign of being on anybody's side as he worried and jerked himself about the office, though I have since found it exciting to consider why two writers touched now and then with genius should be at odds with each other. God knows there was enough militant mediocrity to tilt at in Dublin in those days. But, going further, may it not be that Brendan was resented by that crowd as an outsider, in that the size of his talent made him an awkward Gulliver among even the most distinguished Lilliputians? Behan, like Kavanagh, is a minister of the

* A manuscript written before Behan's death; in the possession of Mrs Beatrice Behan. This is the first appearance in print.

genius of ordinary people. He has tapped their spirit and everyday mystery, while those enemies of his sought to quaff superior notions which really gave them nothing but big empty heads the morning after, every morning. It was too much to expect them to look up to Brendan, who would probably claim that genius and the common man are standing hand in hand in some arcane way all around the world. More simply again, perhaps it was that he was just highly provocative. Any, some or all of this would make it understandable why he had such militant enemies. Whatever the reason, the animosity towards him was so extraordinarily fierce as to tease a man's wonder for ever afterwards. At the time, it led me to take an extra interest in him, and I am now in a position to record that, when Brendan was poor and worse than neglected, I used to provide him on and off with writing paper, and the 'makings', as he called them – tobacco and Rizlas for rolling smokes. He was often dressed on such occasions in working overalls, splashed with paint, as if his workmates had celebrated his marriage to Literature by showering him with spots of paint instead of confetti. Having once obtained the paper – for writing, not the Rizlas – he would rush away as if driven by all the muses of Heaven towards consummating his acquisition by getting something down on it in writing.

All that was before I had read a word of Behan's writing. Then, one morning in the magazine office, I found lying on a shelf a manuscript, dusty and cast in a bottom corner, which was later to grow into *Borstal Boy*. Spots of magic in it held me. Here was somebody in the hunt. From that morning on, I looked on Behan as a potential winner with a chance of achieving greatness perhaps in the future. Whenever our paths crossed, I would call across to Brendan – in a pub, usually, or a café – 'Don't forget *Borstal Boy*.' In the end, though he never complained, I think this habit of mine made him raging, as if I had become his literary conscience nagging him to go home and do some writing. When a short poem by him appeared in *Envoy* I made sure to tell him I thought it uncommonly moving. He was very hard on himself, however: he said it was a crib, a bit of a translation of an Irish poem he had come across. I remarked, 'That doesn't matter.' What I meant, I suppose, was that it took taste to crib such touching lines, and what I meant even more was to encourage him.

Tough was Brendan's other name at that time. When he found himself without a place to sleep, he would, it was said, wreck a pub, so as to get himself arrested and lodged in Store Street Police Station for the night. This toughness of his was subject of the very first conversation I ever had with Brendan, if I may go back to that. 'Synthetic toughness' was his expression for it – a front, similar to the haughty manner adopted by some people to keep a hurtful world at bay. However that may be, it is perhaps worth mentioning what Behan, a man who has been in battle with bullet and broken bottle, thinks of the more notorious side of his own character. Certainly, his prison life in England alone might have thrust hardiness on him, for, he once told me, non-political prisoners used to assault him in the exercise yard in order to ingratiate themselves with the prison warders. About his time in Irish prisons, the only thing Brendan ever told me was that the warders used to make complaints in these words: 'Behan, you're too dogmatic!'

A common concern at the sight of social justice being impeded put Behan and me on the same side. We were never short of symptoms even in the freshness and inspiration of Ireland. Police spies at every corner; inferior people in high places; naturally superior persons in low places; decent people living in ditches with an old sack for a roof; equality of opportunity in the education system: all the signs were there in such abundance that no ancient Turk would ever stand for it, though it might do Brendan and others some good to consider whether the attainment of independence was in itself such a giant move towards a more just social order that politicians may be forgiven for resting on their predecessors' oars. Still, in Ireland today, despite the clergy's crusade for more justice, merit is compelled to yield to money to an extent probably not paralleled anywhere else in the civilised world. In brief, Brendan and I were agreed that one of the massive trends of history – the advance towards social justice – needed a helping hand in Ireland. We ought to have been natural allies, but while we diagnosed the same disease we prescribed entirely different medicines. It is enough for me that Aquinas declares that laws which cause injustice are not laws at all, but rather a species of violence. On top of that, recent Popes in their encyclicals provide enough radicalism for anybody. Brendan, I understand, still believes in straight socialism.

People I have some respect for wish to persuade me to denounce Behan and his ways. 'Did you hear what he did on television?' or 'Did you hear the Métro, the Paris Underground, nearly had to shut down over Behan?' Usually it is something worse. My reaction is to temporise, hum and haw, and end by saying Behan has some talent, and that that is a lot to be going on with. I could add that not every young angry literary person is an impostor; and that Behan's career so far, despite its unfortunate side, amounts to a victory over weighty odds.

NOTE

Owen Quinn, Irish dramatist.

# The Fear of Dying*

## BEATRICE BEHAN

The fear of dying began to preoccupy him. I heard him ask George Kleinsinger,[1] 'George, do you believe in a life after death?'

And George answered, 'I don't know, Brendan. Just enjoy life while you can.'

I wondered whether Brendan was seeking reassurance from George, not just about an afterlife, but about himself as a writer, for there were times when he would ask, 'Do you think I'm fooling everybody, George? Do you think I'm just a fake?'

'You're a natural, Brendan', George would say, 'Maybe you're not blessed with a literary style, but what you give is spontaneous and comes from the heart.'

'George, you're kidding.'

George wasn't argumentative. He would just say, 'If you think so, Brendan. How can I know your innermost thoughts?'

I began to be fascinated by this strange hotel, to be drawn, as Brendan was, to George's bizarre apartment. Even Brendan felt sorry for the mynah bird when it dirtied George's music sheets and had to be confined to its cage, and for the tropical fish which some foolish friends of George's poisoned with the wrong food.

The Chelsea was an unusual literary enclosure. One assumed that James Baldwin and Arthur Miller and Arthur Clarke were preoccupied somewhere in the hotel with their writing, yet at the same time I suppose I shouldn't have been surprised when a girl in the hotel propositioned me, an encounter which alarmed me but amused Brendan, or that George, a kind person, should have befriended a homeless Jamaican girl, abandoned by her boyfriend, until she had her baby, or even that Rae[2] should offer to become the baby's godmother.

When Brendan's seizures began again there were days when he was so ill he could not leave his bed nor eat the food I cooked for him. These attacks of epileptiform occurred only when he was withdrawing from alcohol, usually after a bender. And yet, for my sake and his own, he was hoping to cure his thirst forever. He had sought out Perry Bruskin on his return to New York to ask, 'Where's Alter?' But Alter Weiss, the man he had

---

* *My Life with Brendan* (London: Leslie Frewin, 1973) pp. 220–6. Editor's title.

come to regard as his possible saviour, was dead. Brendan's last hope seemed to have gone.

One Sunday morning he sent Rae and me in search of a book on how to stay sober which he had seen advertised. We couldn't find the book in any shop in the Village. When we got back to the Chelsea Brendan was lying on the floor, the bedclothes from our spare bed around him.

I knew at once he had suffered another attack and had fallen, pulling the clothes from the bed with him in his struggle. I asked Rae to call a doctor.

A Dr Max Tasler, who had been contacted through a friend of Rae's, arrived and gave Brendan a sedative. He told me he thought Brendan would be all right. But he had no sooner left the apartment than Brendan took another seizure.

I rushed out of the room and down the corridor, calling to the doctor to come back. Brendan was screaming, his body twisting grotesquely on the bed. I held him down on one side, Dr Tasler on the other, until he lay quiet.

'He can't be left here', the doctor told me. 'I'll have to call an ambulance.'

They took Brendan to the University Hospital, not far from the Chelsea. Rae and I took a taxi there early the next morning. We asked George if he would come with us.

'Gosh,' said George, 'I'm a bit of a coward, you know. But I'll think it over.'

We were waiting in the lobby of the hosptial when George arrived. 'I'm glad you've come', I told him.

Brendan was in a semi-private ward with three other patients, but he refused to stay in his bed. Just as in Dublin and London, he had tried to walk out wearing his pyjamas, but the staff restrained him. We found him shouting for a drink.

He had discarded the trousers of the hospital's regulation purple pyjamas and was trotting around the corridors with his lower half naked. George tried to persuade him to return to his bed.

'They won't let me read', Brendan complained. 'They won't give me a fucking drink. And the bastard in the next bed won't stop snoring.'

'Brendan,' George pleaded, 'you can't walk around the hospital with no pants on.'

'This is no hospital. This is the fucking "Gorman".'

I knew he was talking about Grangegorman, an old-established mental hospital in Dublin.

'Don't be silly, Brendan,' I told him. 'It's not the "Gorman".'

'Oh, Jesus, Beatrice,' he cried, turning on me, 'you've committed me.'

I kept assuring him he was not in the 'Gorman'. I looked despairingly at Rae and asked her to call Dr Tasler to come and help.

Brendan had started ringing for the elevator, which didn't arrive because he was pressing the 'up' instead of the 'down' button. George had grabbed another patient in the corridor and entreated him to tell Brendan he was not in a psychiatric unit.

'Sure you're not', said the patient to Brendan. 'This ain't no nuthouse. It's just a hospital, Mister, and I'm just a patient like you.'

'It's a fucking puzzle factory', wept Brendan.

Max Tasler arrived. Although he endeavoured to convince Brendan that the University was a general hospital he was no more successful than the rest of us had been.

'Look, Brendan,' he said, 'we'll give you a nice quiet room to yourself where you can read, and there'll be no other patients to disturb you.'

He took us in the elevator to an upper floor and showed us a room with a splendid view of New York City. Brendan said he would stay if Dr Tasler got him a drink.

'Okay,' agreed Tasler, 'I'll get you a beer.'

Brendan changed course again. 'I don't want your fucking beer. I just want out of here.'

He was beyond persuasion. Max Tasler just shrugged his shoulders and told one of the staff to fetch Mr Behan's clothes.

When Brendan had dressed we went down in the elevator with him. It was crowded and suddenly Brendan glimpsed, behind the passengers, a patient lying on a stretcher. He screamed at the attendant to stop the elevator. We scrambled out at the cafeteria floor.

Brendan, followed by George, went looking for a drink, but only soft drinks were served in the cafeteria.

'Give him anything', whispered George to the woman behind the counter.

She was about to pour an apple juice when Brendan caught sight of a waitress filling a vinegar jar from a pitcher. He grabbed the pitcher from her hand and drank the contents down.

'Jeez,' she exclaimed, 'look what he's done!'

Brendan was pulling a face. 'It's kind of bitter, George.'

Dr Tasler had followed us into the cafeteria, and I told him what had happened. 'Gosh,' he said, 'he's got a stronger stomach than I thought.'

We got Brendan into a cab and drove back to the Chelsea. But before we could escort him into the hotel he made a sharp turn left in the direction of the Oasis.

'No, Brendan!' I cried.

But there was no restraining him. He was still talking incoherently, but as soon as he had taken a shot of Napper Tandy, his term for a brandy, he came lucid and began to talk sensibly.

I knew he was starting another drinking bout. I knew I would have to put him to bed when he was hopelessly drunk. I knew that he would wake up unnaturally sober in the small hours, and that the next day would see him drinking again with the pattern repeating itself. At all costs I must get him home to Dublin.

I was worried about my pregnancy. I didn't want to stay on in New York until the baby was born. Brendan had tried to persuade me to sell our house in Dublin, which was in my name, and settle in America, but I was just as determined to return to Dublin and equally determined that he should return with me.

It hurt me to realise how heartbroken he was leaving the city of his dreams. He stayed sober during those last few days so that he would see New York as clearly as on our first visit. But I had turned my face against the city in which he had betrayed me. I had forgiven him, but my forgiveness rested on the hope that we could begin our life anew in Dublin.[3]

As we sailed out of the harbour I saw Brendan gaze longingly at the city we were leaving. I dismissed his fears that he would never see New York again.

## NOTES

For a note on Beatrice Behan see p. 68.

1. George Kleinsinger, American composer. See references to him in *Brendan Behan's New York* (London: Hutchinson, 1964).

2. Rae Jeffs. For a note on her see p. 109.

3. Behan had had an affair in New York with a girl who was infatuated with him.

# My New Role*

## BEATRICE BEHAN

Terence Chapman was the most understanding doctor I had met. He became Brendan's friend and Brendan confided his problems to him. It was pathetic to listen to him those mornings as he gripped the doctor's hand, talking in an interminable monologue, his hoarse voice coming as it were from a body already dead.

Life with him was tolerable if I avoided arguments. At night he would bring home his IRA friends and they would sit up until the small hours, talking, drinking and exchanging stories. When I was too tired to listen any longer I would go upstairs to bed.

Brendan's intervals of sobriety were few, but more disturbing was the

* *My Life with Brendan* (London: Leslie Frewin, 1973) pp. 229–37. Editor's title.

fact that many nights he stayed away from the house. Terence Chapman would tell me that Brendan used to arrive on his doorstep early in the morning, dirty and dishevelled, for an insulin injection. The maid would announce, "There's a drunk at the door, doctor.' But the children would invite him in and he became their special friend. He would ask for a drink, and invariably he would be given tea.

One morning, Suzanne, Terence's small daughter, presented him with a poem she had written:

> Flow on sweet river!
> Flow on to join the sea,
> Where fish are swimming in and out the reeds.
> Where sharks are lying amongst the weeds.
> Where many shells are found lying on the ground.
> Waiting there patiently all day, all night. . . .

And Brendan wrote to her,

Suzanne, *a chara*,[1]

I was delighted and complimented, as a writer, to receive a copy of your poem, 'The Sea'.

Your mention of the shark reminds me of Hollywood. Everyone there has a swimming-pool and you might wonder why, when they have the whole beautiful Pacific Ocean stretching along the coast for one thousand miles.

The answer is the shark, who every year kills a couple of hundred people. Here 'the sharks lying among the weeds' don't stay among their weeds, but swim straight into the beach attacking and savaging anything or any person that comes in their way.

Anyway, thanks for the poem, and if you write any more, or I should say when you write some more, don't forget a copy for

your loving Bawdy Boy,

Brendan

Brendan began to imagine that I didn't understand him as a writer. 'What you want me to be, Beatrice, is a fucking suburbanite. Into the office at nine in the morning and walk the dog along Sandymount Strand after tea.'

It wasn't true. I respected him as an artist, but I was losing hope in the struggle to stop him drinking. Whenever Terence Chapman suggested that he should enter an alcoholic home Brendan was quick to agree, but then he would invent a dozen excuses as to why he shouldn't.

I came into the front room one Sunday evening that August to find him stretched on the sofa, half dozing. The radio was on and I heard a high tenor voice singing.

> A hungry feeling came o'er me stealing
> And the mice were squealing in my prison cell,
> And that old triangle went jingle-jangle
> Along the banks of the Royal Canal.

It was unmistakably Brendan's voice. He looked at me sadly.

'Is that really me singing?'

'It's a recording of the play.'

He began to cry. Perhaps it was the emotion of nostalgia that overcame him, a memory of better days; but most likely it was the realisation of how sweet his voice had sounded then, and how broken it was now.

It was Brendan who had released my father from the institution to which I had committed him. If friends now wanted me to commit Brendan it was because he had become a pitiful object in their eyes, collapsing in public places, helped out of the roadway, dumped on my doorstep by taxi-drivers.

One morning he was taken unconscious from the house to Baggot Street Hospital. Yet when I visited him five or six hours later he had recovered sufficiently to be able to sit up in bed and talk to me.

If he was a legend in this hospital, I knew he was also a handful for the staff. The matron would tell him, 'I do wish, Mr Behan, you would wear your pyjama top.' When he wore his pyjama top he discarded his pyjama trousers.

He would talk to the other patients for hours on end, and if there were children in the hospital he would read stories to them. He so disliked formalised religion that the sight of a priest or clergyman would drive him down to the hallway. If the hospital staff asked him what he was doing wandering downstairs in his pyjamas, and sometimes out of his pyjamas, he would tell them, 'I'm running away from these fucking Druids.'

Some of the nurses were afraid of him. 'I didn't call you a whore,' he would shout at them, 'I told you to shut the door.'

In the evenings it was the custom for the nurses to recite the Rosary. The patients in the ward would take it in turns to deliver a decade. When it came to Brendan's turn all they would hear was a mumbled, 'Fuck off.'

Mortified, the nurses would stop their prayers and leave the ward.

Even in hospital Brendan played the showman. He was circumcised in Baggot Street soon after our return from New York. And, although his circumcision was one of those matters which was not mentioned afterwards, the occasion was one of hilarity for him. 'Not tonight, Josephine', he told the nurses in the operating theatre.

He was unkempt when they took him to Baggot Street, and the nurses found it difficult to get him to wash. His friend from the Fianna days, Bill

Finnegan, the barber who was now a taxi-driver, would cut his hair and shave him in the hospital.

'Do you know Brendan well?' a staff sister asked Bill one day.

'I suppose so', Bill answered. 'That's what has me here, isn't it?'

'Would you do anything for him?'

'I suppose I would.'

'Then make him take a bath.'

'I'll try', said Bill.

'If you can get him to take a bath,' said the sister, 'then I'll know you're a friend of his.'

Bill coaxed Brendan into agreeing to the bath. 'Right', said Brendan, hauling himself out of his bed. 'Fall in and we'll have a bath.'

They went down the corridor to the bathroom. Bill filled the bath and Brendan took his pyjamas off. Bill, who remembered Brendan as an athletic youth, was shocked when he saw his friend stripped. Although Brendan's stomach was swollen, his body was wasted and his shoulders and arms were painfully thin. Bill may have been shocked, but it was a sight to which I had grown accustomed, dressing and undressing Brendan. I knew that only his tough constitution had enabled him to endure the onslaught of his illness.

Bill hadn't the heart to ask Brendan to do more than stand in the bath. He soaked a sponge under the tap and squeezed the water over Brendan's body.

'We're doing great,' said Brendan. 'Like an ass under a ton of turf.'

Bill told him to step out of the bath and he dried him down. 'My goodness,' said the staff sister, when he brought Brendan back to the ward, 'you've done a great job.'

As long as he was with Bill I felt Brendan was in safe hands. Often Bill would drive him home and join us for a meal. Brendan tried to eat, but it was seldom more than a show. One night when he invited Bill home for supper I served chicken and ham to Bill and gave Brendan what remained of a duck I had roasted. Brendan toyed with the duck, then flung it across the floor.

'Why did you do that?' I asked him.

'Because it's too fucking hard to eat.'

Bill, who was always embarrassed by these scenes, told me he had enjoyed his meal.

'For Jaysus' sake,' said Brendan to him, 'never praise the food you get from anyone else. What you get in your own house is always the best.'

'Then tell that to Beatrice', said Bill.

'Is there more roast duck?' Brendan asked me.

'No,' I told him, 'but there's some bacon.'

'Why is there no roast duck?'

'Because your friends have been here and eaten it.'

'Why didn't you give them the fucking bacon and keep the duck for me?'

He was hard to please. He would fling the crockery across the room as quickly as the food. When I bought plastic beakers to avoid somebody being injured by broken glass he complained. He made a point of insulting me whenever guests were present. He would talk about my father and tell them he had been a 'croppy hunter'. And then, when he had made as many abusive remarks as he could think of, he would cry.

Between his drinking bouts and his spells in hospital he managed to keep faith with Rae[2] and the taping of his New York book.[3] 'Are you sure you can go on, Brendan?' Rae would ask him in our front room in the mornings.

He would nod his head. 'If you want me to.'

I knew he liked Rae and didn't want to disappoint her. By November the book was almost ready and with this progress I noticed a lifting of his spirits as though, in spite of himself, he had achieved what he believed was beyond his reach.

Rae was a comfort to me in these, my last days of pregnancy. Brendan's periods in hospital during these months would have depressed me even more had it not been for Rae's encouragement and the fact that I was looking forward so intensely to the birth of my child.

I was filled with a wonderful expectancy. In the evenings I would sometimes visit my mother and talk to her about my hopes for the baby soon to be born. And Brendan, in his sober moments, which had been few indeed in the months past, shared these hopes.

One Saturday evening, very close to the baby's birth, Celia,[4] Rae and I went into town to a cinema to see *Days of Wine and Roses*. It wasn't the most appropriate film; it was the story of an alcoholic whose wife also became an alcoholic. Halfway through the film the screening was interrupted by an announcement that President Kennedy had been assassinated. I remembered advising Brendan not to accept the invitation to Kennedy's Presidential inauguration in Washington. He still kept that invitation on the mantelpiece and we would show it to visitors. My reasons for discouraging him then had been to protect him from the rigours of another American visit.

The assassination cast a shadow on our evening. As we drank in a pub in Baggot Street later, Rae remarked, 'You seem uneasy, Beatrice.'

We arrived home before Brendan. He came in later, quite drunk, and rambled on about John Kennedy. He was shaken by the news of the assassination, but it had given him another excuse to drink. He had brought his old friends, Charlie Joe Gorman and Paddy Kelly, with him, and when he found there wasn't enough to drink he was furious. He had ordered supplies from a local pub, but when there had been nobody at home to accept them the publican's boy delivered them next door. The neighbours sent them back promptly to the pub.

Thank God, declared Brendan, he had shown enough presence of mind to return home with two dozen Guinness.

We sat around talking in the living room, Brendan and his friends, Celia and her friend Seamus, Rae, Petronella[5] and I. They were concerned about me because I told them I thought my baby was almost due, but I assured them that first babies weren't usually born in taxi-cabs.

During the long night Brendan would ask me, 'Are you all right, Beatrice?' In the small hours of the morning he remarked, 'There's one bottle of stout left. You'd better have it.'

It was a gesture on his part. For Brendan to decide that somebody needed a drink more than he did was unheard of.

He had fallen asleep by the time Rae had begun to time my contractions. The others were anxious to get me to the hospital. 'I'm in no hurry', I told them.

Rae made cups of tea and cut sandwiches for everybody. Towards five in the morning my contractions were more frequent. Celia said, 'You'd better get ready to leave, Beatsy.' Somebody woke Brendan. I asked him where he would stay while I was in the Rotunda, for I knew his fear of being alone at night.

'I'll stay down the road in the International Hotel.'

'Fair enough', I told him. 'But I know you won't.'

'I've already booked a room.'

I guessed he would spend his nights in the homes of his old IRA friends or in the taxi-cabs on the rank beside the hotel.

We plied into Seamus's car and he drove us to the Rotunda. Rae, Seamus and Celia stayed with me in the hospital until daybreak. A few hours later I remember being wheeled into the delivery room and a doctor remarking, 'You'd better have a shot, Mrs Behan.' I told him no, but he insisted.

I remember waking up and bursting into tears as a nurse placed a tiny pink bundle in my arms. Through my sobs I asked her, 'Is it a boy or a girl?'

'It's a girl, Mrs Behan.'

Our first child had been born on 24 November 1963.

Later that morning Brendan arrived. He had been in the Black Lion pub in Inchichore, next door to Bill Finnegan's house, telephoning the hospital continually. He bought drinks for the customers before he left.

His first words to me were, 'Well, Beatrice, how are you getting on?'

He peered at the baby. 'She's very nice', he remarked. 'But isn't she very small?' Suddenly he took her in his arms. 'She's a real little Miss Mouse', he declared.

Before he left, he promised, 'I'll be back again and I'll bring you a few bottles.'

He came back later, wearing a clean white shirt and a dark tie which he had borrowed from Bill Finnegan. He had washed and shaved and his hair was neatly combed. He took another look at the baby and asked, 'What are we going to call her?'

I suggested Christina, after his grandmother.

'No', he told me. 'I don't like that name at all.'

We went through other names, and then I suggested Blanaid, after Granny Me.

And Blanaid it was.

I spent ten days in the Rotunda and every day Brendan came to visit me, smuggling in bottles of Guinness on every visit. I found my room so comfortable after the turmoil of Anglesea Road and I was so unaccustomed to attention that I asked the doctor, 'Do you think I could stay on for another few days?'

'My goodness, no, Mrs Behan. We've got to get you up and out of here. We need your bed.'

Before I left the hospital, Blanaid's christening was held in Westland Row church, where both Brendan and I had been christened. Brendan, I was told, arrived when the ceremony was almost over. I don't think he intended to be late, but when Bill Finnegan drove him to the church and he saw the television crews waiting outside he sent Bill to tell the others he was on his way, while he loitered beside the taxi and made every excuse to avoid appearing before the cameras.

When the christening party arrived at the Rotunda and the champagne bottles were uncorked the hospital admitted television cameras for the first time.

Brendan really began celebrating at a dinner party which followed at the Dolphin Hotel. Bill's wife, Maureen, who was sitting facing the glass door of the restaurant, looked up to see Brendan walk past without his trousers. Bill rushed out to find Brendan swearing at the embarrassed staff in the hotel foyer.

'What's wrong?' Bill asked him.

'No jacks paper', Brendan complained. He was shouting for the manager, brushing aside porters and receptionists who tried to placate him.

Bill led Brendan back to the gentlemen's toilets. On the floor lay Brendan's overcoat, among the scattered banknotes which had fallen from his pockets.

When I returned home with Blanaid I was ready to face reality. It would be rough, I knew. Not that Brendan spent much time at home. I had made an arrangement that Terence Chapman would call to the house in the mornings to give Brendan his injection, but this was haphazard because some nights Brendan would not come home.

If I had to look after Brendan and our child at the same time I decided that Blanaid must come first. Brendan was now the second person in my life.

This was my moment now. I had shared Brendan's successes in the theatres of the world. I had been happy to stand by on so many occasions and say to myself, 'This is Brendan's night.' Now I knew that for a woman the first cry of her own baby is more unforgettable than the applause of a dozen first nights in the theatre.

I wondered if Brendan would understand my new role.

### NOTES

For a note on Beatrice Behan see p. 68.

  1. Gaelic for 'friend'.

  2. Rae Jeffs. For a note on her see p. 109.

  3. *Brendan Behan's New York* (London: Hutchinson; New York: Bernard Geis, 1964).

  4. Celia Salked, Beatrice Behan's sister. She created the part of Teresa in *The Hostage*.

  5. Petronella O'Flanagan, Irish journalist.

# A Portrait of Brendan Behan Drinking Life's Last Bitter Dregs*

## MAX CAULFIELD

I had come to Dublin on the most improbable of missions – ghosting an 800-word article by the celebrated Brendan Behan. My editors in London had recognised that it would take too much talking – and too much luck – to get him to write it himself, so they had assigned me to write it in his stead, choosing me, I suppose, because I am Irish (I come originally from Belfast, capital of Protestant Northern Ireland).

It had, of course, never occurred to me that once I had arrived in Dublin there might be any difficulty in just finding Behan. I experienced my first sense of disquiet during the first evening when, accompanied by a local reporter, I drove to Behan's house in Ballsbridge, a red-bricked, terraced affair with silver-painted railings. This reporter had been asked some weeks earlier to contact Behan on my behalf.

'Have you talked to him?' I asked. 'Have I talked to the bloody *Pope?*' the reporter exploded. 'And I've been up to the house five times! Not that Beatrice [Behan's wife] has been much help. Personally,' he added viciously, 'I think he's dead and she's got him buried under the floorboards.'

We got into the house only by making a terrible din on the front door, for

\* *Fact* (New York), III (Jan–Feb 1966) 19–25.

there was neither knocker nor bell. We were eventually admitted by a Mrs Rae Jeffs, sent over by Behan's publishers to help get some of his outpourings down on paper. 'You're terribly unlucky', she began. 'He just went out that door no more than five minutes ago.'

And that set the tone for the evening. Wherever we went – and we visited no fewer than a dozen pubs – we had always just missed Behan. More surprisingly, I detected from the atmosphere in many pubs that he wasn't welcomed in them. Once again one began to be aware of the deep, ancient, welling sadnesses and longings of Ireland, a country that desires an elegantly-suited, Harvard-educated young millionaire like Kennedy as its true embodiment – rather than a wild, drunken, caustic iconoclast. For a country that has possessed many more Brendan Behans than John F. Kennedys, this is perhaps an understandable, if regrettable, attitude.

Still the search had its moments. I particularly enjoyed it when we ran into one of Behan's pals at the Bailey. Oblivious to the fact that it was now 7.30, he said with composure, 'I was to meet him here at four o'clock.' He added, 'You'll find him in Neary's or McGovern's for sure – he's got the mother with him.'

At Neary's they hadn't seen him for four days, and at McGovern's they hadn't seen him since before Christmas – since before the time he had received last rites after being found lying in the Stillorgan Road.[1] At Flood's they suggested we should try Peter's, but of course Peter's didn't have him either. But they promised they would have, later that evening, 'the father and the mother'.

In the Toby Bush, the publican declared, 'God help you, I wouldn't have him in here at any price!' A man at the bar echoed, 'I wouldn't have him at all – not if you gave me all the gold of Solomon. Now Stephen, the father, *there's* a decent man for you.' 'Oh, Stephen's grand all right', agreed the publican, apparently happy to be able to say something good about at least one of the Behan family.

Armed with the knowledge that not all Dublin felt quite as warmly about its greatest living writer as might have been expected, we duly returned to Peter's to find, to our astonishment, that the promised developments had at least half-developed. It almost wrecked one's faith in Dublin's inefficiency. For there, sitting half-dozing, all by himself, breathing heavily, a battered old hat on his head, was Stephen Behan. I noted a fine teaky old face broken by an almost Roman nose. We introduced ourselves and Stephen remained dignifiedly impassive. He did indicate, however, that he had no objection to having his glass recharged.

Stephen Behan seemed a sturdy, kindly old man, but when I asked him about his famous son, he said, 'I'll have nothing more to do with him. I no longer recognise him.' (The explanation for this, as given to me later by a friend, was 'Stephen will insist on arguing with Brendan on a man-to-man basis, and then when he gets beaten and they have both lost their tempers, he'll shout, "That's no way to talk to your father!" ') 'He won't work!'

added Stephen bitterly. 'He won't stop drinking!' 'That's what I'm here to do,' I said, 'make him work. Can you tell me where he is?' Stephen waved a pudgy hand in some vague direction. 'Oh, now ...somewhere there. But I tell you, he's no son of mine.'

There seemed no point in resuming the search, particularly as we had no further clues and even more particularly as Peter's appeared to be slowly filling with Behans or their kin. The pub gradually became so full of Behans or semi-Behans that it wouldn't have surprised me to learn that Dublin was inhabited by no one else. I found them a jolly and intelligent crew, ready to talk on any subject from atomic bombs to the final destiny of the working classes and the disgustingly high price of drink these days. The light of dawn was clarifying Dublin – and it's a city that desperately needs clarifying – when I finally quit the clan, and by then I was hardly conscious...

I awoke in the steam heat of my hotel room, vaguely remembering that I had been told that if I got to Ballsbridge about midday, I'd catch Brendan sleeping it off. Since I had decided to be respectful of his talent to the utmost, I put on a St James's suit and a Christian Dior tie and padded my way downstairs to where a hired Mark III Zodiac waited at the hotel entrance. I drove to Ballsbridge, parked fifty yards from the house, and sat reading a Sunday newspaper. It was about 11.30 and I would not dare disturb Behan until midday. I had been waiting less than five minutes when a chauffeur-driven Mark II Consul drew up outside the Behan home. Knowing that Brendan usually had himself driven round the pubs in just such a vehicle, I leaped from my car and raced towards the house, arriving on the steps just as Rae Jeffs, followed by Beatrice, came down them. I literally bumped into Beatrice at the gate. 'Oh!' she said, startled, and I noticed that she'd shut the front door behind her. 'Is he in?' I demanded of her, pretty fiercely I'm afraid. 'Rattle the letter-box', she said. 'Forgive me, we're just off to Mass.'

I could hardly believe that my luck had turned as I tapped gently on the letter-box while they drove off. There was no sound from within. So I tried a slightly louder rattle. Then I tried a real bang. Aeons later I heard a long, wailing sound from somewhere inside the house, as though I had aroused a Gaelic Minotaur. I rattled the letter-box like mad and again I heard the strange howling noise. This time, however, I thought I detected an interrogatory note in it and, putting my mouth down to the mail chute, I roared my name into the long, gloomy hall. I listened to my voice echoing away ridiculously and I wondered what the devil Behan would make of it if he were in the condition I supposed him to be in.

I don't recall just how long I stood there waiting for some sort of a sequel. I was about to give up and go away when I heard a scraping sound from the far side of the door. The door suddenly came ajar and there stood Behan, and he was the most terrible sight I think I have ever witnessed. His hair was matted as a bloody Gorgon's; his chin bore at least a week's growth of stubble; his right eye was almost completely closed and full of suppurating pus; the left was wholly bloodshot. He was wearing a dirty grey shirt and nothing else: I could see white hairy legs and, when the wind caught the shirt, his genitals. He gave me a strange look and said, 'Come in.'

I followed him into the front sitting-room where he collapsed on a high-backed chair. 'Where is it?' he said. 'Where's what?' I asked, mystified. 'The whiskey, man, the whiskey!' he said impatiently. 'I haven't got any whiskey', I said. 'Didn't you say you came from Coffey's?' 'No.' 'You bawled it up the stairs.' 'I bawled my name up the stairs', I said. 'I don't even know what the hell Coffey's means.' 'Jasus Christ Almighty', said Brendan Behan, and lapsed into silence.

I began to explain my mission and he kept staring at me as though I were a drunken whelp or an adolescent dope fiend. Then he said, 'That's a right la-di-da accent you've got for a Belfastman.' 'It's talking on London 'phones that does it', I explained.

He changed the subject so rapidly that I blinked. 'Look in that thing', he said, indicating a French eighteenth-century sideboard that had its right door almost off its hinges. I searched but could find nothing more lethal than two bottles of tonic water. Behan almost raised the roof with a loud oath. 'She's always hiding the stuff. I'll skin her, declare to God!'

He collapsed back into the chair and I thought he had fainted. Suddenly he opened the pus-laden eye. Then he waved a trembling hand towards the stairs. 'Don't think I want to make a skivvy of you, but would you get me me trousers?' he asked. 'I'll do it for you,' I said, a little resentfully, 'on the understanding that if you ever find me in your condition, you'll do the same for me.' 'You can depend on it', he promised.

I climbed the stairs and entered the back bedroom. It was no lady's boudoir, need I say. Everything was crumpled and all over the place. There were signs on the sheets and mattresses of where Behan had nearly set the house on fire, and manifestations of a lack of control. I journeyed up and down the stairs three or four times to pick up an odd sock or to look for his boots.

Having transformed himself into a semblance of respectability, Behan picked up a top-coat and put it on. It was an odd-looking coat. It had been grey originally, I think, but it had now become a checkerboard of spilled egg and dried Guinness froth mingled with things that could only be guessed at. And thus, clad more truly like a down-and-out than any genuine down-and-out I have ever seen, he marched out to the street. He staggered to the car and got in, and I got in beside him and asked, 'Where to?' 'Go on until I tell you to stop', he instructed.

Conversation with Brendan Behan under ideal conditions might easily have been an enjoyable experience. Wits like Groucho Marx claim to have been his friend, but other men of sound judgement like Kenneth Allsop claim that he is 'an awful bore', a view based primarily on Allsop's recollections of a tour of London pubs when Behan's most witty performance was to stand in the public bar excreting into his trousers. Even at the best of times, his thick Dublin accent would have been an obstacle to full understanding. But now, the victim of a colossal hang-over and of the illness that would carry him off within the next month, Brendan Behan verged on the inarticulate. Most of the time he didn't say anything. He seemed to have great difficulty breathing and gave me directions with simple hand waves.

Yet even *in extremis*,[2] he could not remain entirely silent. As we drove towards Mount Street Bridge he said something which I took to mean. 'We killed fourteen English officers at that corner.' 'The Battle of Mount Street Bridge', I added flatulently, and then threw in a few more details. 'Begod, you know more about the subject than I do', he said sharply. 'I ought to', I said. 'I've just published a book about it all.'[3]

He indicated a turn, then with another wave of the hand ordered me to stop. We had drawn up outside a church. 'Is it altar wine you're after?' snarled Behan. 'Next door', he added in a croak.

I threaded the car through the milling crowd, many people stopping to gaze into the car as though into a cage at the zoo. From the way the girls giggled, it was clear that they recognised Brendan; from the way they shot away hurriedly, it was clear they feared Priapic attentions. Hurriedly I drove the car another few feet, and then, spying a narrow pub tucked in beside what might have been the parochial house, I halted. There was an agonising cry from Behan and yet another oath. 'God's curse!' he said fiercely. 'The bloody thing's closed, wouldn't you know?' He was like a man fooled by a mirage. In a while he flicked his hand and we moved on again.

I have rarely seen an individual so completely thwarted in my life. Contrary to its reputation, Dublin can actually be as dry as Scotland on a Sunday morning – or at least until such time as the churches have disposed of their last clients. We tried some half-dozen pubs or hostelries but all were firmly barred. Even the Bailey refused to admit us, despite my plea that I had 'a dying Brendan Behan outside'. (I little guessed the truth of those words.) For a while I thought Behan had been licked, but I ought to have known better. A turn of his fat little hand and he had me driving down a narrow street towards the Dolphin Hotel.

Behan began to cough fiercely as I accelerated the car. He had been coughing on and off for some time now, but I had not given his apparent agony much thought. It sounded much like the usual smoker's – drinker's noise. But suddenly up from his inside gushed a flood of black bile. I stopped the car immediately and Behan at least had the courtesy to attempt to wind down the window and deposit his load overboard – a task, I regret to say, that proved quite beyond his capabilities. I could only sit there miserably listening to the man choking, coughing, and spewing. In a quiet interval I murmured, 'Can I help you?' only to have him gasp, 'Never ask a man that. Unless you're a bloody fool.'

Conscious of my St James's suit and my Christian Dior tie (I checked anxiously to find out whether either had benefited from Behan's spasm), I gazed stonily ahead. A knot of spectators had collected some twenty yards away. I had to wait until Behan had stopped retching and coughing before I drove past those wondering stares and drew up outside the Dolphin. Behan was a filthy sight as he staggered away into its interior, bound for the gentlemen's lavatory. I handed the porter ten shillings and asked him if he could arrange to have the car cleaned for me. 'Poor Mr Behan', he said. 'And he such a fine man when he's sober.' 'He hasn't had a drink yet', I said.

The great man emerged from the lavatory some minutes later and without a word or gesture lurched toward the hotel bar. Here a small group of residents, two men and three women, were seated in a half-circle round the big open fire and conversing rather loudly. They immediately fell still when the apparition of Behan smote their eyes, and glanced distastefully at him when he shouted at the barman, 'A bottle of brandy, Jim!' 'We aren't opened yet, sir', said Jim, continuing to wipe his counter. 'Will ya give us a bottle of brandy!' snarled Behan menacingly and Jim, obviously thinking better of his refusal, jammed a bottle of three-star Hennessy on the counter. I went and brought it back and Brendan uncorked it dexterously enough and then poured out about half a tumblerful for himself. He left me to fend for myself. Then he bawled, 'And a glass of Guinness!' He drank some of the brandy, then some of the Guinness. And after that he seemed to regain a new lease on life. He gazed inquiringly at the stony group around the fire that was now ignoring both of us rather obviously. Then he shouted, 'When they put on me play in East Berlin!'

He waited to make certain he had them hooked, then launched into an incomprehensible tale of what had happened to him in that unfair city, ending up with a flood of fluent German that surprised me as much as his sudden vomit had a few minutes earlier. When he had finished, the group around the fire was entirely silent. But I could see that he had beaten them. One of the women ventured a thin smile at him. Behan, satisfied with his victory, turned and favoured me with his attention.

'What about the article?' I said. 'You don't expect me to talk business without a drink?' he said plaintively. 'You've just had one', I said. 'Let's get out of here', he said, fairly soberly. 'We can't talk until I've had a few under the belt.'

We got back into the car, which had been well cleaned by now, and once again I allowed myself to be directed by Behan on what appeared to be a down-and-out's tour of the backside of Dublin. Round and round mean, nondescript streets we drove until I finally found myself passing

St Catherine's Church in James's Street. 'Have you any idea what happened there?' asked Behan, jerking a thumb towards the church. 'I have', I said. 'That's where they hanged Robert Emmet.'[4] 'Bejasus, you're a right one', he said and I thought he was a trifle nonplussed. He fell silent again, then after a few hundred yards indicated that I should turn right. He made me halt outside yet another church and I looked round inquiringly for a pub. Behan squeezed round in his seat and eyeing me balefully asked, 'What happened there?' I turned and looked at the church, seeking vainly for a clue. Its façade was old and crusted but offered no help. Disdaining to guess I said, 'I haven't the faintest.' Behan's face split wide in a great triumphant grin. 'Well, that's where they baptised Wolfe Tone,[5] don't ye know!' 'I didn't', I said. 'You can drive on now', he said, satisfied.

I drove him up into the North Side and I ventured a remark or two about literature. 'What do you think of the other Irish writers writing now?' I inquired. 'There's no one in the place writing but meself', he said, closing the subject.

We went in and out of two or three unusually scruffy pubs – in each of which Behan insisted on drinking in the *public* rather than the saloon bar – and I detected a curious thing about the man's drinking habits. His order was always tall and impressive, but he would never finish the stuff. I didn't know what to make of it. Finally I decided that he was now merely seeking amelioration of his hang-over and not further intoxication.

'I go over to London sometimes', he said when we had climbed back into the car for the umpteenth time. 'Do you meet any writers there?' I asked. 'I met Nancy Spain and Godfrey Winn', he said. 'Why those two?' I asked, astonished. 'They're writers, aren't they?' 'Well, I suppose so', I agreed. 'But they're terrible lightweights, surely. Hardly in your class – and I say that without any intention of flattering you.' 'You needn't worry about flattering me', he said.

Making conversation with him continued to be difficult. He appeared eager to reserve what energies he could still summon for those moments when he was actually in a pub and could hold the floor in front of an audience. I was glad to note that his condition had much improved and was just congratulating myself on getting away so lightly when suddenly, as we drew up outside yet another pub, he began another agonising bout of retching and coughing, followed by severe vomiting. This time, he made no attempt to wind down the window but simply allowed his load to discharge itself all over the car's interior. I wanted to be physically sick myself, but decided that the sight of both Brendan and myself in such desperate straits would constitute a blow from which Irish letters might never recover. I took a grip on myself until Behan had entirely spent himself. Then I followed him into the filthy pub.

I had had more than enough of him by now, yet having suffered so much I was reluctant to quit without getting my story.

'What about the article?' I asked him again. 'The article!' he snarled. 'Can you think of nothing else? Haven't you time to sit and drink and behave like a human being? We'll get round to the article in plenty of time and you needn't worry.'

He cadged a cigarette from a man, lit it, took a few puffs, and then threw it to the floor. A second or so later, he cadged another cigarette, again took a few puffs, and again threw it away. Within seconds there was a pool of cigarette butts at his feet.

'I used to work for *The People*, you know', he said. 'What? For old Sam Campbell?' I said. 'Up in Belfast', he said.

As written, this seems like a brisk interchange. In fact, Behan got it all out with difficulty and only over a period of minutes. I said nothing and after a while he added, 'They fired me.' 'They must regret that now', I said. 'I had this job, you see', he said. 'They'd be running some dirty story over in London, "Confessions of a Striptease Queen" or something like that, and they'd have to change this for the Dublin edition because of the censorship. This time they were running a story about contraception in the London edition and this was all right for Belfast, but for Dublin they decided to run the life-story of the Pope. Anyhow, I got the two mixed up. I put the life-story of the Pope in the Belfast edition, which sent all the Protestants into a frenzy, and I put the contraception story into the Dublin edition. Jasus, it was fierce enough.' 'You're as well out of newspapers', I said.

It was about the last coherent attempt at amiability between us. I was absolutely sick and tired of the man by now – and of his squalid pubs. Yet I couldn't see how I could let go. Every time we got back into the filthy car and I viewed the mess he had made and the disgraceful state he himself was in, I felt I was being punished in some way and that this would save me years in purgatory. Awful pub after pub swam past my glazed consciousness, and to my dying day I shall see Behan slumped over his mugs trying to sing a drunken, maudlin song or discourse boastfully about his genius.

And yet in between his madder moments there were short gleams of rationality when a sudden softness and a sensitivity and a kindness would show themselves, and I would feel that Behan was really just 'playing the Irishman'. He must have felt it was expected of him. He might easily, I guess, have really hated it.

Once I asked him about the terrorist Irish Republican Army, now outlawed. 'They're not likely to start trouble with the English again I suppose?' I said. 'That's a bloody stupid question', he said. And implying that all Northern Irishmen were traitors, he added, 'If I knew would I be likely to tell *you*?' 'I thought you might,' I said, 'as I don't live in the country any more.' 'There's something wrong with your thinking, too', he said.

And so I drove on in silence.

Finally he told me to drive him to the home of his half-brother, Andy Furlong.[6] He had been drinking fairly steadily for several hours by this time and was, if anything, in an even worse state than when I had first picked him up that morning. But he did manage to admit as we drove along, 'You always need money. There's always the rent and the rest. So we'll do the article.' 'When can we get started?' I asked, 'Any time now', he murmured. 'Any time now...' It was all said in a slurred and drunken way, but it sounded like music to my ears.

Andy Furlong left us alone in the sitting room, facing each other in two easy chairs on either side of a big fire, while he went away and came back with two glasses of whiskey, neither of which he offered to Brendan. 'Can we get down to work now?' I said to Brendan. 'I'd like to catch the evening plane back to London.' 'You're in too much of a hurry', said Behan. 'What are you going to pay me?' 'I've been told to tell you seventy-five guineas', I said. He rose unsteadily to his feet and I saw that his brow was as black as thunder. 'I want a hundred!' he roared. 'And I want it in notes and no telling Sean Lemass [Ireland's Prime Minister].' 'I can't promise you a hundred,' I said, 'and the accountants will never pay it in cash.' 'Then tell the bloody accountants to write the article themselves', he snarled. 'I'm sorry but I can't help it,' I said, 'but I'll see what can be done when I get back to London. Anyhow, let's get the article down, eh?' 'Ring them up!' he said shortly. 'There's nobody there on a Sunday', I said. 'Ring them at home!' he demanded. 'You can believe me if you like it or not', I said, 'but I don't know their home numbers.' 'If you want the bloody article, you can bloody well ring them up', he said. I could see that he was in a genuine rage now. 'I'm sorry', I said. 'What do you take me for, a bloody fool!' he roared. He glared at me with such a fierce intensity that I recognised that he was not only drunk but really did feel insulted. For all I knew, too, he had abruptly come to realise his own inadequacy in the face of an actual invitation to get down to work. Perhaps I hadn't handled him very well but at least I had told him the truth, and I had not tried in any way to cheat him or beat him below his price. Back in London, no doubt, they would agree to pay him what he wanted, although they would never agree to pay him in cash, of course. Meanwhile, what could I do but sit there quietly and wait for him to work off his rage and then resume negotiations again?

I had expected him to sit down in his seat again. Instead, lurching violently and angrily, he vanished out the door. I sat and waited for a while – waited, indeed, even after Andy Furlong had gone searching for his errant half-brother. Then I got to my feet and walked towards the sitting-room door. Andy and his wife were just coming along the hall from the kitchen.

'I'm sorry about all this,' said Andy, 'but we'll have to put him to bed. He won't do the article for you in his present state.' 'Would he do it in any state, do you think?' I asked. 'I'm sure he would,' said Andy, 'but we'll have to put him to bed now.' 'Well, thanks anyway', I said, 'but I'm bloody well fed up.'

I drove towards the Dolphin Hotel, conscious all the way of that great, horrible mess swimming on the floor just beside me, desperately trying to pretend to myself that I didn't really care about it, that I didn't feel disgusted, that I didn't think that Behan should have known better. He had talent, the great idiot, and yet I was glad I wasn't him. And I was glad I didn't have whatever was bothering him.

And yet I was slightly puzzled, too. How was it that he wasn't already dead? Surely if anybody else had been going around behaving as Brendan Behan had for the past few years, he would never have survived as long. For despite his great drunken bouts, despite his innumerable sojourns in the hospital, and despite his obvious lack of interest in even the most rudimentary rules of health, Brendan Behan seemed as if he might go on forever.

But as the next fortnight would show, in this – as in probably much else I had decided about Brendan Behan – I would prove to be singularly lacking in judgement.

### NOTES

Max Caulfield, Irish writer.
1. See 'Brendan Behan Injured', *Irish Independent*, 30 Dec 1963, p. 1.
2. In the last extremity; at the point of death.
3. Max Caulfield, *The Easter Rebellion* (New York: Holt, 1963; London: Muller, 1964).
4. For a note on Robert Emmet see p. 68.
5. For a note on Wolfe Tone see p. 23.
6. Rory Furlong. See his recollections of Behan, p. 283.

# Funeral Oration of Brendan Behan*

## MATTI O'NEILL

In speaking these few words in response to a request by some of his old comrades, I hope I am also expressing, however inadequately, the

* Delivered at Behan's graveside, Glasnevin Cemetery, 23 March 1964. This is the first appearance in print.

sentiments of all Brendan's friends in all spheres of life whether they be writers, dramatists, poets; be they Irish, English or French. Whether they be European, American or Asiatic. Whether they hail from the North Side, or from Crumlin on the South Side. Be they from far-off Dunquin or from distant Carraroe.

Many of those legions of acquaintances would be more worthy of this honour than I, and certainly most of them would do it more eloquently. I can only plead that I am a Dubliner myself as Brendan was. That I served with him in the IRA in our formative years. That we shared the same hopes, the same struggles, the same prisons, and the same internment camps. I say this, not in any spirit of bravado, but simply because I think that it is a comrade of these days that Brendan himself would prefer to carry out this sad honour over his grave. Because I humbly submit that these were the two influences which make the name of Brendan Behan resound from radio and television all over the world at this moment. The first great influence was his native Dublin. Dublin with its literary memories of Joyce and O'Casey, both of whom lived within a stone's throw of where Brendan was born and reared. Dublin with its pity, its poverty and its slums. Dublin with its weeping and its laughter. Dublin with its proud memories of all kinds of struggles. Ninety-eight. Emmet, whose supporters hid in the cornfields not far from where Russell Street now stands. Dublin, with its memories of '48, its Fenians and Invincibles, its Martin Murphyism and its great un-christian lockout of 1913. Dublin of the Starry Plough and the Citizen Army; of the Proclamation of the Republic, and the burning GPO. The Dublin of the convening of Dáil Éireann. The Dublin of the burning of the Custom House and the Dublin of the more tragic burning of the Four Courts and the Hammond Hotel. All this had burned into Brendan's bones, and ripened in his blood from generations of Dublin ancestors who had handed it down as the fireside lore of his childhood.

The second – and, in my view, even greater – influence was what was called the new IRA of his formative years. If there are some things, above all others, which Brendan would like to be remembered by – I dare to say it, because I feel he would have it said – they are the secret drillings, the parades, the daredevil exploits; Borstal; imprisonment, both in England and in our homely Mountjoy (pardon the description, but I think Brendan would have liked it), in Arbour Hill, and in Tintown on the Curragh.

On these years he based the main part of his writings. The history of Ireland in these years, written by professional historians, can never be understood without the deep insight, the human glow, the apt vividness which Brendan infused into all this history which he himself had lived.

Others may deal more fittingly with the writer and the poet; the rich, complex, many-sided personality. To us, who lived with him through this disturbed epoch, and shared his trials, it is not just the Dublin wit, which lightened many a dark hour in the early forties. It was the universal element. The great sympathetic humanity, and, if I may say so, the sorrow of things which lay behind and deeper than all this wit. Behanism to us is not merely play-writing, or play-acting. It was a man-to-manism. A courageous comradeship in the hour of danger, and in the hour of need. A great light has gone out of our lives forever. Can we still hear the echoes of that strong, inimitable baritone voice as it sings,

> Wrap up my green jacket
> In a brown paper parcel
> I'll not need it now any more.

#### NOTE

Matti O'Neill, an old IRA friend of Behan and a trade-union official.

# The Man Brendan Behan*

## TIM PAT COOGAN

Bars of one sort or another played a large part in the life and death of Brendan Behan.

He first saw his father through the bars of a prison, or rather his father first saw him, because he was a babe in arms at the time; and his exploits as a result of his fondness for bars of another kind helped to make him a world figure.

Naturally his antics made him unpopular with some sections of his contrymen, but it should be remembered that he was a man who as a boy spent long Sunday afternoons learning to make bombs in Killiney, Co. Dublin, and the greater part of his impressionable adolescence in British jails surrounded by convicts.

It's difficult at this stage to say what posterity's verdict on his work will be. It seems likely, however, that empirical, torrential, heartwarming, brilliant, but slightly undisciplined as it was, it will have the unusual fate of failing to outlive the memory of the artist who created it. He was completely self-educated in the broader sense and was a good French and Irish scholar.

* *Evening Press* (Dublin), 21 Mar 1964, p. 9.

I once heard him described as being 'like a barrel of porter. Full of goodness, heady, not to be taken in excess and with sediment that should not be stirred up.' It was an apt description.

He seemed to live by balanced excesses, never doing anything in the way or in the quantities that everyone else did things.

He liked swimming for instance and stayed in literally for hours until his body was often blue with the cold.

On the Aran Islands, where he was probably the most popular visitor they ever had, his popularity survived an incident on Kilmurvey Beach when he dashed past a group of bathing girls and plunged into the water stark naked saying, 'Close your eyes, girls, I'm coming through.'

At Seapoint or at Killiney one remembers the great shaggy head bobbing about in the water, picturesque verbiage emanating therefrom, and crowds of small boys sitting around the extraordinary man when he lay on the sand afterwards. He seemed to love children and to be loved by them.

Although his general attitude towards authority was 'If there's a government I'm against it', he had too much perception and charity in him to be truly bitter.

The only time I ever heard him speaking really venomously about anyone was the time Billy Morton brought over the Liverpool police band to Santry. He cursed the Liverpool police from a height that day – showing me a scar on his forehead which he said he owed to an encounter with Liverpool's police in his teens.

He had the true Dubliner's almost diseased clarity of vision when it came to summing up situations or characters. But with him part of this ability was wasted owing to his inclination to see a bookie's tout as a decent man because of his job, whereas a banker or a professional man was one despite his position.

Here lay his strength and his weakness. On the one hand his writing was like his slumland speech, fresh, uninhibited, strong and compelling. Despite the fact that on the night of *The Quare Fellow's* premiere in the Pike I heard critics say 'Ah yes it's enjoyable all right, but it won't do. It's not a play', he was hailed as the saviour of the British theatre.

In person he had that indefinable personal magnetism that is sometimes called 'star quality'. It makes news. It makes people pay to see, read or hear its possessor.

But this is what killed him. A heavy drinker he was at first delighted by fame after the success of *The Quare Fellow*. The adulation, the flocks of predatory journalists, the celebrity treatment by a country that had once imprisoned him, the thing got out of hand. And the novelty of changing, without changing himself, from being an impossible outsider to the arch insider of his decade, a man about whom it was a conversational necessity to be informed, started to wear off.

The public image not so very different from the private one gradually overwhelmed the man, who could at various stages discipline himself enough to go away to the West to write saying 'the only thing a writer needs is sobriety – and a quiet room to work in'.

The flood of new writing was overtaken by new stories about the writer 'dropping pound notes all over the floor of the pub…and then he said–' …the court appearances, the increasing visits to hospital. The great Catherine Wheel of his life and talent was beginning to burn itself out. People began to shake their heads and say, 'He'll kill himself yet', first unbelievingly but gradually with what we now know to be a prophetic accuracy.

Most Dubliners, even those who disliked him, felt saddened when they heard that he had died, the public image has been diluted, with regret for a very lovable, wayward, talented man, who improved either in private or in public with acquaintance.

In private I found him first of all the man who repelled me by saying nasty things about my father, because he had been instrumental in locking up a friend of his in connection with a tommy-gun, and then attracted me each time we met subsequently for years afterwards making atonement through some pleasant little anecdote about my father which he would have picked up somewhere, until I eventually came to have a liking and sorrow for him equally and strongly.

In public I found him to be the object of one of the two most unusual and spontaneous outbursts of applause I ever witnessed. This was at the conclusion some years ago of the film *The Quare Fellow*, in which he was interviewed by Eamonn Andrews,[1] when the audience gave a terrific clap. The only other time I ever saw this happen was at the end of the film of Queen Elizabeth's wedding – a touch which poor old Brendan would have enjoyed uproariously.

## NOTES

For a note on Tim Pat Coogan see p. 194.

1. See the text of this interview p. 142.

# Brendan Behan: Vital Human Being – a Memoir*

BRYAN MacMAHON

As the newspaper is thrown onto the porch, I lever myself out of bed, slip on my dressing-gown, open the door and crouch to reach for the daily ration of news. The tang of a snowy Iowa morning brushes my face and ears. As my fingers tighten on the paper I see the face of Brendan Behan look up at me. I read the heading 'Wild Boy of Irish Letters is Dead'...then 'They mourn him in the pubs and theatres of Dublin, the wilful but gifted son of Erin who once said, "In the Dublin of my boyhood to eat was an achievement, but to drink was a victory over circumstances."'

Brendan Behan dead! A rent shows in the cloth of being. I look for a long time at the photograph, at the lion-like but cherubic face, at the gapped mouth, at the hair that could on occasion be curly and wilful. Hidden in the mouth is the quicksilver tongue now silent forever. I return to my bedroom. Turning on the radio there again emerges the same image of the dead High Priest of Paddywhackery and Whiskey – 'Arrested in four countries . . . denied the right to march in the traditional St Patrick's Day Parade he . . . .' At last it seems that even by his own standards Brendan has got a bad press. For he so often declared that for a writer the only bad notice was an obituary notice!

In all the Shillelagh-swinging over the coffin of Brendan Behan, there is something missing, and that something is the essence of this immensely talented, lovable, and sincere man.

I knew Brendan Behan. I don't claim to have been an intimate of his – for all in all I cannot have been more than ten times in his company. But on first meeting I found that we had some kind of chemical affinity for one another such as happens when two stranger terriers meet, sniff each other, and then go off romping happily together.

I first met him about nineteen or twenty years ago in the office of *The Bell* in O'Connell Street in Dublin. *The Bell*, a literary monthly, had been founded by, among others, Seán O'Faoláin, Frank O'Connor, Maurice Walsh, Peadar O'Donnell, and Ernie O'Malley (great men all!) with the object of 'letting Irish life speak for itself'. It was the opportunity many of

* *North American Review*, 1, n.s., no. 2 (Summer 1964) 60–4.

us country and small-town writers needed, and in the pages of *The Bell* (it is now defunct) we were welcomed by the editors O'Faoláin and O'Connor, who proved stimulating toastmasters. Even yet, *The Bell* continues to exercise its influence: a recently published posthumous novel of Michael Farrell ('Gulliver' of *The Bell*) is certain to be widely discussed when published on this side of the Atlantic.

This afternoon I speak of, I stood in the office chatting with Paddy Farrell, the clerk, who constituted most of the office staff. I was talking about some proofs of a story of mine to be published in a forthcoming issue. The muted traffic of O'Connell Street was a faint droning coming from below us. Then the door behind me banged open and I sensed a huge presence directly behind me. I smelled paint. I heard stertorous breathing. I started at the clatter of a paint tin as it was slung into the corner to my left. Out of an eye-corner I saw a paint brush with bristles gobbed with red oxide follow the paint-can. A hoarse Dublin voice began to shout, 'Tell O'Faoláin that I'm finished with painting Butt Bridge and I'll be so-and-so-ed if I ever handle a paintbrush again!' Still I did not turn. I watched Paddy Farrell's forehead corrugate in doe-like anguish. The voice behind me stopped. I knew I was being sized up. I spoke noncommittally to Paddy and straightaway the voice roared, 'You're MacMahon up from Kerry for the so-and-so football match!' I turned to see Brendan Behan – up to this unknown except as a released Borstal lad.

'O'Faoláin means well!' he said in a more restrained tone, 'but I'll be so-and-so-ed if I'll paint bridges any longer!'

'C'mon away!' he said to me. We went downstairs and out into the street. As I listened to his good-humoured ranting, I learned that O'Faoláin, with his keen eye for the significant individual, had interested himself in securing employment for the ex-Borstal boy. And here let it be clearly understood that Brendan's 'crimes' were political ones, occasioned by the presence of the stupid and arbitrary border that divides Ireland and constitutes the only obstacle to final reconciliation between Britain and Ireland. Perhaps also O'Faoláin, who himself had been on the losing side in the Irish Civil War, felt that in Brendan's case the 'back breeding was good' and that as nephew to rebel Peadar Kearney, composer of the Irish National Anthem, there was good stuff in the wilful Brendan. If at this stage Seán O'Faoláin had foreseen the literary resources of this turbulent youngster he was truly prophetic.

Brendan and I walked for some time in O'Connell Street. The sun shone. He was an amazing talker – it was as if talk had been stoppered up in him for years. He was telling of his arrest and trial in England.

'So this ould geezer of a magistrate looked over his glasses, and says to me, "Young man, how did you get into this country?" "By plane", says I. "By parachute?" "No, by umber-ella!" "Umbrella!" "Yeh, me grand-father had a noble umber-ella with powerful ribs to it – 'twas in the family for seven generations. We were flying over London an' I says to the pilot, 'Let me out here, mate.' So he slides back the door an' I opened the brolly an' out I stepped. This was an umber-ella that'd hold up an elephant. I landed in a park near a statue of... Lemme see what the statue was of ", says I to the magistrate.'

'I thought yer man'd get a stroke', Brendan went on. 'But 'twas I got the stroke...in Borstal.'

He howled with laughter as if possession of explosives were a trivial matter and his subsequent incarceration (he was too young to get penal servitude) were excruciatingly funny.

Then suddenly serious, 'The solitary confinement near drove me crazy', he said; 'I was never made to be alone.'

Idly I said something precious which he was to recall for me many years later. 'The genuine artist is crazy and has a hard time of it pretending to be sane: the phony artist is sane and has a hard time pretending to be crazy.'

He went on word-painting for me those tragicomic pictures which were later to be incorporated in *Borstal Boy*. As he talked I could not help experiencing the intense sense of humanity inherent in this then unknown Dublin man.

Later, when again I met him, I found that he was proficient in Gaelic – he had learned the language from fellow internees in the Curragh. Under a roaring exterior he hid a keen love of his country and the things indigenous to his own soil; when he had won fame (some would call it notoriety) he spoke out unhesitatingly in favour of his own people when it might have been materially of benefit to him to keep his mouth shut.

He had the nimble tongue of the Dublin man. He *spoke* literature – a torrent of never-ending observations informed with humanity close to the reality of the Dublin streets. I listened to him one night in O'Neill's pub in Pearse Street. His *Quare Fellow* had been alternating with my *Song of the Anvil* at the Abbey Theatre down the road. As I go to Dublin only a few times a year, he had heard I was coming and had left word with Seán O'Riada, then leader of the little Abbey Theatre Orchestra and a man who has profoundly developed Irish traditional music, that I was to contact him as soon as I reached the city.

This was the time when Brendan could hardly walk a hundred yards without attracting a crowd of observers and admirers. As I didn't feel quite up to being one of such a host, I didn't get in touch with him. Later in the week he met me and quietly taxed me with forgetting his invitation. We adjourned to the tavern. He was 'on the dry' at this time. I watched him narrowly: behind the mask of gaiety I fancied I saw in him the human unsure person we all more or less are.

To my son Jimmy, then a young graduate, he was kindness itself. He listened with patience to my son's young ideas he himself had long since sloughed in the light of bitter experience. All the while he quipped and roared greetings to the people entering or leaving and reminisced in a manner that was truly memorable.

His lively mind was fully evidenced in a short film which showed him being interviewed by Eamon Andrews, a Dublin man who had risen to the very top of British radio and television. The story goes that the interview was shot with little or no rehearsal, probably in a pub in Dublin. How the Dublin cinema audiences roared as Brendan glibly held his interviewer (this is precisely the response that the good interviewer evokes) at bay! I cannot quote verbatim from the film, but memory of part of it goes like this.

'Are you a Catholic, Brendan?' 'Certainly I'm a Catholic – a bad Catholic.' 'Have you any regrets for having taken part in the subversive business in Britain?' 'I'll tell you – if you fight for the liberty and unity of a small country – you're an anarchist: but if you go bombin' for a great power, you're a patriot. It all depends on the size of the country in question.' I can still see Brendan's eyes narrowing and his tongue rolling in his cheek before each reply. And I can hear the Dublin movie audiences roar approval for a fine performance.

Because he was a city man bred and born, I think that at first he must have had the true citizen's distrust of the open spaces of rural Ireland. To the average Dublin boy the land beyond the Red Cow, a famous inn near suburban Clondalkin, is *terra incognita*, where hefty, hairy Culchies (or yokels) armed with clubs clump around the bogs in search of well-behaved 'gurriers' or city lads. This mind-barrier of Dublin Brendan broke by his contact with the country lads with whom he was interned in Ireland during World War II. He spoke Irish fluently – his play *The Hostage* was first written and produced in Irish. He visited the Irish-speaking districts of the west coast (as, indeed, Dylan Thomas had done before him), and when he portrayed a country man he did so with true understanding.

After his release he and his fellow internees for a time found it difficult to secure employment. So they banded themselves together in a type of co-operative unit: carpenters, plumbers, plasterers and painters, to tender for reconstruction work. The first big job they secured was the reconstruction of Derrynane House, County Kerry, residence of Daniel O'Connell the Liberator, who won Catholic Emancipation for the Irish in 1829 (*vide King of the Beggars* – Seán O'Faoláin). On the beautiful but wild stretch of coast in which the house is situated, Brendan, the painter of the group, came fully face to face with the countryside which a true city *gamin* instinctively fears. By a coincidence the old parish priest was a namesake, Father Behan, and this served to prove to Brendan that the west of Ireland was after all inhabited by people with whom he had much in common.

I had other contacts with him which provided subjects of common interest whenever I met him. On the invitation of Ben Kiely,[1] the writer and literary editor of the *Irish Press*, Brendan and I each contributed a weekly column to the paper. I did a piece called 'MacMahon on Monday', dealing mainly with subjects of rural interest, and Brendan contributed a midweek column in which he described the magical gab of 'the old wans' in the pubs of Dublin. With a recurrent catch-cry of 'Trew for yew Mr Being' he caught these toping old folk with rare skill – these pieces helped to provide much of the material in *Hold Your Hour and Have Another*.

About this time also on the invitation of Micheál Ó hAodha of Radio Éireann, I had designed and scripted a radio programme called *The Ballad-makers' Saturday Night*, which built up a big listening public. Submerged in correspondence (the ballad is all-powerful in Ireland), I got out from under the programme to let other hands take over. Among the first to do so was Brendan Behan, who contributed almost forgotten ballads of Dublin City. I can still hear him sing the ballad he later incorporated into *The Quare Fellow*:

> 'In the early mornin' the screw was bawlin'
> 'Get up you bowsy and clean out yer cell!'
> While that ould triangle, it went jingle-jangle
> Along the banks of the Royal Canal.
>
> In the female prison there are seventy-four wimmin
> And it's with them there I would like to dwell
> But that ould triangle, it goes jingle-jangle
> Along the banks of the Royal Canal.

As written these words look robust but innocuous enough: as sung by Brendan they were electrifying. The electricity of his presence pervaded Ireland as a whole and caused total strangers to say to one another without preamble or introduction, 'He's on the wagon again – he's making a great fight of it surely.' This is the classical allusion, a common Irish struggle more literary than real, dating back from the 'Whiskey you're the Devil' of the Clancy Brothers to 'Raftery and the Whiskey' and even to the dim past in which the Irish invented whiskey or *uisge beatha* – the water of life. Coming as it did at times from the mouths of many of the great half-million-strong army of young Irish who have voluntarily given up all alcohol, there is implicit in the reference the real voice of understanding. In his day Brendan did what we shall charitably call dramatic things – but somehow it seemed that, after the initial shock, the Irish again and again forgave their wilful but supremely human son, and engulfed him in their affections. I cannot ever recall his being publicly condemned: he must have earned occasional censure, but somehow or other I cannot now recall a single instance of it. His capers were interpreted in the light of his Borstal experiences and his diabetic condition, and invariably the Irish reaction was 'The poor devil – what harm is he doin' but his own?'

John Donne in a characteristic excess of wisdom spoke of 'a strenuous virtue or a strenuous sin'. Brendan would I feel have liked the quotation. He had a great deal of the playboy to his make-up, which mingled with the shrewd realisation that it was good business to interrupt his own plays by shouting at the actors from the stalls and even going on stage to fool it up for a while, or to sing, like an ordinary street busker before the crowds queuing outside the theatre. But all in all he brightened the scene and gave entertainment to a pretty drab world.

In the bygone Dublin that breathed the spirit of Jonathan Swift there lived an old ballad-maker who called himself Zozimus. He sat on a stone near the Four Courts and rattled off balladry about St Patrick and Pharaoh's daughter, 'who lived contagious to the Nile': in this Dublin too lived a termagant of a fishwife called Biddy Moriarty, whose tongue was considered invincible until conquered by Daniel O'Connell by the simple trick of using a terminology of abuse with which she had scant acquaintance, so that when she was called a downright parallelogram, a barefaced hypotenuse, and a wall-eyed rhomboid, she was left gasping like one of her own codfish. In the Dublin of recent years there also lived a picaresque writer in Gaelic called Pádraic O'Conaire who often climbed the railing of St Stephen's Green to pass the night sleeping amid the ducks that nest in the island in the mid-park lake. Somehow Brendan Behan managed to fuse together the spirits of Zozimus, Dan O'Connell, Biddy Moriarty and Pádraic O'Conaire. What emerged was a marvellous and vital human being who played the pipes for a scintillating while and then fell silent.

It was night. I strolled downtown towards the central business section of Iowa City. From East Washington Street, the place below twinkled like a Christmas tree. Frozen snow crunched underneath my boots. *Tom Jones* was showing at the 'Varsity'. This March night Brendan Behan was being cried for in Dublin, and for once the hack obituary phrase, 'he was loved by all classes and creeds, by gentle and simple', would seem to be appropriate.

Passing a bookshop I saw something that made me pause. Half the window was bare of books and on it had been placed a square of black crêpe paper. In the middle of the black paper stood a half-empty glass of beer with a deadman bottle beside it. On an ash-tray was a half-smoked cigarette, its long ash grey – dead. A copy of *The Quare Fellow* and a much-handled photo of Brendan Behan completed the display.

I stayed looking at the display for a long while. It was a fair tribute in the American manner. About me the street was empty and the smell of pizza and coffee was strong in the frosted air. Then I smiled: the beer bottle was British Bass, a drink that, due to an alleged anti-Irish statement by one of the directors, the IRA had tried to outlaw in Ireland. 'Will I change it?' the girl in the bookstore asked when I told her of it. 'No,' I said, 'Brendan would have liked the irony of the tribute.' So we let it stand.

PS. Air letter from my son Jimmy:

Down beat Cavan today in the Football League semi-final – Kerry are playing Dublin next Tuesday. Brendan Behan (I know you've heard) died – I went to his funeral with Sean O'Briain – it was an extraordinary funeral – not so sad (people knew his premature death was inevitable), but it was an extraordinary combination of people. When the remains were being removed from the Meath Hospital, Jimmy Hiney the ballad-maker struck up the Rosary from the midst of the theatrical and poor Dublin assemblage – it's like a passage from the Gospel. They are still talking about him here and will be for a long time to come.

### NOTES

Bryan MacMahon, Irish writer.
1. For a note on Benedict Kiely and his recollections of Behan see p. 267.

# Was Poet, Comedian, Rebel and Lover of People*

### PROINSIAS MacAONGHUSA

Brendan Behan once said that the only bad publicity was an obituary notice. This then is not an obituary. For I have no wish to give bad publicity to a friend of many years' standing who gave me more amusement with stories, attitudes, songs and witticisms than any other person I ever knew.

Brendan was a funny man. He was a real natural comedian. No one enjoyed his wild antics more than himself and he got special delight from embarrassing the pompous and the proud. I knew many Brendans. There was Brendan the flamboyant playboy barracking his own plays in London and New York. There was Brendan the tough drinker swapping stories of burglaries and fights with criminals in snugs. There was Brendan the anarchist who would break and batter all before him without a thought for the consequences. There was Brendan who walked in badly broken shoes all the way to Donnycarney to M. J. MacManus's funeral on a wild wet day.

* *Sunday Independent* (Dublin), 22 Mar 1964, p. 7.

He did not have the price of the bus but he felt he had to be there to honour a great man. There was Brendan the Irish speaker and poet singing and drinking and talking to his friends in Carraroe and in Dunquin. There was Brendan, the rebel, shooting at policemen in Dublin and placing bombs around Liverpool. There was Brendan, the successful writer whose books sold in tens of thousands within days of publication.

And they were all real men. Brendan was a revolutionary. In his life he rebelled against all the accepted rules of society. For a man with his Republican and socialist background it was natural for him to join Fianna Éireann, and, later, the IRA. Borstal was his secondary school, the Curragh Camp his university. Those two periods as a political prisoner and his other experiences in jail, the men he met there and the books he came across for the first time influenced him more than anything else.

He met the Republican leader Mairtin O'Cadhain in the Curragh. He taught him to speak Irish well and Brendan later wrote brilliantly in that language. But the rebel remained. He was never fooled by peasant worshippers and he wrote stingingly of those who spoke Irish for what they could get out of it.

I remember once going to see Brendan in Baggot Street Hospital for *Time* magazine. They wanted quotes for a light article. Brendan had just announced his intention to give up the drink. 'Look, you sit down and read a paper. I'll write the quotes, the funny remarks I am supposed to have made. I know what that crowd want', he said. And he did.

He wanted to work for Dr Noel Browne in the 1959 election. Browne supporters were a little worried at the impression Brendan would make as a canvasser. 'Look, I am not going to canvass for Noel. I'll go around looking for votes for MacEntee. That should be enough to get Browne votes. I'll denounce him on every doorstep', he declared.

Brendan loved life. He loved people. He loved Dublin and he loved the Gaeltacht. He hated no one. He knew nearly every gangster and bowsie in Dublin, yet he himself was a most gentle person. He was considerate with the weak and above all he adored children. The last conversation I had with him consisted of talk about his little daughter and mine and the different ways they reacted to life.

Britain, which he once invaded, loved him, France admired him, Sweden adored him, America lionised him, Ireland never knew where she stood with him. Ireland and himself were lovers, jealous and suspicious of one another.

Brendan was against cant and hypocrisy. 'I stand for the abolition of the village idiot', said Lenin, 'and that is what I stand for too', he once said. That may sum up his life: a boisterous, roaring crusade for personal freedom and a battle against codology.

Brendan always stood by his friends. He let no one down in a real sense. He lived a gay, wild, extravagant, loud life. He never counted the cost. He died a far too early death. But who will cast the first stone? Is it better to die young having led a full life and leaving behind a handful of good books, a couple of first-class plays and a half-dozen fine poems than to die quietly at four score leaving behind a mere handful of dust?

NOTE

Proinsias MacAonghusa, Irish writer.

# Tribute*

## MICHEÁL Ó hAODHA

I knew his prowess as a ballad-singer and his extensive repertoire, many of which he learned from his mother, and when I suggested that he might like to sing in the programme he was delighted. In fact, he scripted the Dublin sections of the programme. That was before he was known as a writer.

We produced his radio plays *Moving Out* and *The Big House,* which was first produced by BBC, by whom it was commissioned, and then *The Quare Fellow,* which I myself produced.

He also had a number of short stories broadcast, some read by himself.

I believe he had the spark of genius all right. Whether he quite fulfilled all his promise in the few short years he worked is a matter of conjecture.

I regard *The Quare Fellow* as his greatest play. It was a powerful indictment of capital punishment, the most powerful document against it I have ever known.

* *Irish Times* (Dublin), 21 Mar 1964, pp. 1, 9.

NOTE

Micheál Ó hAodha, the Radio Éireann producer and Director of the Abbey Theatre, speaks of his early association with Behan in *The Ballad-makers' Saturday Night* on Radio Éireann around the early 1950s. See also his Introduction to *'Moving Out' 'A Garden Party.' Two Plays by Brendan Behan,* ed. Robert Hogan (Dixon, Calif.: Proscenium Press, 1967).

# He Ran Too Quickly*

### SEAN O'CASEY

I did not know him personally and, in fact, I never saw him, but I recognise the fine talent he had.

One thing Brendan Behan never did was to exploit his own talents. He should have settled down and rested and not bothered about running around. You simply can't do this all the time, and he was very much in the same mould as Dylan Thomas.

There is something peculiar in the Gael or the Celt. When he decides to go along the 'Primrose Path' he runs too quickly. This is what Brendan Behan did. He died too quickly.

Our daughter knew him as a delightful, kind, charitable, humane chap, a delightful type of man.

* *Evening Press* (Dublin), 21 Mar 1964, p. 1.

### NOTE

Sean O'Casey (1880–1964), Irish dramatist. Behan highly respected O'Casey, and in a letter to the Editor of the *Irish Times* (Dublin), 29 Aug 1961, p. 5, he said, 'I do not include myself as a man of equal stature as Sean O'Casey.'

# He Was So Much Larger Than Life†

### FRANK O'CONNOR

I remember the day I was first conscious of knowing Brendan Behan. It was outside the Four Courts and a dishevelled-looking tough said, 'I know

† *Sunday Independent* (Dublin), 22 Mar 1964, p. 7.

you. I saw you once with Kavanagh. What the hell are you doing here?'

'I'm on a jury', I said. 'And you?' 'Oh, giving evidence for a fellow that's up for pucking a Guard. I only got out of jail this morning. But he's a civil servant. He has to defend himself.'

I got away from him for fear he might take the notion of pucking me instead of a Guard, but a couple of hours later I met him again.

'Well, how did you get on?' I asked. 'Ah, I only told the oul' Judge what the Guard said to us, and what I said to the Guard before I pucked him, and he said, "Oh, don't continue, Behan! That's quite enough! We can take the rest for granted." ' Soon after, a Dublin solicitor with more imagination than lawyers usually show, pleaded that Brendan's system was upset by the sight of a Guard's uniform.

I cannot say I really liked him until after the arrest of Alan Simpson[1] for the production of *The Rose Tattoo*. A little group of us were waiting outside the theatre for the arrest of the cast – a handful of theatre-lovers, some newspaper men and a lawyer or two, came to see fair play.

Brendan had managed to get a box and was delivering a long speech in which he said quite truthfully that the country was being depopulated, and all the Government could do was to prosecute a harmless company of actors. Then he sang 'Se Fath Mo Bhuartha' with real feeling. The goat, which was a principal character in *The Rose Tattoo*, emerged on to the lane, and he shouted, 'Never mind the goat! Bring out the——peeler!'[2]

He sent up to Mooney's at the bridge for a dozen of stout and distributed it among his audience, saying, 'Mind the bottles! They'll come in handy for ammunition.' I enjoyed watching Brendan's glowing face, and later he and I went off for a drink together. I remember thinking, 'That man is twice life-size.'

Later I read *The Quare Fellow* and reviewed *Borstal Boy*[3] and was astonished again, because under that turbulent exterior there was quite clearly the soul of an altar boy. I described *Borstal Boy* as a deeply edifying book because the impression it left on my mind was of someone who, like Mangan, was condemned 'to herd with demons from hell beneath' and who had emerged with his essential purity and sweetness intact. Later, I noticed that even in Dublin, where no one's reputation is safe, people everywhere told stories of his goodness as freely as of his wildness.

A doctor who was attending him described how he would be rung up by the Guards in the middle of the night and have to bail Brendan out, but by the following evening Brendan would be on his doorstep with apologies and the bail money. Someone else told how he cashed a small cheque from Radio Éireann, then bought a bottle of port and gave a shilling to a small boy to take it to the house of a sick woman.

The same doctor described two old men with cancer who had shared a ward with Brendan and were still alive, six months after they should have been dead, waiting for him to call and cheer them up with his songs and funny stories.

A poet described how Brendan had left him outside a house to pay a call and how when he entered the house a half hour later he found Brendan sitting by the bedside of an old woman in her last agony, singing in a low voice to her with tears streaming down his face.

One heard the other sort of story as well, of course: the poet described Brendan later, beating his head with his fists and shouting, 'Why should a —— like me be left alive and a grand woman like that die?' But he added, 'That was Brendan putting it on; there was no put-on about the man I saw singing by her bedside.'

It was the goodness people remembered about him. He wasn't only twice the size of life, but it was our life that he enlarged – the things we enjoy and value. It was curious to think that when we were trying to present to the world a sophisticated, prissy view of ourselves the man who represented us best was forever in jail or hospital.

It was a disaster that he could not have had some success at home such as he later had abroad. With literary friends like Benedict Kiely[4] and Francis MacManus,[5] he did not have to apologise for the altar boy in himself, but theatre directors and censors could not see it. He was bitterly hurt by the banning of *Borstal Boy*, but for a reason our censors would not understand.

'The people whose opinions I care for', he said, 'are simple people who can be taken in by fools like those. What can they think except that I'm a bad man?'

It left him open to the flattery of England and America, and I am afraid he vulgarised that small, pure, absolutely genuine, gift of his, or allowed it to be vulgarised. I took care not to see or read *The Hostage* because dramatic critics in Ireland and America recognised it as a jazzed-up version of a story of mine,[6] and I did not want to see my work travestied by an English producer.

It was typical of Brendan abroad that in that silly book *Brendan Behan's Island* he gave a false account of how he came to write it. In a Dublin pub he put on no such airs. 'Ah, sure, of course I stole the —— thing.'

I wish I had it in my power to suppress *Brendan Behan's New York* with which we are threatened.[7] It will not be New York and it will not be Brendan. I should be happier to think that some young writer was gathering up the hundreds of stories about him that are circulating at this moment in Dublin and that would tell scholars and critics a hundred years from now what sort of man he was and why he was so greatly loved.

## NOTES

Frank O'Connor, pen-name of Michael O'Donovan (1903– ), Irish novelist.

1. For a note on Alan Simpson see p. 118.
2. Reference to the song 'The Peeler and the Goat'.
3. Frank O'Connor, 'To Show That Still She Lives', *Chicago Sunday Tribune*, 1 Mar 1959, p. 3.
4. For a note on Benedict Kiely see p. 267.
5. For a note on Francis MacManus and his recollections of Behan see p. 312.
6. 'Guests of the Nation.'
7. *Brendan Behan's New York*, with drawings by Paul Hogarth (London: Hutchinson; New York: Bernard Geis, 1964).

# Great Man*

## SEAN KENNY

Behan was a great, wild talented man, and should be accounted a true brother of that company, making him one in the true tradition of Ireland's poets and writers.

It was an immense experience to work with him. He had an extraordinary ability to break down all conceit and preconception even among a fellow-artist. He probably had more friends and critics than anyone else. His work in the theatre had a fantastic impact.

It came at a time when the English so-called *avant-garde* theatre was taking itself seriously. *The Hostage* came blasting in with irreverence one night and changed all this. For this Brendan must be thanked. It was a great privilege to work with him.

* *Evening Press* (Dublin), 21 Mar 1964, p. 9.

## NOTE

Sean Kenny, Irish stage-designer.

# Greatest Dublin Jackeen*

## HUGH LEONARD

In Dublin, which is a small city, it takes only two writers to form a literary clique. The trick is in getting them to talk to each other. Perversely, Brendan Behan and I were on non-speaking terms for years, until someone took the trouble to introduce us. Thus was ruined a beautiful enmity which began one morning in Parson's bookshop on Baggot Street Bridge. Brendan and I were both nursing separate and independently acquired hangovers. He lurched up to me and muttered, 'What day is it?' Mistaking his legitimate enquiry for satire, I snarled 'Fuck off' and ran out of the shop, hotly pursued by Brendan, who stood at the door shaking his fist and roaring hoarsely, 'That's nice! That's lovely! That's gorgeous fuckin' language!'

An amnesty was declared when we were formally introduced in the Brazen Head a few years later. Brendan, who, when sober, was shy of strangers, was sitting quietly at a table, and I asked him what he was working on. He said, 'Nothin' at all. I'm off the hard stuff, and as soon as I can give up the stout as well, then I'll get down to work.' A few days later, he went to a formal luncheon where some joker poured gin into his tomato juice. Within a matter of a few weeks, after the resultant binge, he ended up in hospital. It was the story of his later life. Wherever he went, there was always someone who wanted to see the dancing bear in performance.

My first opinion of Behan's work was not high. I was fortunate enough to see the Abbey Theatre production of *The Quare Fellow* (or *Fella*, as it was then called with true inverted pedanticism), which was a travesty by any standards. It was not until I later read the published text that I realised what a very formidable play it was. Behan's personality and upbringing made him incapable of self-pity or of approaching any question seriously, no matter how grave the issues involved. In many ways he was the greatest living example of that rare creature known as the 'Dublin jackeen': a being who is by tradition bawdy, witty, irresponsible, fiercely loyal, iconoclastic and withering, yet who is riddled with unexpected demarcation lines beyond which is perdition. He also possessed an artist's sensitivity to a ruinous degree. I believe that he wrote *The Quare Fellow* unself-consciously and truthfully. It never occurred to him that he was breaking down old

---

* *Plays and Players* (London), XI, no. 8 (May 1964) 43.

dramatic barriers or that his play might be construed as an indictment of capital punishment: he was telling a story about prison life in the only way he, Behan, knew how. Then, later, he found himself suffering the fate of the silent comic, Harry Langdon: people began explaining his art to him. A born writer was libelled as a cunning writer. Suddenly, Behan – who knew damn all about so-called dramatic art, but could write like an angel – was hailed as a master craftsman and satirist. Not only did he pay for his fame with ill health and the attentions of parasites, but a worse fate overtook him: he became self-conscious.

In *The Hostage*, one could almost see Behan trying to be all the things his professional discoverers and explainers insisted he was. A later play, given in Irish and supposedly the basis for *Richard's Cork Leg*, was no more than a series of dirty jokes, strung together with wit and desperation. Not that it matters: one good play more than justifies any writer's existence, even if its author is to die at the hands of cerebral idiots and beer-spiking Joxers.

In Dublin, Brendan was regarded as a 'drunken bowsie' by the middle classes and with veneration by the lower orders. Whether he will go down to posterity as a wit or as a writer (as far as Dublin is concerned) is still a moot point: for in Ireland 'characters' are loved, but playwrights are suspect, and it was not until England applauded that most of the Irish critics began to back-track furiously in Behan's direction. But the real trouble with knowing Brendan, although slightly, is that the man tended to swamp the writer. One can still see him at a patriotic pageant, watching St Patrick overthrowing the pagan idols, and roaring out wildly in full and handsome approval 'Good oul God!'

There is a fine, if little-known, play by Jack B. Yeats called *In Sand* in which a man asks that his epitaph be written in the sand of the seashore, to be duly washed away by the sea. But through a chain of accidents the epitaph is not so easily forgotten and, in fact, outlasts any marble monument which might have been erected to his memory. I think, as a Dubliner, the same epitaph might serve for Behan. It is simply, 'We have the good thought for you still.'

NOTE

Hugh Leonard, Irish dramatist.

# Brendan Behan: 'Uproarious Tragedy'*

## ALAN BRIEN

Brendan Behan first came to ad-mass fame as the 'television Irishman' when he sang his songs, cursed his curses and flapped his arms before the uneasy eye of the BBC camera.

He leaped into pop fame like an egg into a fan. He was a one-man Beatle quartet – an omelette served up from a mixed bowl of Gilbert Harding, Dylan Thomas and Michael Collins.

Theatre critics and discerning play-goers had for some time known a different – if sometimes disturbingly similar – figure, the author of *The Quare Fellow* and *The Hostage*. He was one of the first dramatists on the British stage to open the steps leading into an underworld where a new and alarming repertoire of characters introduced themselves.

He forced us to watch men at the end of their tether, men facing death and humiliation and loneliness with humour and spirit. Behan cared about men at work – and his definition of work included crime, politics, drinking and unemployment.

*The Hostage* was, in his phrase, 'an uproarious tragedy'. In this he came nearer to his public image when he created that roaring outing of a broth of a bhoy, that wild Synge-song in an Irish stew, which carried audiences away on a frothing wave of talk and song.

Sometimes, in private and with his friends, he still wore the glowing mask of Battling Brendan. I remember a Dublin night when he insisted upon giving me the pleasure of his voice raised in rebel ballads. Knowing the English reluctance to listen to the voice of ancient independence, he took the precaution of linking his little finger through the top button of my waistcoat. The concert began, and went on and on and on. After half an hour I unslipped my waistcoat and went to the kitchen for a drink. Two hours later, I returned to find Brendan, eyes closed, still crooning into my watch pocket.

There was also Brendan the defier of illness and denier of mortality, who exposed his body and brain to punishment beyond the call of duty. He had several deathbeds before he died, and never flinched on any. I remember

* *Sunday Telegraph* (London), 22 Mar 1964, p. 19.

in the Middlesex Hospital waiting, guiltily, for last words for a newspaper. For hours he had not moved, then came a faint stir.

'Brendan', I whispered 'Do you never think about death?' He sat up, like an enormous Pooh bear in a sheet like a toga, 'Think about death?' he shouted. 'Bigod, I'd rather be dead than think about death.' It was an epitaph worthy of a permanent place in the *Oxford Dictionary of Quotations*.

There was also (though many may find it hard to believe) a shy, insecure Brendan who was worried and embarrassed by the headlines he could also command. If he was reluctant to write, if he began each new play with the author's curtain speech, this was not through arrogance or vanity. It was because he was deeply suspicious of his own talent, and sought continual reassurance of his abilities. He never believed what we critics wrote about him – but we were right and he was wrong.

I cannot think of anyone who has made me blush more in public. I never knew him as an intimate, but only a few close friends have ever given me warmer, richer, more lasting pleasure in private. The anaemic veins of the British theatre will be thinner and poorer for the loss of his 100 proof spirit.

### NOTE

Alan Brien, English drama critic. See his review of *The Hostage*, 'Political Pantomime', *Spectator* (London), CCI (17 Oct 1958) 513–14.

# Rich in Talent and a Great Personality*

## BENEDICT KIELY

The first time I met Brendan Behan? It's a difficult question to answer because there were so many hectic and happy times that every one of them seemed to be the first.

But I think the first time in time (so to speak) was one day when I was walking along St Stephen's Green to meet in the Shelbourne Hotel a group of people that turned out to include Anita Loos, Ria Mooney and Maire MacNeill and her husband.

On my way Anthony Cronin[1] stopped me, introduced me to a stout, lively young man about four years younger than myself, whom I already

* *Sunday Press* (Dublin), 22 Mar 1964, p. 6.

knew by sight and hilarious reputation, and pointed out that there was a temporary shortage of funds.

Possessed of some silver and a pound, I made two fair halves of the silver, but preserved the pound, unmentioned, in case I'd have to do the decent in front of the nice folk in the Shelbourne.

The episode is interesting as a light on the lot of the young writer in Ireland or, perhaps, anywhere else.

The three of us between us couldn't have mustered two-fifths of the price of a Prize Bond. It is even more interesting for the light it throws on the sort of X-ray insight Brendan had; for some time afterwards he said to me, 'I liked you, you Northern —— you, because I knew you had a pound in your pocket.' He couldn't see into my wallet but he could see into my mind.

To say that, after that, our friendship ripened would be to use a laughably weak word, for anything that had to do with Brendan had more of thunder and sudden sunshine in it than of any gradual process leading to the content of harvest.

M. J. MacManus, my predecessor on the *Irish Press* and one of the world's finest gentlemen, was a close bond between us, for M. J. ('Joe') had first put Brendan into print when Brendan was in the Curragh, and I took up where Joe left off and James Pearse McGuinness (an old companion of Behan) carried on the process by making possible what proved to be a precious and most unusual column.

What nights there were upstairs in the White Horse, while that column was in the making, with Brendan at his acts: Toulouse Lautrec walking on his knees; or with his jacket shawlwise over his head as the Poor Old Woman who developed the walk of a queen; or making the sort of speech that should be made by a prospective candidate for the Dáil;[2] or doing any one of the thousand things that were all Brendan.

Those well-reared writers of the English papers who seem to get hysterics when a man falls off a barstool, write a lot about wildness and turbulence.

Etiquette may be calmer where they drink their pale ale. But his friends of my own vintage remember much laughter and kindness and a deep wisdom, and the slow sadness of the later years as ill-health left its mark upon him.

One night in the Horse when I was helpless with laughter I may claim that I said in the presence of witnesses, 'When he [*missing words?*] he'll shake them. He'll also make a lot of money.'

He did that, indeed, and in a most extraordinary way and gave to the world the treasures of one of the richest personalities I have ever encountered.

In all humility the world has reason to be grateful and I offer these few hurried words as part of my own payment of a deep debt. There is a lot more to be said about him.

NOTES

Benedict Kiely (1919–    ), Irish journalist and writer.
 1. For a note on Anthony Cronin see p. 29.
 2. The Irish Parliament.

# This Man Behan*

## DAVID NATHAN

Of all the times I've spent with him perhaps the finest was a few days in
Paris about five years ago. We had eaten well one April night, warm like
the Paris nights they write songs about, and afterwards we sat down outside
a café.

We had passed a poster advertising an exhibition devoted to foreign writers
and artists who had lived in Paris during the thirties.

Brendan himself had lived there in the late forties, always broke and, as
he put it, 'calling upon American, English and Irish pilgrims on their way
to Lourdes to exercise a little charity'.

But that night he was full of food, success and money. Theatre
Workshop's production of *The Hostage* was the hit of the Paris International Theatre season. Brendan's picture was in all the papers and he
had an endless supply of the audience he always needed when he was
happy.

Anyway, there he sat, sipping occasionally at a brandy, and talking
about the things he believed in like 'more food, cheaper drink, better roads,
smaller bombs, softer beds and free coal for old people in winter'.

He was also in favour of public schools for 'they provide the educated
classes such as meself with endless amusement'.

Suddenly he remembered the poster and started composing a Lament to
the thirties. It began,

> I absolutely must decline
> To dance in the streets
>     for Gertrude Stein,
> And as for Alice B. Toklas,
> I'd rather eat a box of
> ——ing choclas.

* Extracted from the *Daily Herald* (London), 21 Mar 1964, p. 3.

Later he used the lines as an introduction to one of his records but little of the Lament survived. Some of the rhymes were rough and some were unprintable and most were forgotten.

But one or two sang their way into the memory and to our astonishment – but not Brendan's for he had seen what was happening – were greeted by applause from a crowd of St Germain writers, artists and journalists who had stopped to listen and by now had spilled out into the roadway.

And that is how I like to remember him. Not the bleary-eyed mumbler hurling insults in a bar, but the laughing story-teller with the gap-toothed smile who was a far greater writer than he ever was a drinker.

And a far greater man than either.

NOTE

David Nathan, English journalist.

# Deckhand on Collier*

## MAURICE RICHARDSON

I first met Brendan Behan in 1950 in Dublin, during Horse Show week. He was then twenty-eight, fresh-faced, very handsome, almost pretty. He was wearing nautical costume because he was supposed to be a deckhand on a collier that had been chartered for some doubtful enterprise plying between Dublin and Belfast; it seldom, if ever, put to sea. He produced from his seaboot a short story he had written about the painted corpse of the dearly beloved friend of a publican lying in state in a bar parlour. I don't think it was ever published, but it showed distinct signs of talent.

He wasn't then as roaring and boisterous as he afterwards became, but he had enormous natural charm which you could sense immediately. He gave off a powerful current of warmth and vitality and sympathy like some very friendly animal who knows all about you by intuition. He kept this quality after he became a success and on his periodical raids on London you could feel it coming through the alcoholic haze that generally surrounded him. Unlike most lost people, he was never a bore, always capable of making instant contact.

* *Observer* (London), 22 Mar 1964, p. 3.

NOTE

Maurice Richardson, the *Observer* television critic. See his review of Behan's *Confessions of an Irish Rebel*, 'Behan on Tape', *Observer* (London), 7 Nov 1965, p. 27.

# He Squandered his Life*

## JOAN LITTLEWOOD

Brendan was caught between love for, and mockery of, obsolete myths. His personal suffering and loneliness gave the world some of the finest laughter medicine of the century. Already in his last notices the greatness of the man was undervalued.

He was a fine scholar as well as a glorious clown, a man who translated Marlowe's verse into Irish and improvised his finest ballads for the street-sweepers and lonely vagrants of every city in the world. He squandered his life and his genius, but he took the world out on a spree with him. Theatre Workshop will put on *The Quare Fellow* in his memory as soon as we can.

* *Observer* (London), 22 Mar 1964, p. 3. Editor's title.

NOTE

Joan Littlewood, theatrical director and founder of Theatre Workshop. She staged the first London productions of Behan's *The Quare Fellow* and *The Hostage*.

# Behan: a Giant of a Man, Yet Gentle*

KENNETH ALLSOP

Brendan Behan's rogue elephantine talent drowned in a whiskey glass. He was an alcoholic, a big man helpless as a baby in need of its feeding bottle, who pretended to be a jolly, convivial gargler.

He always had to push the boat out to avert being stranded alone on the bleak island of his own memories and fears.

I knew Brendan well, and had paddled along behind him in the spray of his drinking bouts in London, Dublin – where he died last night – New York and sundry scatterings of pubs elsewhere.

Now, more than sadness I feel anger that he is dead – anger that the creative bounty that was rich as yolk within his huge humpty-dumpty frame was so systematically addled in booze.

But, really, it's pointless to rue all the surge of unwritten books and plays that were there where *The Quare Fellow*, *The Hostage* and *Borstal Boy* came from. For like Dylan Thomas, who also committed suicide by drink, he was the man he was and had to do what he did.

There were two reasons why he was compelled to drown his troubled heart. He was Irish as one of his own gamy stage characters, and success and celebrity forced him to stay permanently in the glad rags of the roaring boy, the terror of pale suburbanites, the tosspot who always tossed his pot farther than anyone else.

But behind the clown's mask – if Dylan had, in Dame Edith Sitwell's words, the 'face of a fallen angel', Brendan's, with that delicate broken nose and tangled curls, was that of a ruined Caesar – was the unbearable knowledge of what he had done.

Of course he had been an IRA gunman. But it was not until I was with him in New York last spring that I learned the true source of Brendan's anguish. In 1942 he came to Britain with bombs in his suitcase to strike a militant blow for the freedom cause he then passionately believed in.

The terrorist squad he was working with dropped a bomb into a pillar-box in Liverpool and it exploded and killed a young woman and her baby who were passing.

* *Daily Mail* (London), 21 Mar 1964, p. 7.

It was not only something he could never forget, but something he could never bring himself to remember if there was drink there to swill it over.

He said to me recently, when describing how he had once fired a pistol at a policeman in a 1942 Dublin battle, 'Only a lunatic boasts of taking a human life. Essentially I'm a very gentle and amiable person.'[1]

But behind the roistering boisterousness and the bellowed anecdotes, songs and aphorisms was a man with an appetite for living greater than his thirst for drink.

The only people he hated were those wet blankets who try to quell and diminish the blaze of life. He believed ferociously in kindliness, and he would punch anyone on the nose who advocated violence.

He was, indeed, a gentle and amiable man. More than the loss of the books he never wrote, I shall feel that henceforth there will always be an empty chair at the feast.

## NOTES

For a note of Kenneth Allsop see p. 92.

1. Cf. 'I reflected on the sadness of Irishmen fighting Irishmen or indeed, I'm ashamed even now to say, of men fighting men or men fighting women or women fighting women anywhere, because at heart I'm a pacifist' – Brendan Behan, *Confessions of an Irish Rebel* (London: Hutchinson: 1965) p. 51.

# The Behan*

## WALTER HACKETT

Brendan Behan has gone just as he predicted he would.

He said it and he meant it, and he was sober when he said it.

He said it to me at the Purdy Kitchen, a pub in Dun Laoghaire, just down the coast from Dublin. That was in 1962.

I asked him why the critics kept insisting he was the Irish equivalent of Welsh poet Dylan Thomas.

He looked at the rain that was lashing in from the sea, and took a long drag of soda water.

'We had nothing in common other than the fact we both got drunk in public and made spectacles of ourselves.

'However, like Thomas, I may go out as sort of a cumulative result of my excesses.'

* *Washington Post*, 22 Mar 1964, Show Supplement, p. G–1.

That was the quiet-voiced Behan being himself, not the gregarious, blustering, pugnacious, loudmouthed, four-letter-word, sarcastic, publicity-seeking, drunken Behan that people liked to read about.

Actually, Behan was a soft touch for anyone who needed advice or a handful of shillings. He was intelligent, literate and had a knowledge of English, French, American and Irish literature that many a professor who teaches those subjects does not have.

I knew him for only about seven years. There was one long span when I lived almost around the corner from him in Ballsbridge, a Dublin suburb, and we used to meet in various places, such as Herbert's news store, the dry-cleaning shop and at Ryan the butcher's – all in that area – and several times he came to my flat on Merrion Road.

Once he rode 125 miles in a taxi from Cork to Kruger Kavannagh's guest house at tiny Dunquin in County Kerry, where Ireland slides into the sea. He took that ride because he thought 't'would be grand to have a few jars and some fine conversation' with Kruger, who used to work on newspapers in Springfield and New Haven, and me.

It wasn't that I saw him every day or every week. None of his friends or acquaintances did, for he had a way of disappearing, not so much to get drunk as to do some soul-searching.

I remember one raw winter morning. I was trying to track him down. There are 733 pubs in Dublin. He was barred from roughly 725. I looked in Davy Byrne's in Duke Street. He wasn't there, nor was he across the way at the Bailey, where he was admitted through a benign form of literary sufferance. I went down Grafton Street past Trinity College and to the second floor lounge of the Pearle, across the street from the *Irish Times*.

I asked for Behan. Sean the barman said, 'You're three drinks behind him.'

I hit pay dirt in the bar of the Dolphin Hotel. There he was – Himself – dressed in his 'uniform' of an old tweed suit, open-collar shirt and heavy walking shoes. He was reciting in French something from François Villon, while the barman and patrons looked on apprehensively and courageously.

Behan greeted me effusively.

He had been drinking.

'Just a drop to keep up me flagging circulation.'

He introduced me as a 'Yank professor come to lecture at Trinity College on the moral aspect of Marco Polo as he affected the Irish literary scene from Moore through Synge and O'Casey'.

Then, unbidden, he recited 'Me Undergraduate Days at Dear Old Oxford, the Protestant Annex to University College, Dublin'.

'Let's take a ride in that big green American car of yours', he said.

On foot we threaded our way through the traffic, some of it horse-drawn, of Georgian Dublin's back streets. A pair of coatless urchins leaped around us like dirty-faced dolphins.

'Ah, Brendan, would you not have a few coppers for us?'

Behan roared something in Gaelic, dipped into his pocket and gave each a two-shilling piece.

'It brings me back to me own tenement district days in Dublin,' he said, 'when not a bloody penny could I rub against the next one. I had a great penchant for thinness in those days, for many a time I had an empty belly.'

Suddenly a wrinkled gnome of a man darted from a pub.

'Brendan, it's a word I'd like with you.'

The man outlined an improbable plot for a play. Behan listened politely, for basically he was not a rude person.

We walked through the rain. 'Who was that?' I asked.

'Never saw him before.'

We cut over to Stephen's Green, and at his insistence we stopped into a famous food and wine shop, where the manager wears striped trousers and the clerks speak in cultivated tones.

In a loud voice, Behan asked for hummingbirds' wings in aspic. A man in a hacking jacket, burly and obviously Anglo-Irish, made a snide remark.

Behan's mood changed. He hit the man with a left jab and a right cross. The man went down like a rag doll. I grabbed Behan and eased him out.

Behan probably held the all-time modern Irish writers' record for getting into fights, most of which he managed to win. That same day he described his style as being 'more like Mr Rocky Marciano than Sugar Ray'.

After one Dublin brawl, when Behan appeared in court, be insisted upon defending himself in Gaelic. The judge dismissed the case. He had forgotten his Gaelic.

Before we got to my car, Behan reminisced about the seven months he spent in Paris as a house-painter. His reason for going to France was to perfect his French and at the same time be close to the libraries at the Sorbonne and National Archives, and there he read French literature.

'The French are very civilised. You can break up a café and as long as you pay for the damage you're perfectly welcome to come back the next night and do it all over again.'

'Now we'll drop in on Ben Kiely', Behan announced. Under the name of Patrick Lagan, Kiely writes for the *Irish Press*. Under his own name, he is a steady contributor to the *New Yorker*. He has been known to take a drink.

At the paper Kiely's secretary said in a small 'reefeened' Dublin accent, 'Mr Kiely's out doing research.'

'Tell him I was in and was accompanied by the late Horace Greeley, and that we're both going west', Behan said.

We looked for Kiely in one pub where Behan was not *persona non grata*. A youngish, ragged man, carrying a violin and bow, said to us, 'Excuse my temerity, kind sirs, but I am without funds.'

Behan gave the man two pounds, bought him a larruping big drink of whisky and said to me, 'Put that in one of your stories and I'll give you a bust in the jaw.'

The violinist played 'The Kerry Dance'.

'There's never any lack of characters or situations or conversation in this city', Behan said to me. 'Take that man – if I were to use him in a play, American critics would say I was creating a caricature of a Dubliner.

'I write about the people I know, and I record how they talk and act and how they smell with the liquor and stale, sour sweat coming out of their pores.

'And under it all, I try and show the black and sardonic streak we Irish have, something that underlies our humour.'

He told how he was painting the outside of the *Irish Times* (he is a third-generation house-painter) and at the same time was writing a three-a-week column for the newspaper.

'Old J. M. Smyllie, the editor, would say to Jack Jones, features editor, "Has Behan turned in his copy?" and Jack'd say, "No, he has not indeed" and with that Smyllie would come to the window, throw it open, and yell up at me, standing on the scaffolding, "Behan come up here and write your story. We're close on to deadline."'

We got into my car and started up Baggot Street, then on to Merrion Road and he talked all the way. I asked just how much rewriting was done on his books and articles and plays.

'Ah, an ocean of new words,' he said, 'but despite what you read, I do it myself, naturally with the help of editors and directors. And what's wrong with that?

'And where would Tom Wolfe have been without Max Perkins, also James Jones? There are some critics who would try to make me out nothing but a literary poseur. If they don't understand what I am and what I'm trying to say, the hell with the whole bloody lot of them. I'm not trying to please them, only meself and the people who read and listen to what I have to say.

'I haven't reached my peak yet, Give me time. Oh, if only time will hold out for me, I'll be happy.''

He motioned me to stop and we gave an old lady in a black shawl a lift.

'Relax, mother,' he said, 'for here I am a Texas millionaire and this man (nodding toward me) is my chauffeur.'

'I know your face from the pictures in the press', she said. 'You be a good boy.'

At his insistence we kept on to Dun Laoghaire. 'I'm making a public appearance', he said. 'Inside, they are holding a national songfest. My appearance is sort of a sneak preview. I'm in fine voice.'

I refused to go in. He swaggered his way toward the hall. Now he was not being himself. Now he was being a swaggering Behan.

The followiing morning I read about it in the Dublin papers. He had gone on stage, where he had sung and danced and told stories. Three strong Christian brothers had escorted him from the stage and firmly eased him out, but not into oblivion.

There must be a lot of talk in Dublin, also all over Ireland, about Himself and his doings, which were legendary before he died. Even those in Ireland who didn't like him never underrated him.

# My Friend Brendan Behan*

## CATHAL GOULDING

Brendan Behan was a kind of person that I don't think attached great significance to what he said or did. But there was to my mind, in a lot of things, he was responsible, particularly in Republican circles and in different working-class and left-wing circles in Ireland for, say, a kind of an awakening. I wouldn't say that wouldn't have come out and it would, certainly, but he helped to develop it, you know, the kind of attitude, a more radical attitude in Ireland because Ireland was a very stuffy place in a sense. It wasn't stuffy from the point of view of getting drunk or fighting or drinking or singing or something like that; that was quite all right. But from the point of view of personal freedom of our people it was, and still is, and still is bad enough when you consider there is no such thing as divorce in Ireland and a lot of things like that. So, he had a lot of things to say too about the attitude of the Irish revolutionaries; he was very critical in particular about *The Hostage* and other things like that. You see he always did at the same time, although he didn't criticise, he didn't, what we term 'knock it'; he didn't. His criticism was criticism of something he thought necessary. He wasn't a kind of destructive person; he didn't want to destroy it; he wanted to, say, readapt itself or if you like, realign itself to the true ideals of Republicanism, and in Ireland, when it was originally introduced here in, say, roughly about the 1790s, 1780s. It was a very radical thing indeed; and coming as it did after the French Revolution, and to some extent, developing on the same lines like the American Revolution. People

* Extracted from an interview taped in Dublin on 15 September 1977. This is the first appearance in print.

like Wolfe Tone and Thomas Addis Emmett and these other people were much more radical types of revolutionaries than most people, say, like the French revolutionaries or the American revolutionaries. Their attitude was that the people who really mattered in Ireland at that time were the people with no property. Well, the French Revolution didn't take into consideration the people with no property; it was the lower middle classes who were in emerging industrial positions and weren't about to accept any longer the dictates of the aristocrats. The American position was, to some extent, slightly different but at the same time it was people who were developing a new country, like say, mostly engaged in some kind of agricultural pursuits in some shape or form, and trade, and were resentful of the burden of taxes and other kinds of regulations that were put on to restrict them in this development. And they weren't fighting for freedom of the Indians, anyway; and there were plenty of other people like the Blacks and poor white people that weren't considered. But Brendan's whole attitude was to, I suppose, create resentment to some extent to what he said; even to his friends. And then, from that position, to try and make them do a rethink on it. There are lots of little things – *The Hostage* to me was a very deep kind of study of the whole situation in relation to living and trying to exist in Ireland, particularly when you consider the people who had struggled in the physical sense and the actual return. I don't say that they want us any special place; they didn't, but they were just as discarded as were ordinary people, the ordinary people in this country.

Brendan was writing all the time. When he was about twelve years of age he wrote some articles for an Irish magazine. Now, the only place that they could get any copies of them would be in the National Library – would be in the 1930s, say, if they had any copies. I remember in 1939 he wrote a poem; that was one of the first poems he wrote. That he was in a paper called the *Irish Democrat*. Now, there has been so many *Irish Democrat*s; at the present moment I couldn't tell you which one it was. I also remember reading in prison lots of things he wrote, different short stories and things like that, and novels and things, and none of them were published. He wrote a play called *The Landlady*; that was his first play. I think one of the first books or stories he wrote was called 'The Execution' and then there was one called 'Green Flags' or something like that; more or less a life-story. It was a kind of an autobiographical thing, something on the same lines as O'Casey's *Drums under the Windows*. I don't know where that is either. And then I remember reading long ago *Richard's Cork Leg*; he wrote it in Gaelic; it was *La Breá san Roilg*. But there was one piece that he wrote which I think was a masterpiece. It was a translation of a very old Gaelic poem called *Cuirt an Mhean-Oidhche*, 'The Midnight Court'. Frank O'Connor did some translations of it in a book called *Kings, Lords and Commons*. When Behan was in the 'glasshouse', that's the military detention barracks, he did a translation of the *Cuirt an Mhean-Oidhche* there and I think it was one of the best translations I ever read. It is certainly better than O'Connor's, because O'Connor wrote his translation to be published and therefore it wasn't as bawdy or as earthy as the original Gaelic poem.

Concerning Ulick O'Connor's claim that Brendan was a homosexual. We used to go to a place called the Catacombs in Dublin, and it was just after the war and Dublin was kind of fairly wide open town at that time, beause you had lots of American servicemen coming over here on leave. There were still many of them who had not been demobilised in Europe or in England and owing to the shipping situation there was loads of meat here, things like that, that were plentiful and cheap. England was starved of meat, butter and stuff like that. We had a brewery here that was in full production all the time and we had plenty of whiskey and if we hadn't whiskey we had poteen, home-made spirit. American soldiers came over for a good time. When they got their leave they came over to Ireland and it was wine, women and song. So, apart from the official pubs and places like that, they developed kind of shebeen; not really anything that was organised or commercialised, but it was a kind of a spontaneous thing. And the Catacombs was placed down off Fitzwilliam Square and it was in the old basements of these Georgian houses. I'd say people were beginning to get a bit trendy about these old basements and, oh, say an artist or some person would talk about a poet or a painter or something and would do them up, limewash them, all brick-vaulted ceilings, and all this kind of wine-cellars where they used to keep the bottles – kind of a maze of passages and things like that. And they got them for a very small amount of money; rents were cheap enough then and these places were for nothing. If the landlord got the price of a drink a week out of them, he thought he was getting something because nobody would live in them; they were rat-infested and everything. But they took these on and then what they'd do is they would have 'hoolees'[1] as they call them, you know the pubs would shut and they'd have parties in them when you would buy a few bottles and bring them back and you'd always know there'd be somebody there, or if there was nobody there, well, the door wasn't shut anyway. The people who owned the place or who rented the place would be back sometime and they wouldn't mind, so you could bring somebody there. If you had a girlfriend you could bring her there and nobody bothered. You found a place for yourself then afterwards you had a few drinks or you had a few drinks before or whatever. But it got to the stage where you had maybe homosexuals and people who weren't indulging in any kind of sex whatsoever but just went there for a singsong, like a party. Irish people are very partial when they get drunk to singsong, a bit of music, things like that; that's mainly what it was. But there was everything; if you wanted it it was there. And Brendan used to go there and Brendan wanted everything. He would never let anything go by that he wouldn't try at some stage or another. And I know for a fact that on many occasions he had women there. But I never knew him to have a man there; but I know that there were plenty of homosexuals that went there and had their homosexual relationships with each other, whatever it may be, and that was it. That was one of the things that put O'Connor on. Now I was in prison with Brendan Behan and if a person is ever sex-starved anywhere he has to be sex-starved in prison, and I never knew him to indulge in homosexual activities with anybody in prison. If he did, it would have been well known. Actually it was McCann, I think, that first of all discovered the Catacombs episode. Then O'Connor got on to that; then he went to America to trace up Brendan's activities in the States, in New York particularly. I just can't remember the name of the sailor lad that more or less gave him most of this information in the States. That's, I think, the situation in relation to where O'Connor got most of this information.

At the time of *The Hostage*, Brendan wasn't active in the IRA anymore, and the police knew that of course. His picture used to be in the papers in England and in America and in France and other places like that, and he had written *Borstal Boy* and had become more or less famous. And he said to me, well look, if the police are ever looking for you and you're trying to dodge them, you can sleep in my house, you see. So I said, fair enough, that's very good. One day I was going home and my son met me on the road; he was very young at the time, about twelve or thirteen, and he said the police are up in the house. When they came up he had gone out the back door. They didn't mind; they let him go away. They were waiting for me to come home but I didn't go home. I went down to a house we had at the time. So I decided to go up and see Brendan then. I went up and he was there. I said look I have a put-up place at the moment I don't need. But he wouldn't let me leave the house; I had to stay there that night. He gave me the key then and all the time that he was there. We were there for about, I suppose, five or six months before he went to America. And when he went to America I was in the house on my own. That was very handy for me because it was a house and the neighbours knew that I was staying there beforehand; they didn't attach any importance to me. It was just somebody minding the house for Brendan and it was a very good cover. And then he was in great form about going away, but I noticed a tremendous change in him when he came back from America. He hadn't been drinking for nearly twelve months before he left Dublin, and when he came back from America he was really bad and he never really broke. He tried on a number of occasions but never really got rid of it, he never kicked the habit then. He always came back to it; even sometimes he might stop in a hospital too, and he had some very stupid people he thought were friends of his who would take him drinks in the hospital.

We never lost contact with each other really, never. But from the time I came home from England in '59 up to the time he died, I would say, once I was out I was nearly in daily contact with him; certainly most weekends we used to go somewhere together, even if it was only spending three nights a week looking for him to find out where he was. But he was one of these fellas that money didn't mean anything to. I've seen him going into these brothels, you know, we haven't many of them in Dublin, but very unofficial and very low-class places. But mostly there was one place called the Continental Café that was run by a woman, Fawcett was her name. She was born and reared in Dublin but her people were Italian, I think, and with her son used to run it between them. But the girls from the streets used to go in there and you could always buy drink in it, even till late at night, and they used to serve it to you in cups and saucers so that when you are drinking if the police came in, well, you could drink it real quick and you had an empty cup. But there were no glasses in the place and they'd mix the drink with orange or something like that. Brendan used to go there very often; I often went there myself. But I remember one night looking for him all over the place and eventually finding him in Dolly Fawcett's; Dolly Fawcett's we'd call it. He was sitting down at the table and he was drunk and he had just received a cheque for two or three hundred pounds, probably was royalties or something from America from *The Hostage* or something like that. I said to him, what about going home. Ah, he said, we'll go home but he says I'll bring my friends. I said fair enough, I don't mind. But I said I haven't room for them all. There were about maybe four prostitutes and their bodyguards, or business managers or whatever you like to call them. So I said well I haven't room for them all. So he said, ah it's okay, we'll get a taxi. So we arrived home at his house, knocked on the door, Beatrice is in bed asleep. Well, she is in bed, anyway. So I called her, she gets up and comes down and opens the door. I said, well we've arrived as you know. I expected her to say get out of here. I have a few friends, Brendan said. Bring them in. So we went and sat in the parlour and she went up and put a coat on and came down and she made tea. She got glasses and poured out drink for his friends. She knew who they were; she knew we brought them from Dolly Fawcett's, that they were prostitutes and business managers and everything else. Now I felt that that was a great thing. She knew he was on his way out, like there was nothing she could do with him. She was doing the best she could and the fact – like she used to say, I don't care who they are or what they are and I don't care how much they steal from him as long as they bring him home. That was that, you see. Like to see her at three in the morning; her man was missing for three days and I arrived home with him with three or four prostitutes and she pouring our drink, making tea and sandwiches for them.

Brendan was like a brother. A brother that was very, very hard to put up with for the last year of his life, because he had become too bad. I don't mean bad in himself; he wasn't a bad person by any means. But his alcoholism had taken over completely and there was very little of the human Behan left in him for the last few months anyway. You could say that he was disgusting really, like in lots of ways. It was only when he would come out in the morning time and may be getting down to the hospital for an injection for the first hour or two after that that he resembled the person he was at all. He used to come down here; my mother knew him from a baby and nursed him, and he would come in here – our older people, like they wouldn't use language like we use. But Brendan would come in and he'd start swearing and using rough language and my mother would say now you stop that or I'd box your ears. And he'd stop; he wouldn't say any more, he'd never even though he was very drunk, he wouldn't. But she used to get him and she would, say, make a bowl of soup and she wouldn't let him leave until he drank the bowl of soup because she knew he couldn't have eaten anything for days. And he used to be, he had that awe of her, that kind of little bit of respect for somebody who had slapped his bottom when he was young, and had given him a penny or something like that, that when she said you do that he'd do it, and it was amazing to see that. In the last year of his life there was one time there in the beginning when he became famous he loved to go to places like Luggala Castle[2] and dine with Lord Browne[3] and, say well, he was invited to Jack Kennedy's inauguration and he'd met this body and that body and he'd name names you see. Well, when he really got sick, he went back looking for people that he hadn't met for years and years and years; he came back like to what he came from and other people like, say, the Guinnesses and all these kind of people that were big in the theatre and so forth; lots of them would love to say and do say, they were great friends of his. But lots of them didn't want to see him then, for a start, but certainly he went back to that, he did. He came back – it was funny to see because he hadn't been in this house here. We came to live here, say, in the late thirties, and he had been, used to be, in and out of this house and he had gone out to Kimmage in 1938–9. That's when they went out to Crumlin rather, and when he went to Crumlin we used to meet each other in town more or maybe I'd go over to his house and the odd time he'd come over here. But then when we got to be quite adult and got married, I never went out to his mother's house much and he never came to my mother's house. But immediately in that last eighteen months or so of his life he started. It just happened like one Christmas; we used to come here, my brothers and I used to come here and have a drink with my father who was an old man, and they used to come here. And one Christmas he rang up Christmas Day. Can I come over? – and he came over; himself and Beatrice came over. Well, that was, I suppose, the second to last Christmas before he died, and the next Christmas after that he was too sick to go anywhere. But he came over here, I think it was Boxing Day or the day after that, like around Christmas. But he used to come here and when he came here my mother used to fight him for being dirty and wash his face. She'd go to the bathroom and she'd get a towel and wet it and she'd wash his face and comb his hair. And he loved that, even though she'd fight with him and she'd tell him he was a blackguard and he was a drunkard and wasted his money and all that. He knew that she liked him and that's why she was doing it. But the last few times he went to hospital, well the last time he was in hospital he couldn't pass water; he was on drip and kidney machine and all these things. To be quite straight with you, it was better that he died then; it was better because his liver was – he wanted to die too. He wanted to die. I couldn't really say, you know, when I started to read up, the first thing that annoyed me about O'Connor's biography was the picture on the cover. You see the picture on the cover was an exact replica of a beer-bottle label and I said this in the review, if you remember.[4]

From the time that Brendan was very young he was very conscious of the inequality of people in the world, and he was very conscious of the fact that so many people were exploited, victimised and discriminated against. He was very, very cynical about lots of things; but he always was very, very vocal in attacking hypocrisy, whether it was religious hypocrisy or political hypocrisy or anything else. I remember even years and years ago his insistence on the fact that we in the National Liberation Movement in Ireland weren't simply looking for a change of flag or green pillar boxes instead of red pillar boxes or whatever it might be; we were looking for a social system that was going to deal with people justly and equally and that where people would have a chance to develop as human beings. And also when he saw something that was wrong and people wouldn't admit that it was wrong, like cover up, many people do for, say, sentimental or other reasons, he was very, very vitriolic. For instance, one time there the Republican movement, our movement in Ireland here, was noted for its factionalism and things like that; all the splits and things like that would happen, he would say, how we never agree on any little thing. I remember just after the war there was an old prison, his father and my father were in prison, called Kilmainham Prison, and a number of people formed a committee because some developers wanted to buy the site and knock down the old prison that had been vacant; since about 1932 it hadn't been used. And the developers wanted to buy this and knock it down and build an office block or something there. And a lot of these people got together and they protested about this and they formed a committee and the corporation or whoever it was that owned the thing allowed them to take the prison over and renovate it and clean it up and put in new bars for the drunks and they made a kind of a national museum out of it, national liberation museum out of it. When the committee was in formation, a lot of people were invited to it. I wasn't particularly interested in preserving prisons, neither was Brendan; but at the same time he was saying what we'd do and people would have to collect money and subscribe and this sort of thing. So Brendan said to him, 'Oh by the way, is this a Republican committee?' he says to the chairman. 'Oh, yes, Brendan, this is a Republican committee.' 'Are you sure this is a Republican committee?' 'I am, yes', he says. 'Well let's prove it,' says Brendan, 'let's prove it.' 'How can we prove it?' says the man. 'Let's have a split.' Nothing that was Republican would ever. And it is true, the committee was only going for six months and it was split, there was a split. I think that the humanity in a person, I suppose, it was one of the things he saw, before many of us saw in the movement, like how essential it was to have a kind of socialist outlook or perspective, if you like. There was no point in us in Ireland, say, pushing the British out if we put in a government that was going to do the very same thing as the British were doing.

Brendan was a very warm kind of a person and either hated you or he liked you and he could fight with you tomorrow; it wouldn't mean anything. He could fight with you three times in one day – like Myles Na Gopaleen.[5] Him and Brendan were great company for about fifteen or twenty minutes and then suddenly they'd explode. Both of them were alcoholics, and they would fight with each other, you just couldn't tear them apart, and then maybe in an hour's time they'd be together again. For about fifteen or twenty minutes Brendan could reef you asunder today, and tomorrow it was as if nothing ever happened. And some people who did very bad turns on him, certainly there is a lot of people in this town, and in a few days' time it doesn't matter. But I think that he was a person who was a great human being with a great attitude to people in general. He would go to a tinkers' camp and talk and sing with them and drink with them, get drunk with them. Well, I can do that too to some extent; but I always have this kind of idea in my mind that I've got to watch my step. I do this but he wouldn't care; he'd fall down drunk at the fire, say, and was quite content to trust them with him that they wouldn't abandon him or leave him or something like that, which in most cases they wouldn't, because I think it's like the way my mother used to treat him. It's like when you get on that wavelength with them they treat you as one of their own.

## NOTES

Cathal Goulding, a Dublin contractor and an old IRA friend of Behan. Cf. 'Cathal Goulding, a very dear friend of mine whom I had known since childhood. We had known each other almost from the time we were born. We had been in the Fianna Boy Scout Organisation together and joined the IRA together, had been thrown out of it together and had been taken back in it together' – Brendan Behan, *Confessions of an Irish Rebel* (London: Hutchinson, 1965) p. 64. Goulding is also the subject of the chapter entitled 'Special Watch Prisoner' in Beatrice Behan's memoir of her husband, *My Life with Brendan* (London: Leslie Frewin, 1973).

1. House dances, usually associated with drinking and bordering on a 'wild party'.
2. For a note on Luggala Castle see p. 180.
3. Of the Guinness family.
4. Cathal Goulding, 'From the Reverential to the Scurrilous', *Hibernia* (Dublin), 7 Aug 1970, p. 11.
5. For a note on Myles Na Gopaleen (Brian O'Nolan) see p. 85.

# My Brother Brendan*

RORY FURLONG

I never met Brendan at any time when he didn't give me money. A few bob [shillings] now would be ten pounds. A lot of money then, say, around the sixties. And he did this for a lot of people. I know people who would come to him and they would say we haven't got our electricity bill paid – fellows who were forever coming to him, and he would say, right, and he would go down himself with them to the ESB and he would pay the bill there and then. But he wouldn't give them the money in case they go off and drink it. And he would pay their rent too – for people living in flats and in corporation houses. He'd pay up all the rent for them. And this is all forgotten; people who don't know any of this, any of this so-called research with regard to Brendan never brought that into the public eye, never let the people know the humanitarianism of Brendan. You could go on for years and years and years speaking about what he did and the good he did for people. He was a very delightful man. I attribute the fact that he died so young – it wasn't from drinking, in any case. A lot of people said, I read critics who have said that his talents got dried up and this put him on to drink. That's another lie, because his talents hadn't dried up at all. It was this illness that was scraping on him and would bring him to hospital. Many times I brought him myself into hospital.

Not many people know the fact that it was the people, the children, of Crumlin, with their pennies and their shillings who put a plaque on 70 Kildare Road in bronze, which was designed and executed by John Behan, the sculptor.[1] And John was so proud of it that he wouldn't even allow our own people to put it in position; he had to put it in position himself. He felt proud of the fact that he was asked to design this. I personally asked him to design it and he did it. This, in other words, was done by the poor people of Dublin. And this is where, if there's going to be any recollection of Brendan Behan by the people of Ireland, it will come from the poor people. It won't come from, as he described himself, the intellectuals. He is highly appreciated in Cork City, where there are people down there always willing to do something. He is also appreciated in Dublin because he had so many real genuine friends here – more friends than a lot of the people he knew in the early 1960s.

* Extracted from interviews taped in Dublin on 29 and 31 January 1978. This is the first appearance in print.

On one particular day we went up to visit one of his poor friends and one of the little girls, she was about twelve, came dancing over to Brendan and she said Brendan we are making my confirmation on Thursday. Confirmation is, well you know, anyone who has read 'The Confirmation Suit' will know what confirmation is in Ireland, particularly Roman Catholic confirmation. He said now isn't that grand; on Thursday you're making your confirmation. It is, she said, it's lovely Brendan, but I don't think I'll have a new dress. Well, Brendan said, for one thing, he said, you will have the best dress in the school, and he said, you will have shoes, a handbag and everything, and a coat, he said, everything that goes to making your confirmation – and I'll buy you also a silver medal. And he took this child's mother there and then, immediately down to the centre of the town and into Arnott's, in Henry Street, and bought the best, the very best outfit that could be bought for any little girl who will be making her confirmation at any day. The mother said it cost him about sixty pounds to rig the child out; and sixty pounds would have been then a lot of money around 1959. And he did that. This would sound a bit maudlin, but these are things that stay with me and that I have told you before. The people whose bills he paid, the number of children he bought shoes for.

Brendan would sing and sing until the cows come home. He'd play a song on a mouth-organ beautifully. You see a lot of people forgot this. Actually, his real start, his first start came on a children's programme on radio when he played, I think it was sixpence it cost him, the harmonica. They called them harmonicas at that time; we call them mouth-organs. That was his first appearance, I would say, in public. He was about eleven years old when he played the mouth-organ. I remember quite well because outside of that he couldn't play. He wouldn't be able, he would never be on the bloody radio. But he was on radio all right, when he was about twelve. Did it all on his own. He played jazz and swing and everything else. But this is how we came to, one of the reasons how we came to do this record.[2]

Anybody who knew Brendan as well as I knew him and his way of life as well as I knew him would know full well that he wasn't, in any manner and means, bisexual, homosexual; he was heterosexual, the same as the rest of us. Not that there is anything wrong, as he would have said himself – being homosexual or even bisexual, because in our poverty days, I mean, in his poverty days, some of our best friends in Dublin were homosexuals, some of our very best friends were homosexuals. Just because Brendan would throw his arms around me or you and kissed you; they do that in France and the continent all the time, all the time, and this was one of the reasons, I think – I've written to the, on that occasion I wrote to the newspapers denying it most emphatically, to the three Irish national dailies, and I denied that emphatically.[3] Not because I would have been worried had he been a homosexual; I don't think that this, when it was written, I don't think it was written with malicious intents. I think it was just written from the point of view of sensationalism more than anything else, or if not sensationalism, false information was given to Ulick O'Connor. I believe that; whether Ulick believes it or not, I don't know. But he never had any time to apologise to me except on one occasion when, after my letters to the papers, I was on a programme on radio with Ulick O'Connor and he asked me, before the programme, not to have a confrontation. He said please Rory, don't have a confrontation tonight. So what could you do? I didn't want to have a confrontation because I thought at the time that the less publicity of this kind of writing, gush, with regard to Brendan, the less it got the better. I don't think it made any great impression on the book, on Ulick O'Connor's book or on the people who read it because I have yet, among all the people I know, have yet to meet one who would ever dream of saying such a thing of Brendan. As a matter of fact, not only of Brendan but any of Brendan's friends either.

### NOTES

Rory Furlong, Behan's half-brother. He is the only one of Behan's brothers who still lives in Dublin. The recent unveiling of a plaque on 14 Russell Street to commemorate Behan inspired Rory to write a short play entitled *The Street*. It was broadcast on the Canadian Broadcasting Corporation on 25 March 1975.

1. See 'At the Unveiling of a Bronze Head of Brendan Behan', *Evening Press* (Dublin), 9 June 1975, p. 3.
2. 'We Remember Brendan Behan – Our Own Dear Laughing Boy', Midnite Records (Ireland) AM 304. (An album of songs by Sean Og McKenna, Noel Carrol, and Liam Rowsome; with sleeve-notes by Rory Furlong.)
3. See Rory Furlong, 'New Book on Brendan Behan', *Irish Independent* (Dublin), 29 July 1970, p. 8.

# Behan's Mother Wasn't There*

## CLARE BOYLAN

When the curtains opened at the Abbey last night the stage was set with prison walls and bench, and alongside a large portrait of a strong-jawed young Irishman hung bold white lettering which spelt out the words 'Borstal Boy'. Brendan Behan's documentation of British prison life was having its premiere in a packed house.[1]

* *Evening Press* (Dublin), 11 Oct 1967, p. 3.

It seemed as though the whole world was there. Only the one woman who knew Brendan better than anyone else was missing. Kathleen, the mother of Brendan, lay in her sickbed last night at the Meath Hospital.

Kathleen Behan has been in hospital for three months now. She was put there by a motor accident, just three days before the death of her husband. When I spoke to her yesterday evening, she said she had read the script of the play, and had examined the poster for *Borstal Boy* many times.

'I'm very happy about Frank McMahon's adaptation of *Borstal Boy*', she told me. 'It's very, very good. I'm sure it will be a great success. It's a grand treat for Beatrice, too.

'Brendan was such a great man, God rest him. His sense of humour was with him from the day he was born and never left him to the day he died. He was full of fun and love and songs, and that's what *Borstal Boy* is all about. People are going to like it. They all need a good laugh, don't they?'

Kathleen Behan unfolded the poster and took another look. 'I like that picture at the bottom – just like him. I think it was taken shortly before he died.

'Come here till I tell you a story about Brendan when he was a little lad. I just want you to see how little he changed.

'He was five years old when this happened, and we were living in a tenement. He toddled out of the house and rambled in next door, where a neighbour was giving breakfast to her family.

'She had just put on some eggs to cook when she saw this extra *little visitor* coming in, she sat him down, she couldn't afford to cook an egg for little Brendan, so she poured him a cup of tea and buttered some bread for him.

'Brendan sat for a while staring disconsolately at his plate, not touching a thing. When the neighbour said to him: "Have you lost your appetite, child – will you not eat up your breakfast?" our little Brendan looked at the lad beside him and said, "Hello egg."

'Even at that age, he had more sense of humour than most men develop in a lifetime.'

Although Kathleen Behan has not been able to be present at any of the rehearsals for *Borstal Boy*, she is well acquainted with the man who represents him in the play.

'Niall Toibin was a great friend of Brendan's. He could hardly play the part if he didn't know him. Niall knew Brendan better than anyone, and I'm glad it's he who has the part. I believe they have a grand young man playing Brendan as a young chap, too.'

'It's nice to see Brendan remembered. He was a man that loved everyone. He was always good to the old folk and he loved little children. When he used to throw pennies for children, and later on it was shillings and half-crowns, he used to get anxious in case some of the little ones wouldn't manage to get any of the money.

'I always liked *Borstal Boy*, because it's Brendan as he was to me – forgiving and good-natured. *The Hostage* was great too, but *The Quare Fellow* was a little bit sad, I think.

'My favourite part in *Borstal Boy* is where he's serving at Mass. Brendan used to be an altar boy, you know. I hope to God I get well soon so I can see the play before it moves from the Abbey.'

## NOTE

1. Frank McMahon's adaptation of *Borstal Boy* was presented at the Abbey Theatre, Dublin, on 10 October 1967, during the Dublin Theatre Festival.

# Brendan*

## BRIAN BEHAN

Ah Death where is thy sting-a-ling-a-ling?

*The Hostage*

'What do I think of Brendan Behan?' The lorry-driver looked worried for a minute. 'Oh I know, the big fat Irishman that was always getting drunk on telly. Well, he's a lad. Isn't he?'

Was this all there was to brother Brendan? Was he just the poor man's drunken Beatle? The crown prince of the never-ending booze-up? The press wrote big headlines that said nothing. The biggest thing about their stories was their complete lack of knowledge about Brendan. Why did he kill himself; a man who loved life? Loved to swim, play Rugby football and above all, read. Hidden behind a waterfall of beer was a man who could no longer live in a world where all the things he had fought for came to nothing. A disappointed man. Yes, disappointed in the failure of the Republican movement. Disappointed in the collapse of the left-wing world that looked upon Stalin as our father and Russia as our Mecca.

For my brother was first and foremost a rebel. He really fought for the things he believed in. And that made him different. He came out of a house

* *Spectator* (London), CCXIII (17 July 1964) 77–9. Forms chapter 30 in his autobiography, *With Breast Expanded* (London: MacGibbon and Kee, 1964) pp. 200–8.

that never took poverty or oppression for granted. My mother rocked him to the air of Connolly's[1] rebel song:

> Come workers sing a rebel song,
> A song of love and hate,
> Of love unto the lowly
> And of hatred to the great.
> The great who trod our fathers down,
> Who steal our children's bread,
> Whose greedy hands are ere outstretched
> To rob the living and the dead.

My mother sang not just of hatred, but of the blessed day to come when the darkest hour would herald the brightest dawn.

Our kitchen; seven of us; my mother scrubbing and singing. Proudly she lifts her head and belts out the end of her song.

> And labour shall rise from her knees boys
> And claim the broad earth as her own.

My brother was a rebel with a thousand causes. When the Italians invaded Abyssinia, our Brendan sang, 'Will you come to Abyssinia will you come, bring your own ammunition and a gun.' When, in my ignorance, I sneered at homosexuals he turned on me like a tiger and told me to keep my dirty ignorant thoughts to myself. Although he was only fourteen when the Spanish Civil War broke out he moved heaven and earth to get out there.

From the very start our Brendan was the favourite son. Good-looking with a head of dark brown curls; he easily captivated my Granny who worshipped the ground he walked on. He was to lack for nothing in a street where money was counted in halfpennies and pennies. Bengy we called him and from the start felt a little in awe of this disturbing creature who could cut you up with his tongue or his fists, as he chose. Yet running through Nature's abundant cup was a thin line of poison. For years he suffered with his nerves which caused him to stutter. He overcame this eventually but even years later when he became excited back it came. Underneath his ebullience he was a quivering mass of too much feeling. Feelings deep, raw and violent that were liable to explode at the slightest provocation. Then like a mad stallion he couldn't bear to be bridled by anyone.

He first wrote for the Republican paper *An Phoblact*. How proud I was of his work in print. Yet I remember, I fought him that night because he taunted me about my silences.

Brendan was as Dublin as the hills and loved every stone of it. On my father's side the Behans stretch back ten generations of Dublin bowsies. My granny Behan was a tenement landlady, fat, black, and powerful as any man. Thanks to the survival of the fittest the breed was short, stocky and hardy. Brendan could have lived to be ninety if he had chosen to. From my father came his love of people, from my mother his idealism. Good, uncomplicated Da, who always has a ready excuse for anyone's transgressions and in whose stubby little hands are the work of a lifetime. Fierce, wolflike mother, who would rouse a brigade of the dead to fight for freedom. Out of these two came Brendan. Brendan, who challenged everything to the death and then burst out laughing as he was finished doing it. Brendan, who in his youth could keep you entertained for hours acting and mimicking and making up outrageous stories about anyone he despised. One time there was a mother in the road who was driving everyone mad boasting about how she'd sent her darling boy to Lourdes to walk in the Holy Procession. According to Brendan she'd sent him equipped with a pair of wooden hands, which he wore piously clasped in front, while he picked pockets with his real ones.

One of our uncles was the owner of an old Dublin music hall, the Queen's. He would often send us free passes and it was great for us boys sitting in the stalls amongst all the posh customers watching plays like *The Colleen Bawn* and *Arrah na Pog*. It's small wonder that Brendan took so well to plays and play-writing.

But like everyone else he had to work for his living, and my mother's call changed from 'Brendan you'll be late for school' to 'Brendan get up for your work, your father's just going out.' He followed Da as an apprentice to the painting trade. Not just a brush hand but sign-writing and decorating. He joined the union but only attended one or two meetings. A labour Republican, he saw more in direct action than long-winded resolutions. And all the while we were splitting asunder as a family. My brother Seamus was off to fight Hitler while Rory joined the Free Staters and supported de Valera's neutrality. I was a Marxist and looked down my nose at Republican adventurers.

One night Brendan came home to tell us that he had denounced the capitalists in his union branch for 'driving along the Stillorgan Road in their brothel wagons killing the children of the poor'. Unimpressed I poured cold water on his efforts and he went away hurt and dismayed.

Yet the family feeling has never completely dried up. It still warms my heart to remember the long letters Brendan wrote me from Borstal when I was in Malin, telling me to keep my heart up and remember it couldn't last forever.

In the intervals when we were all at home together I never saw him but he was writing. Sitting up in bed, typewriter on his knees, he never thought of food or drink till he was finished what he was doing. Then he would come down to a great bowl of soup. Worn and unshaven he looked a proper Bill Sikes.

In the main we were afraid of him. It wasn't just that he could be cruel and biting, he had an unpleasant habit of putting his finger right on the truth. So that when you had a conversation with him it was like walking in a minefield, a single lie could unleash a desperate bang.

At length he burned his paintbrushes and determined to live as best he could amongst the left-bank Parisians and the arty set in Dublin. He had never had much reverence for toil. One time he was made foreman over some painters doing out a hospital. My mother sent me to pick up his money for fear it might vanish in some pub. When I got to the job I proudly asked where my brother, the foreman, might be. 'Ah,' said the painter, taking a swig at a bottle of Guinness, 'you mean Brendan man, he's one of the best. Jasus if we only had him on every job. He's out there now singing with the cleaners.' And there he was sitting on some laundry baskets between two charwomen, drunk as a monkey's uncle. He was great for organising a job of work. As the painter said, 'It's seven hours for drink and one for the work and if that interferes with the drink we'll get rid of it.'

I woke one morning to see the special police tearing our house apart. Brendan had shot a policeman and they told my father, 'Let him give himself up, Stephen, or he's a dead man.' My father, who had fought in the IRA with some of the specials, pleaded with them not to plug our Brendan. Two days later Brendan was sentenced to fourteen years.

By now our house had become notorious as the local Kremlin. When Brendan came out of jail after doing about three years he found that my mother's life was being made miserable by the neighbours who were having a persecution by gossip campaign, calling her a Communist cow and other such pleasantries. He soon put a stop to that by going round the streets knocking on doors and informing all and sundry that he intended having an early Guy Fawkes night and burning down the house of anyone maligning his mother. Then off we went again into the night with my mother begging him, 'Brendan love, take care of yourself.' My mother was convinced by now that he was mad. Not mad in the loony sense, but mad with spirit and too much feeling that knew no bounds. Mad in the sense of too deep perceptions, of second sight almost. Mad in the sense that one minute he could be prickly and truculent and impossible to communicate with, and the next cuddly and loveable as a teddy bear.

He had a real feeling for old people. Once on a visit home I went to see my aunt Maggy Trimble. 'Ah Brian,' she said, 'your Brendan, God love him, was here yesterday in a great big car, and he nearly tore the house down knocking. "Brendan," I says, "what's wrong?" "Nothing", he shouted, "Get your coat, you and me mother are coming out for the day." "Oh Brendan," I said, "I'm too shabby, look at the cut of me, I can't ride in that big car." He only roared like the town bull. "To hell with poverty, we'll kill a chicken." And out he dragged me Brian. And away the three of us went up the mountains drinking and eating to our hearts' content. Ah, God love him for thinking of an old woman.'

My mother has always had to be ready for anything. Another time he whipped her out of our kitchen, pinny and all, and the next thing she knew she was on the plane to England and a weekend at the Savoy. One night we were knocked up in the early hours to find three beautiful women bearing an unconscious Brendan into the kitchen. They laid him on the floor with all reverence while my mother ran crying round her poor cock sparrow, roundly abusing the three young women.

His friends ranged from a Dublin composer who haunted our kitchen just to hear my mother talk, to gunmen just out of jail who drank morosely and long while they talked of various nicks and mushes. When it came to ideas Brendan was always a stirring stick. He never accepted Communism, it was too cut and dried for his liking, and the idea of party discipline was anathema to him. But like many writers who came out of toil and travail he supported the Russian Revolution, believing it would eventually bring world freedom. Like us all he longed for the day when we would establish a new world free from hunger and poverty. In his case it was more a longing for the big rock candy mountains, a kind of tired man's heaven. He longed to go to Russia but never made it. During the Cold War the C[ommunist] P[arty] couldn't get enough tame clods to visit Russia and 'report back.' Brendan came to me and asked if I would use my influence to see that he got onto one of these cultural delegations. But the CP would never have risked sending him. They couldn't be sure what he would say when he came back, and a Brendan let loose in Red Square would have hastened Stalin's heart attack by a few years. Brendan ranted and raved about the idiots they were sending, while real men were left behind. He was right, all we wanted were a few castrated scribblers who would see only what we wanted them to see. Brendan had no politics, he made them up as he went along. He used to say the first Communists were some monks in Prague who agreed to hold everything in common long before Marx appeared on the scene.

As he became famous he was sought after by the rich and powerful, but he was a very chancy bedfellow. Once at Dublin airport he told reporters that he had to go to America to earn money to support some ignoramus in the Government who couldn't tell a pig from a rabbit.

When I visited Dublin from England I never sought him out. I'd seen him over here surrounded by what appeared to me to be sycophants and toadies, and I didn't want to seem to be one of them. Also I always had a sneaking fear that he'd think I wanted to sponge on him. Anyway it would have cost a fortune to hold your own with him when it came to buying drinks. I wonder now if he didn't lose a lot of genuine friends through this. Anyway he came twice to see me. Once bounding up the stairs in Dublin shouting, 'Why must you live like a fucking monk? Why can't you come out and have a drink, like anyone else?' I started to get mad, but behind his bluster he looked so unsure and anxious that I couldn't keep it up. Another time he descended on us like a tornado in a Dublin street, and dragging me into the steamship office insisted on booking first-class fares for us all back to London.

During the strike at Shell Centre, he paraded round to see all the pickets, congratulating them on the fight and handing out money to all and sundry. Then he marched in the gate and soundly abused the scabs working inside. After, we went for a drink at the Hero of Waterloo and he told me, 'I'm proud of what you are doing', and he meant it. A blow struck, anywhere, against any oppression or injustice had his full support. Still he felt a bit out of it with the rest of the strike committee. Large, strong and very manly, they were completely different from the people he had become used to drinking with. These were men you didn't fool around with. For a while he tried pressing them to drink with him but they politely refused. He stood silent and worried, he was losing contact with the very people he admired. Suddenly he smiled. A street musician came into the pub with his flute. Brendan stuffed the old man's hat with coins and notes. Then taking up the flute he dipped it in a pint of cider and slowly began playing and dancing. Out into the street he went and began begging from the passing crowds. To the old man's delight he filled the hat several times over. This was Brendan; trying to reach out through a clown's mask into the hearts of humanity.

All the while his world was crumbling. The Republican movement had failed. Ten years of hunger strikes and jails and firing squads had smashed the movement that had set out to make old Ireland free. When all the world was young we thought unstinted sacrifice and fiery faith were sure to win out. But though stone walls could not a spirit break the released Republican prisoners from Dartmoor and Wakefield came back to stare at empty grates or hurry to the pub to relive old battles. Time had passed them by. The clear lines of the struggle for freedom in Russia, in Spain and in Ireland were breaking up. Russian guns at Budapest were blowing the workers' paradise to hell and a grey dust was falling on all the things we had held dear.

Brendan loved humanity; he believed heart and soul in its causes. He believed in the goodness of people. But the causes crumbled and his very success drove away his true friends and left him prey to the flatterers and spongers. Fame and success became his twin headstones. The more he got the less he had. The more he drank the less he understood what had happened to his world. He became harder and harder to put up with. One night when we were celebrating the opening of *The Hostage* he suddenly turned on me and called me a traitorous bastard for leaving the Communist Party. The party he would never join himself. Even so, I know he tried hard to get a grip on things. The last time we met, that is, not surrounded by hordes of other people, he invited me out for a drink but drank nothing himself. He had a beautiful tenor voice and knew all the operas, and he just sat singing to his mother and Celia, or listening to our talk. At closing time he stood outside looking so sad and pathetic that it made me cry to look at him. He took my hand and asked me what was wrong. I couldn't speak. In any case the truth was there in his own eyes. He was done for and there was nothing he or I or anyone could do about it.

Bengy, our most favoured brother, smiled on by Nature and people, was dying. He had all the wild wilfulness of my mother, but with no chain to bind him. Spoilt from birth by an overabundance of talk and flattery, he denied himself nothing. People destroy people. To make a god of someone is to destroy them as surely as driving a knife into their back. Our Brendan would brook no arguments as to what he did or where and when he did it.

Self-indulgence without caring what it does to those around you can be either selfishness or generosity, depending on where you are in the firing line. I remember once at *The Quare Fellow* a man came up to Brendan with his hand out saying, 'I knew you years ago.' Our Brendan loudly told him to 'fuck off out of it'. At the time I felt ill, but then maybe he was right, at least he lived his life without compromise in the way that he wanted to go. Perhaps the world is smaller for mingier people like ourselves. Brendan was above all an individualist in the extreme. A man possessed by demons that demanded absolute unquestioning obedience to his desires and whims. But then disillusion and boredom set in. Struggle will never kill you, boredom will. If there's nothing left to strive for, you collapse like a watery jelly. Standing opposite Brendan are the thousands of lemmings who march on to their deaths without ever doing a single thing to alter their unhappy states. His end is preferable to their mummification. I'm damn sure a world where the Brendans would rule would be a lot better than a crazy, stupid, chaotic one that we live in now. In the end there was nothing left for him to do but die, and like everything he did, he carried it to excess.

Certainly he feared nothing, not even death whose sting he reached out for again and again until it finished him off. He was bored: bored with life and people. He had come to despise most of us and accused the rest of either living in his shadow or waiting to borrow money off him. Restlessly he went round and round and came back to nothing. Why didn't he try writing a long novel? He was too much a person. He expressed himself in what he did and said, much more than in what he wrote. He was too big for his own skin. A lesser man might have peeped out at the world and made notes. Brendan jumped into it and gave that old triangle a mighty swipe. Worse, the press began to praise some of his stuff, even when it was rubbish. He told me, 'They'd praise my balls if I hung them high enough.' Some of his stuff he wrote now just to pay the tax man and the bills. This seems to be the inevitable fate of all those who write for a living. Sucked dry, they have their bones reboiled until every scrap of flesh is stripped white and clean. He wasn't writing better stuff before he died, it was getting distinctly ropy. Cut off from his main source of supply, real people, he couldn't write much about the cavorting set of false-faced bastards who praised his every belch as a sign of heavenly inspiration. But nothing or no one can take from *The Quare Fellow*, or *The Hostage*. I was very proud that my brother wrote them and that my family had added its little bit to make people laugh and cry.

Brendan was like a great storm at sea that lashes up wild waves and rocks the ships at anchor, only to spend itself in some quiet, peaceful valley. There it will drop to a quiet murmur twining its tired arms in the tall pines. Our Brendan is sleeping now, not far from the hills he loved so well. God save us from a world without room for the Brendan Behans.

### NOTES

Brian Behan, Brendan's younger brother.
1. James Connolly (1868–1916), Irish nationalist.

# Shed a Tear for Brendan*

### STAN DAVIES

Brendan, in another and peculiarly induced moment of introspective quiescence, told the Irish novelist Ernie Gebler[1] (who happens to be my uncle) about the endless evenings in Dublin pubs after his release and before he had made his name as a writer.

My uncle at that time (around 1953) had bought himself a country estate in County Wicklow, thirty miles from Dublin, on the proceeds of the sale of his novel *The Plymouth Adventure*[2] to an American film company. Brendan came up unannounced one day to visit him, bounced boisterously into the house yelling greetings to all present, and headed for a full whisky bottle on the sideboard. He swept past Ernie into the room and up-ended the bottle down his throat. He had swallowed half of it when he threw the bottle violently away and retched on the floor, sputtering the yellow liquid out doubled over.

'——ing Gebler,' he moaned in a strangled voice, 'what was in that bottle?'

'Cowpiss', said my uncle. 'You should have asked me but you didn't. I would have told you what it was. We took it from a sick cow to give to the veterinarian for urinalysis.'

Brendan, gasping 'cowpiss', ran outraged at full speed the few hundred yards outside and down the side of the mountain to throw himself in the freezing waters of Loch Dan.

Later, lying down shivering with fever and the thought of his unfortunate drink, he told my uncle, in between interjections of '——ing

* Extracted from the *Saturday Night* (Toronto), LXXIX (May 1964) 16–18.

Gebler' (Brendan's language was not, as is well known, the most polite) the story of his troubles and his drinking after the release from Mountjoy.

He had been accorded a hero's welcome everywhere.

' "Well looka who's here," ' he mimed, ' "if it isn't Brendan, the man himself! Brendan, me son, what'll ya have? Here, give the man a porther, will ya. Give the man a porther." (——ing Gebler.) "Sing us a song, Brendan. Tell us that story of Jimmy Joyce." '

'I didn't need a drink,' he went on, 'I needed a job. But ask them for a job and see what answer the ——ers'd give. (——ing Gebler.) Nothing doing.'

Brendan drank too much in those days, to keep on the good side of the barflies he thought were friends. There are many witnesses to his being a very good conversationalist, the possessor of a rich and beautiful voice and a sparkling wit when he was sober.

In March, the English critic David Nathan told the Welsh playwright Allan Owen, and myself, of an afternoon with Brendan in Paris a few years ago. Nathan, Brendan, Beatrice and a few others had been sitting outside a sidewalk café talking shop-talk about writers. Somebody came out with a stiff pomposity about Fitzgerald. Brendan started a half-hour steady-stream monologue in rhymed couplets beginning,

> There's the pity you have missed
> The sight of Scott Fitzgerald pissed.

Which is hardly poetry. But the comic effect of a half-hour's unfailing stream of small witticisms about Fitzgerald, Hemingway, Dylan Thomas, Shaw, Wilde and all other targets that occurred to Brendan can well be imagined. Nathan said he had never wished for a tape-recorder more in his life. By the time Brendan was finished he had collected a large, presumably English-speaking, audience. All were listening closely, laughing in the pouring rain that no one seemed to mind. They must have thought a half-hour of Behan worth a soaking.

After Brendan had become famous it should not have been necessary, if ever it had been, for him to get roaring drunk to entertain the ignorant. But by that time he was a compulsive alcoholic and it was too late. He would stop drinking every now and then and stay religiously sober for a few weeks or months, during which he would write. Then something would happen to start him drinking again.

He came to Toronto to emcee a variety show in 1960 at the O'Keefe Centre.[3] He had no idea what the show was about, other than that it was a variety show and he was to sit on the stage and wittily introduce the numbers. He was then on the wagon. He went to the first rehearsal and afterwards went to see Eamonn Martin,[4] who was sick at the time.

'The show's a lemon. I don't know what to do. I've signed the contract. I've got to go on stage. But I can't go on stage with a show like that.'

Eamonn knew what he would do, but there was nothing he could do to stop it. Brendan turned up on stage drunk and abusive. Later, after further drinking, he hit a policeman and was arrested.

## NOTES

1. Ernest Gebler (1915– ), Irish novelist; married to Edna O'Brien.
2. Published in 1950.
3. Behan went to Toronto for the show, *Impulse!*, in 1961, not 1960.
4. Behan's IRA friend. See his recollections of Brendan on p. 200.

# Brendan's Confessions*

## RAE JEFFS

It was in the spring of 1957, seven years before his death, that I first met Brendan Behan. He had come to the offices of his London publishers, Hutchinson, to deliver the manuscript of *Borstal Boy*. I knew little about him, except that he was the Irish author of an extremely good play, *The Quare Fellow*, and that he was the star of one of the most talked-about television interviews of 1956.

When I met him, he was standing next to a table, a formidable figure with his unruly hair cascading over his forehead and his clothes arrayed around him as best they could without the help of the wearer.

We were introduced – Brendan's introductions to the opposite sex could hardly be described as formal – and I was asked to give a *précis* of my life up to that very moment. He listened quietly and with genuine interest, interrupting only when he felt I had glossed over an important detail. When he learned that I came from Sussex, he was obviously delighted. Apparently he had been extremely well treated in a Sussex prison, and he had a warm regard for anyone coming from that county.

The introductions over, Brendan, whose thirst took small account of licensing hours, called for a drink. With vicarage garden-party decorum, I inquired whether it would be tea or coffee.

'Do you call that a drink?' he roared, interpolating a stream of unbridled Anglo-Saxon words which would not normally be heard in a publisher's office. And so began the first of my many lessons in nonconformity.

* Preface to Brendan Behan, *Confessions of an Irish Rebel* (London: Hutchinson, 1965) pp. 7–12. Editor's title.

Somehow I managed to get hold of a bottle of whisky, and I returned triumphantly to the office, as much exhilarated by the act of procuring the bottle as the man himself by the act of emptying it.

For the rest of the afternoon I was entertained by numerous stories, which were not altogether easy for the uninitiated to follow, for Brendan had a most captivating way of unexpectedly breaking into song. He had an unlimited repertoire of folksongs and Dublin ballads, which he would sing enchantingly by the hour in a light, lilting tenor.

Then suddenly, without a word of warning, as if on castors, he glided to the door and off down the passage, shouting 'Slan leat'[1] to the wide-eyed astonishment of the passers-by. I raced after him as I remembered the precious manuscript, still not delivered, only to receive the casually imparted information that he had 'left it at the BBC' and he would go and get it. Sometime later I started out to look for him, but I did not have to go very far. I heard his voice coming from the George, singing, somewhat more lustily than before, the same Dublin ballads.

Under the rumbustious bravado, Brendan was courteous, considerate and absurdly generous. Every person in the pub that evening was clustered round him as though drawn by a magnet, and it would have taken a bigger fool than myself not to discover the largeness of the heart that ticked behind the showman's mask.

I had simply started out on a business mission, but in a matter of hours I lived a lifetime. It was a most remarkable experience, and to those who poke the finger of scorn at objects of popular adulation, I can only say it was as though a powerful light had suddenly gone on. It wasn't necessarily that things were dull before, but that Brendan's presence produced an overwhelming current of electricity quite beyond the ordinary. He was not then a world-renowned figure, and his exploits were not yet hot copy for the morning's editions. He was a man being himself, more alive than the rest of us, and our batteries were charged with a borrowed vitality that, for me at any rate, changed the whole conception of life.

Throughout the following year, my connection with Brendan was mainly that of a public-relations officer, and it was in this capacity that I began to pierce through his external ferocity and to discover the innocence, the tenderness and the sensitivity behind it. Before any public appearance he would assume a completely different personality. As we neared the television studios or the newspaper offices for an interview, I could almost see him building up the bricks of the wall that protected him from himself. Beads of perspiration would break out on his forehead, and he would be cruel, abusive and arrogant.

He felt he had to live up to his reputation as the tough IRA rebel, the man who would assault not only others but himself as well, rather than conform. When the strain of impersonation became too much, a bout of drinking would follow. But when he realised this armour was unnecessary, he became almost childlike in his frankness and candour.

With the publication of *Borstal Boy* in October 1958, Brendan's success was assured. My chief recollection of these days is the genuine pleasure that Brendan got from reading the reviews. It was almost as if he was no longer afraid to look in and recognise himself, and I think he was nearer at that time to establishing a real relationship with himself than he ever became again. Perhaps if he had managed it, the self-destructiveness that he carried within him would only have come to the surface spasmodically and certainly would not have killed him. I do not think that he wanted to die, only to stop living the life he had made for himself.

At any rate, at this time he did not snatch for the whisky bottle, nor impatiently throw the clippings down, as I saw him do so many times afterwards. He sat in the chair quietly reading them, unafraid, and was both impressed and delighted with himself. Every now and again, he would point out a particularly good review and say, 'That's what so-and-so thinks of me', and his head would lean a further two degrees toward his shoulder as the grin spread all over his face.

With world-wide acclaim for *The Hostage*, which had been produced by Theatre Workshop in the week preceding publication of *Borstal Boy*, Brendan began to devote less of his time to writing. More and more did he parade the public figure of the irrepressible drunken Irishman, and the newspapers helped enthusiastically. And as the column inches added up, they somehow managed to convey, for the first time, the impression that the end was as inevitable as the end of Dylan Thomas.

With his wife, Beatrice, always a patient and steadying influence, he stampeded through Paris where *The Hostage*, chosen to represent Great Britain and later to win the award of best play of the year, was being presented at the Paris Théâtre des Nations festival.

Still the column inches mounted with stories of brashness and flamboyance, and the hangers-on became more numerous, not so much on account of his undoubted talent, for which life meted out a cruel revenge, but because he was a 'character', a species of man distinctly rare. Repeated demands from both publishers and agents to fulfil his contracts were ignored. His solution of the problem was rather primitive: when he saw the publisher's representative in the street, he would quickly cross over to the other side.

Finally, I was asked to go over to Dublin and be, in Brendan's own words, his 'literary midwife'. Although, at the time, I was unaware that the diversion from my role as publicity manager would be more than a temporary one, I was happy in the knowledge that he had assumed I was the natural choice for the assignment, and that by the end of it he seemed so delighted with the partnership. Some time later I returned with *Brendan Behan's Island* and the slightly ravelled air of having been through labour myself.

Shortly afterwards he came to London, and a drinking bout took place that terminated in a hospital. For the following nine months, Brendan, perhaps too acutely aware of his instability and emotional problems, struggled successfully to resist the temptation of drink. A new seed of hope sprang up inside of him, and he began writing again – a third play – without any help or instigation.

But it was not to last. In America, where he was lionised, he began to drink again, and although he made repeated attempts to stop, he was fighting a losing battle as his physical being and will-power weakened. Still, he knew that working was essential to him – the only force stronger than his desire for drink – so he asked me to join him in New York and help him write the second part of his autobiography.

*Confessions of an Irish Rebel* was recorded on tape during Brendan's last visit to America, and was transcribed and edited after his death. It may, consequently, lack the final polish Brendan would have wished. But it is all his, and no one, I think, will mistake it, or find the hand of a once-proper British lady in it.

Perhaps nothing does greater credit to the magnitude of the man than that he chose to work with a person who held totally opposing beliefs and politics and who came from a country which he had fought against bitterly – both physically and mentally – at no small cost to himself.

Brendan never forgave my being English. But in the final reckoning, he was too big a person to notice it.

NOTES

For a note on Rae Jeffs see p. 109.
  1. 'Goodbye'.

# That Old Triangle: a Memory of Brendan Behan*

BENEDICT KIELY

In the end of all, the hostage, Leslie Williams,[1] rose from the dead in full view of the audience and mocked the bells of hell that go ting-a-ling-a-ling, and in cheery parody of St Paul, asked the grave where was its victory, and death where was its sting-a-ling-a-ling. The victory and the sting are in the sore truth that the bold Brendan, quiet for the first time since he yelled as a

* *Hollins Critic* (Hollins College, Va) II, no. 1 (Feb 1965) 1–12.

newborn babe, has drawn the Glasnevin coverlet over his head and is no longer to be found raising the roof or entertaining the customers in any one of the many places of public resort that lie between the two White Horses: the one in Greenwich Village and the one that Michael O'Connell keeps on Burgh Quay by the River Liffey.

He was, as we say in Ireland, much missed at his own funeral, for he was always one to bury the dead with sympathy but with a spirit that mocked at mortality, and he would have appreciated the verbal slip that made one graveside speaker say that he had had the privilege of being interred with Brendan. He meant interned: and while the dead man in his time had had his reservations about the joys of internment he would, of a surety, have preferred them to the *nox perpetua*[2] of the grave. Dying as a 'lark', he often said, had no attractions for him. It was a lonely business and he was, even to the detriment of his work and health, the most gregarious of men. The one thing he found most wearisome in prison was to be locked alone in his cell: 'There were noises of key-jangling and door-banging. I hoped they would open my door. Even if they were distributing nothing better than kicks or thumps, I'd prefer not to be left out in my cold shroud of solitude. Fighting is better than loneliness.'

Even in prison, where he spent eight years of his short life, he did his best to beat off loneliness, and so much of the best of what he really wrote – not talked about into a tape-recorder when he was sick – is that very odd thing, a shout of laughter from the cell. The name of the prison in North Dublin City where his play *The Quare Fellow* was played out to its end in a hanging, was ironic enough to please him: Mountjoy, for yet further irony abbreviated into the Joy. An ale brewed in that part, his own part, of Dublin was called by the same name as the prison, and an enticing advertisement displayed at one end of Russell Street where he was born, and visible every Sunday to the followers of games in Croke Park which had, once, its Black and Tan Bloody Sunday, said, 'Joy Be with You in the Morning'.

Song erupts from the punishment cells as the curtain rises on *The Quare Fellow*, a song that Behan adapted from a cruder original by another prisoner:

> A hungry feeling came o'er me stealing
> And the mice were squealing in my prison cell,
> And that old triangle went jingle jangle,
> Along the banks of the Royal Canal.

He understood and could make laughter out of the old lag's perverted pride in his record between stone walls and iron bars. One old prisoner says to a novice, 'Meself and that man sitting there, we done time before you came up. In Kilmainham, and that's where you never were. First fourteen days without a mattress, skilly three times a day. None of your sitting out in the yard like nowadays. I got my toe amputated by one of the old lags so I could get into hospital for a feed.' Warden Regan says to a prisoner who boasts that he has been in English prisons, 'There's the national inferiority complex for you. Our own Irish cat o' nine tails and the batons of the warders loaded with lead from Carrickmines aren't good enough for him. He has to go Dartmooring and Parkhursting it. It's a wonder you didn't go further when you were at it, to Sing Sing or Devil's Island.'

His temperament, a comical sight more than that of Lovelace, made light of prison, because prison was familiar to his rebel family and his Irish blood and, in prison as outside it, he had a passion for making mockery of authority. He looked, for instance, in *Borstal Boy* at the Governor of Walton Prison, England, and saw a 'desiccated old-looking man, in tweed clothes and wearing a cap, as befitted his rank of Englishman, and looking as if he'd ride a horse if he had one. He spoke with some effort and if you did not hear what he was saying you'd have thought from his tone, and the sympathetic, loving and adoring looks of the screw, PO, and Chief that he was stating some new philosophical truth to save the suffering world from error.'

Dunlavin,[3] the greatest of all his old lags – called, by the wild comic spirit that made Behan laugh even at those patriotic things that were dearest to him, by the name of a Wicklow village famed in the heroism of the Rebellion of 1798 – expresses his disgust at having to live cell-by-cell with a sex criminal, 'Dirty beast! I won't have an hour's luck for the rest of me six months.' Those who are alive, even though they lie in jail, must accommodate themselves to the conditions of living, and Behan took his durance vile as a priceless part of his experience and all the time intended to use his prison memories when he turned to writing. Once when I complained to him that if things were as they once were the rising cost of living in Dublin would land me in jail for debt he said, with affected horror, 'Don't take from me the one advantage I have in this hard-backed book business.'

His best hard-backed book, superbly done as the scattered, dictated notebooks were not done, was, too, in the oddest way, a continuation of the considerable library written by Irishmen in English prisons or on the run from English law: Doheny, Davitt, Kickham, Tom Clarke, Darrell Figgis, *et alii*. Through his mother's brother, Peadar Cearnaigh [Kearney], who wrote the song, by no means his best, that was to become the Irish National Anthem, Behan was very much part of all that. But no accused patriot adding to that holy scripture 'Speeches from the Dock' – a paper-backed national piety once a bestseller in Ireland – could have permitted himself the humour, the mockery, the bad language of Behan; and the resonant Carlylean voice of John Mitchell,[4] of Young Ireland in 1848, orating rather than writing his classical *Jail Journal*, finds an uproarious *reductio ad absurdum*[5] in *Borstal Boy*.

The Joy, then, was a fine and quiet place compared with the Bog (the long-term Portlaoise Prison in the flat Irish Midlands) and had, because of a kindly governor whose blackthorn stick Behan borrowed and never returned, the name of being easy: easy, that is, until matters went as far as hanging. Then the laughter sourly dies in the cell and the prisoner called Neighbour tells how once for two bottles of stout he took the hood off 'the fellow was after being topped' and how he wouldn't do it a second time for a bottle of whiskey for the 'head was all twisted and his face black, but the two eyes were the worst; like a rabbit's; it was fear that had done it'.

Brendan was in the Joy, not for politics as was his wont, but, like the bold Thady Quill, for 'batin' the police', when the last man to be hanged in the Republic of Ireland went to the drop. With two warders he and the condemned man made a four for handball. He drank the condemned man's daily bottles of stout because the crime for which the unfortunate fellow was doomed to suffer had been done under the influence of that beverage and he could no longer be convinced that Guinness was good for him. When the pitiful wretch asked Brendan if hanging hurt, Brendan assured him, with his own special type of kindness, that he didn't think so but then he had never been through it himself nor had he talked with anyone who had. He was in prison for politics when the original of the Quare Fellow was hanged: a pork-butcher who had murdered his brother and filleted the corpse so skilfully that nothing was ever found. It was one of Behan's more lurid jokes that the murderer had sold his brother as fresh pork to the Jesuit Fathers in Tullabeg. That Brendan Behan, like Lord Byron, woke up to find himself famous overnight, right in the middle of the English debate on capital punishment, was in no small measure due to that hanging; and that was the only good turn hanging ever did him or anybody else. For decent people are as interested in hangings nowadays as they were on the night before Larry was stretched – in public; and think of all the long years during which Tyburn was London's greatest theatrical draw, a popular open-air theatre.

The famous drunken appearance on BBC television came to the aid of the hangman in the popularisation of Brendan Behan, and that was the only good turn drink ever did him. Now that I've raised the question, and since it must be answered, let me say how grossly by the lower-class London papers the drunken legend was exaggerated. It was no news at all that an Irishman should be sober and working. Yet while Brendan did not invite such publicity he did nothing by word or deed to squelch it: he went a long ways further than Samuel Johnson in believing that to be talked about, well or ill, drunk or sober, was the best way for a writer to bring in 'the readies': meaning dollars and pounds. It is the way of the vile world, but Henry James, and others, would have demurred. It is customary and correct to lament the drinking and the waste, as my friends, Irving Wardle, the London critic, and Francis MacManus, the Dublin novelist, have done, but it is also a wonder that so much writing was done in such a short time, not because of the impediment of drink but because Brendan never had any regularly developed habits of work, and being, as I said, the most gregarious of men, he craved company, which in Dublin frequently leads to drink unless you care to join the Legion of Mary or the Pioneer Total Abstinence Association which neither he, myself, nor any of our friends in Dublin ever showed any fanatical signs of doing. The mornings I have been aroused at six or seven to find Brendan smiling at the foot of my bed with the bright idea that we could start the day well in the early bars in the fruit markets or on the docks! There's a sweet story that once when, following his first trade, he was painting a ceiling in the Land Commission office in Merrion Street, and had his head out the window for air and looking at the people, James Sleator, the painter, passed and invited him round the corner for a 'tincture', and Brendan went and never came back, leaving the ceiling half-painted and his kit for anyone who cared to collect it. He painted the flat of the poet Patrick Kavanagh for free but, for laughs, did it, in the poet's absence, a complete and total sable. He had an odd sense of humour. He was also, we must remember, in his final years a sick man with a sickness that craved the sweet heat of drink and that the drink only aggravated.

He was, first and before all, a Dubliner from that restricted area of North Dublin City to which true Dubliners confine the high title of the North side. The rest of the North City is suburbia inhabited by provincials. After that he was an Irishman and a member of the underground Irish Republican Army at its most troublesome period since the bloodshed and burning ceased in 1923. He was, by his own definition, 'a bad Catholic' or, as Irish euphemism has it, a 'lapsed' or 'non-practising' Catholic.

His IRA activities brought him at an absurdly early age to an English prison and a Borstal institution, gave him the makings of his best book, which either as autobiography or as part of the literature of penology has established itself as a classic, and inspired him for various reasons with a healthy respect and a liking for the English people. Although his first feeling, after two months studying and experiencing the brutalities of the warders in Walton Jail, was that he was most anxious for a truce with the British, that not only was everything he had ever read or heard about them in history true but that 'they were bigger and crueller bastards' than he had taken them for because 'with tyrants all over Europe I had begun to think that maybe they weren't the worst after all but, by Jesus, now I knew they were, and I was not defiant of them but frightened'. But later acquaintance with kindlier types – they included sadly enough a decent Borstal chap called Neville Heath later to be renowned, although Behan with splendid restraint does not say so nor fully name him, as the sadistic murderer of two women – made him modify his opinion, and he allows himself that deliberately exquisite understatement 'The British are very nationalistic.' He was, too, always glad and grateful that London Town gave him his first and best welcome as a playwright and that once when on the way through England from Ireland to France he was arrested under a deportation order the British authorities deported him not back to Ireland but onwards to France, paying his fare – a humorous and decent people.

For all previous sharp statements about the neighbours he made amends in the character of Leslie Williams, the hostage, also a voice from a prison, an ordinary young English boy caught fatally and wonderingly in a situation he cannot hope to understand. Teresa, that sweet young country girl, so lovably played by Celia Salkeld, an orphan as the hostage is, tells him that Monsewer, the old mad owner of the house in which he is held, is an English nobleman: 'he went to college with your king'.

> SOLDIER [i.e. Leslie]. We ain't got one.
> TERESA. Maybe he's dead now, but you had one one time, didn't you?
> SOLDIER. We got a duke now. He plays tiddlywinks.
> TERESA. Anyway, he [i.e. Monsewer] left your lot and came over here and fought for Ireland.
> SOLDIER. Why, was somebody doing something to Ireland?
> TERESA. Wasn't England, for hundreds of years?
> SOLDIER. That was donkey's years ago. Everybody was doing something to someone in those days.

Caitlin Ni Houlihan[6] and John Bull have never spoken so simply, so comically nor so wisely to each other as in that passage. And mad Monsewer was, indeed, English, the son of a bishop, and had gone to 'all the biggest colleges in England and slept in one room with the King of England's son' until one day because his mother was Irish he discovered he was an Irishman, or an Anglo-Irishman, which in Behan's misleading definition was 'a Protestant with a horse'. Anglo-Irishmen only work at 'riding horses, drinking whiskey and reading double-meaning books in Irish at Trinity College'. To become Irish, Monsewer took it 'easy at first, wore a kilt, played Gaelic football on Blackheath . . . took a correspondence course in the Irish language. And when the Rising took place he acted like a true Irish hero.' But when he lays down his bagpipes and raises his voice in song, as all Behan's people, including himself, were forever ready to do, his father's blood proves living and strong:

> In our dreams we see old Harrow,
> And we hear the crow's loud caw
> At the flower show our big marrow
> Takes the prize from Evelyn Waugh.
> Cups of tea or some dry sherry,
> Vintage cars, these simple things,
> So let's drink up and be merry,
> Oh, the Captains and the Kings.

Monsewer has a dual, lunatic significance: the house he owns and in which the young hostage is held and accidentally killed by his rescuers is, as Pat the caretaker says, a 'noble old house that had housed so many heroes' and is, in the end, 'turned into a knocking shop'. It is also romantic, idealistic Ireland fallen on sordid, materialistic days, and that a madman of that most romantic people, the English, should in his imagination lead the last Irish Rebellion, playing the pipes and making heroines out of decent whores, would seem to be a fair chapter of our national story. But the house is more than heroic Ireland down in the dumps; it is the world in a mess and God gone off his rocker: the very first stage direction says, 'the real owner isn't right in the head'. Monsewer, in fact, is one of Behan's visions of God, and as he parades, salutes, plays the pipes and sings of tea and toast and muffin rings, the old ladies with stern faces and the captains and the kings, he falls into line with images of the Divinity that appear elsewhere in the plays and prose.

The ministers of religion, because of Brendan's experience with prison chaplains who had to tell him that as a member of the IRA he was excommunicated, seldom come well out of his story. Yet God is, nevertheless, not to be judged by the deficiencies of his servants; and Dunlavin, satirising the higher Civil Servants talking big in the back snugs of pubs in Merrion Row, defends the Almighty against their patronisation: 'Educated drinking, you know. Even a bit of chat about God at an odd time, so as you'd think God was in another department, but not long off the Bog, and they was doing Him a good turn to be talking well about Him.' The same turn of phrase, almost, recurs in *The Hostage* when Meg attacks the canting and quite impossible Mr Mulleady. In a good cause Brendan was never afraid of repeating himself.

The cynical Meg may say that 'pound notes is the best religion in the world' even though the 'chokey bloke' in *Borstal Boy* points out that some men are so miserably constituted that they 'couldn't be 'appy no matter where they were. If they was in the Ritz Hotel with a million nicker and Rita Hayworth they'd find some bloody thing to moan about.' God could sometimes be faltering, as Monsewer was, in his judgements of people, for Ratface, the altar server in prison, looked like 'a real cup-of-tea Englishman with a mind the width of his back garden that'd skin a black man, providing he'd get another to hold him, and send the skin 'ome to mum, but Our Lord would be as well pleased with him, if he was in the state of grace, as He'd be with St Stanislaus Kostka, the boy Prince of Poland, and race or nationality did not enter into the matter, either one way or another.' Regardless, the Maker of All Things had compensatory qualities. Following in a mob the course of the Saviour's Passion around the Stations of the Cross in the prison chapel, the prisoners were enabled, in a passage that is pure Hogarth, to fuse and mingle and exchange cigarettes and even fragments of food. The crooked greyhound men taking the doped dog to the races in one of the best sketches in *Brendan Behan's Island* were respectfully pious enough to warn Brendan that it wasn't a lucky thing to mock religion and they going out to 'do a stroke'. If the law that excommunicated the IRA had not existed and Brendan had been allowed to go to confession he would have missed the sight of one of the nastiest of the warders slipping and falling and floundering in a snowdrift, and shaking his fists in anger and falling and floundering again while the prisoners from their cell windows roared with laughter. Brendan sat down again at his table and, in the terms of an old Gaelic proverb, thanked God and His Blessed Mother for all that: 'God never closed one door but He opens another, and if He takes away with His right hand, He gives it back with His left, and more besides.' Pressed down and flowing over, in fact; and we are back with God as Monsewer, a decent fellow, not quite in control of things. Whose actions even when He doesn't plan them too well frequently turn out for the best. Even the 'lapsed' Catholic comes out in defence of the Old Faith when he tells Hannen Swaffer, the columnist, who has just announced that he is a spiritualist, that Catholicism keeps a better type of ghost.

Borrowing a sentence from the lingo of his beloved Dublin streets, he was fond of saying that every cripple had his own way of walking. It is also true that every writer has his own way of writing, and I have already pointed out how wonderful it was that so much good writing came out of Brendan's gregariousness and chronic restlessness. His great kindly spirit had to express itself in every possible way, and what was writing – if it didn't go on too long – but another form of movement. *Borstal Boy*, *The Quare Fellow*, *The Hostage* and the better portions of the notebooks or sketchbooks are the considerable achievement that he has left us, although one stage direction in *The Hostage*, reading, 'what happens next is not very clear', would seem to indicate that Behan threw his hat (he never wore one) at the whole business of writing and said, 'Joan Littlewood, the dacent girl, will look after that and —— the begrudgers.' Reading your own works, he argued in his sad book on New York, was a sort of mental incest but, as a rule, it is better at least to write them; and to the New Yorkers who have been disappointed in what he had to say about their stupendous city, which as cities go he loved next to Dublin, I keep saying that the book was not so much written as spoken by a sick and weary man into a tape-recorder.

Yet even in the tired ramblings-on of a man who was so close to the grave, there is flash after flash of the spirit that made him the most entertaining companion I have known or am ever likely to know. One night in Michael O'Connell's White Horse when sick with laughter at his antics – (i) Toulouse-Lautrec, by walking up and down the floor on his knees, (ii) the Poor Old Woman, Mother Ireland, with the tail of his jacket over his head for a shawl, (iii) an aspiring Irish politician mouthing every platitude ever heard from an Irish platform and borrowing a few from the pulpit, (iv) Sex in the Abbey Theatre, for which there are no words but only mime and the mimic is now forever motionless – I remember thinking that if he ever got a wider audience he'd make a fortune. I can't claim much credit for the prophecy: it came easy. My sadness is that this great kind comic man held the stage only for such a brief time. We have left, as I say, the plays, including the one-act *The Big House*, effective on radio but a dead loss on the stage, the autobiography, and what was good in the notebooks. To come, there may be yet another piece of dictated autobiography, and the play *Richard's Cork Leg* which, borrowing a title from a very irritated James Joyce, was to be the meeting of all Ireland around the grave of Honor Bright, an unfortunate whore done to death by gunshot on the Dublin mountains forty or so years ago. *The Scarperer* we may dismiss, forgiving as well as we can the person who wrote the publisher's blurb to say that Behan having accomplished this and that, now turned to the novel and made it his own: the sort of praise that can only damage a writer's reputation. But for a delightful brotherly sidelight on the ways of the wonderful Behan family and on the lovable father and mother, Stephen and Kathleen, Dominic Behan's *Teems of Times and Happy Returns* is valuable.

Brendan had a happy boyish belief that you could find a good man everywhere and, being a friendly man, he liked meeting people and being always, in some ways, a boy he liked talking about the important people he had met. He liked being invited to the inauguration of President Kennedy. Who, politics apart, wouldn't have? He liked talking about the late Gilbert Harding, who was a fine man, and about Oona Guinness, who is a great lady, and about John Betjeman who is, anyway, a sort of Irish institution. I detect an ironic flicker of the eyelids, even if by then they were very tired eyelids, when he says, 'As Hemingway once remarked to a friend of mine.' He was vain and proud of his success and eternally talkative. But he was not so much a name-dropper as a friend naming friends, and Princess Margaret and Rosie Redmond, the Dublin whore, were all equally to him just people.

Rosie Redmond we will remember from Sean O'Casey's *The Plough and the Stars*, and I feel that Brendan and certainly his father, Stephen, knew stories about her that even O'Casey had not heard. This is not the place to tell them, yet the mention of her fair name brings me by a most 'commodius vicus of recirculation back to Howth Castle and Environs', to the 'fort of the Dane, garrison of the Saxon, Augustan capital of a Gaelic nation', to the city built around the body of the fallen Finnegan and the more catastrophically fallen giant Haveth Childers Everywhere.

A city, he said, was a place where you were least likely to get 'a bite of a wild sheep', and the test of a city was the ease with which you could see and talk to other people, and New York was the friendliest city he knew. But Dublin was his own town, not the middle-class Dublin that John Mitchell had found a city of bellowing slaves and genteel Dastards, and that Pearse said had to atone in blood for the guilt of Robert Emmet's execution, but the Dublin of the fighting poor who were led by Larkin in 1913 and the Dublin with the everlasting memory of the Post Office in flames. It was the Dublin, too, that the prisoners Neighbour and Dunlavin fondly dream over in *The Quare Fellow*. Meena La Bloom belonged to it, who, with

Dunlavin's help, gave many's the Mickey Finn to a sailor; and May Oblong who debagged the Irish MP on his way to Westminster to vote for Home Rule, and locked him in her room, and neither for the love of her country or his would liberate him until he slipped a fiver under the door; and the patriotic plumber of Dolphin's Barn that swore to let his hair grow till Ireland was free; and Lottie L'Estrange that got had up for pushing the soldier into Spencer Dock. They belong in Joyce's Nighttown and on the shadowy streets that Liam O'Flaherty wrote about in *The Informer*.

Behan's Dublin, too, as the plays show, was as much or more that of Boucicault and the old Queen's Theatre Variety as it was of the Abbey Theatre, except when O'Casey was in possession of the Abbey stage. And his Dublin was my Dublin from 1937 onwards, and with warm brotherliness he once told me that I was one of the few country —— he knew who had enough in him to make a Dublin jackeen. From an early age he had what he called a 'pathological horror' of country people, because to a Dublin child the symbols and exercisers of authority, teachers and Civic Guards, all came from the country, the provinces, and the jungle began where the Dublin tram tracks came to an end. But his heart was too big for one city to contain, and it opened out to Ireland, the Aran Islands, London, Paris, New York; although to the end he had his reservations about Toronto and Berlin – as they had about him.

He would have died and almost did die for Ireland, but he was sharply conscious of the delirium of the brave in the Robert Emmet pose of the dying hero. It was fine to feel like Cuchullain[7] guarding the Gap of Ulster, his enemies ringed round him, his back supported by a tree, calling on 'the gods of death and grandeur to hold him up until his last blood flowed'. But if the only spectators were two Walton jailers, Mr Whitbread and Mr Holmes, clearly Private Compton and Private Carr in later life, and if Mr Holmes was methodically beating you up, then the hot glow went out of the heroism. You could be mangled in an English prison and who would 'give a fish's tit about you over here. At home, it would be all right if you were to get the credit for it. . . . But the mangling would have to be gone through first.' He was brave from boyhood to death, but there were no false heroics about him and he felt that between mangling and martyrdom there should be some satisfactory, poetic and preferably unpainful relationship.

Like Peter Wanderwide – and how Behan would have mocked at me for quoting Belloc – he had Ireland 'in his dubious eyes'. In Irish and English its ballads and classical folksongs were ready to his lips, and when he wasn't deliberately roaring his head off he could sing. At penal work, digging on the Borstal farm, his fork uncovered from English soil a golden apple 'as hard and as fresh as the day it fell there', and biting it surreptitiously and feeling the juice sharp on his tongue he thought of Blind Raftery, the poet, and of the spring coming, after the feast of Brigid, to the wide plains of Mayo. But in the swift switch of humour that was characteristic of him he would admit that digging was an activity he wouldn't pick for pleasure and would tell how his father, Stephen, during a Dublin strike brought him out to help farm an acre of land on ground, at Glasnevin, once associated with Dean Swift. Stephen dug for a bit 'with great function', talked about the land, how his ancestors came from it, how healthy it was, and how if they kept at the digging they might uncover relics of Swift or Vanessa or Stella or Mrs Delaney. But next day, bored, he got a countryman to dig the plot in exchange for Stephen doing the countryman's strike picket-duty. That is a touching, endearing picture of father and son – two rare comedians.

But Brendan was grateful for the golden apple and the good weather. He was always grateful and pious in good weather, and the day he found the apple was the sort of day that 'you'd know Christ died for you'. A bloody good job, he thought, that he was born in rainy Ireland and not in the South of France or Miami Beach where he'd have been so grateful and holy for the sunshine that St John of the Cross would have only been trotting after him: 'skull and crossbones and all'.

As a great swimmer, next to the sunshine he loved the sea: the eastern sea at the Forty Foot, the swimming pool famed in *Ulysses*; the laughter of the western Galway sea which, according to Louis MacNeice, juggled with spars and bones irresponsibly. Brendan did not view it so sombrely. On the Aran Islands, and along the Connemara shore, and in Glenties in Donegal with the Boyles and the Harveys, he claimed he could forget all the cruel things of this world. He wrote so pleasantly of the night, after the licensed hours, in the pub in Ballyferriter in Kerry, in the South-west, when the Civic Guards obligingly sent word that they were going to raid so that the customers could withdraw a little up the mountain slope, taking supplies with them, and drink in peace until the raid was over, 'It was a lovely starlit night and warm, too; and one of my most cherished recollections is of sitting out there on the side of Mount Brandon, looking at the mountain opposite called the Three Sisters framed against the clear moonlit sky and the quiet shimmering Atlantic, a pint of the creamiest Guinness in my hand as I conversed in quiet Irish with a couple of local farmers.'

That was a happy Irishman at home in Ireland. Mount Brandon, as he said with proprietary pride, was called after his patron saint, Brendan the Navigator, who, the legend says, reached the New World before either Norsemen or Columbus and who left to all who came after him the promise of the Isle of the Blest that all mariners might one day find.

'And that', as Brendan said when he finished his sketchbook about the island of Ireland, 'is the end of my story and all I'm going to tell you and thanks for coming along.'

## NOTES

For a note on Benedict Kiely see p. 267.
  1. The British soldier in Behan's play *The Hostage*.

2. Everlasting darkness.
3. The prisoner in Behan's play *The Quare Fellow*.
4. John Mitchell (1815–75), Irish nationalist and writer.
5. Reduction to absurdity; proof of the falsity of a conclusion or principle by reducing it to absurdity.
6. Ireland.
7. Champion hero of a cycle of myths who at the age of seventeen defended Ulster single-handed for four months.

# Brendan Behan*

## FRANCIS MacMANUS

I remember Brendan Behan in the morning, as it were, of his writing life when the dew was still on him. He used to ramble in to see me in old Radio Éireann in the very late forties and early fifties with scripts of short stories and talks and once with a few pages of a play about a man who was condemned to death for boiling his brother. Mostly he was alone. Sometimes he had his half-brother with him or some boozing friend he had picked up in a cattle-market pub before any of us were awake. Alone or in company, he let the whole place know with a hullabaloo that he had arrived. With his gap-toothed grin and his fat round-cheeked country-woman's face he looked utterly harmless, like an overblown cherub.

The uproar was part of the Behan game. He could be docile as any lamb and sober as any judge when we got down to the job of reading and discussing whatever screed he pulled in a ball out of his pocket. But there was always preliminaries – an anecdote or two with appropriate jack-acting, a reminiscence of his time in jail or in France, where he joined the Foreign Legion a few times for a bed and a meal, only to opt out the next morning; or even a song.

Once he arrived with a dreadful looking weblike gash on his chest oozing blood behind the remnants of a belly-open shirt. On his way into town he had passed over Leeson Street bridge and, seeing a few youngsters cavorting in the canal, he had peeled off his clothes and dived in to cool off; an old rusty broken bucket had met his chest. It took a lot of shouting and argument before he would let me apply an antiseptic. On another occasion he barrelled in with his mop of hair shiny and stiff like a gorgon's wig of hissing angry snakes. What had happened was that on his way down

* *Irish Press* (Dublin), 4 Apr 1964, p. 6.

Granby Row – Matt Talbot country – he had found a man varnishing a door, demanded to see his union card, discovered he had none, lumped him in with Matt as a non-union man and tossed the can of varnish up in the air for the sake of the solidarity of the workers.

What goes up must come down. It came down on Behan's own head. By the time he reached my office the varnish had stiffened and he was nearly weak with hilarity. He called it Matt Talbot's revenge.

Hilarity often enveloped him in a gale. Friends were greeted with fusillades of perfectly amicable four-letter words. Girls of every age and shape were kissed. Once in his more rotund days I saw him pretending to buss a very stout, good humoured lady. Their equators prevented conjunction. 'The spirit is willing,' he shouted, 'but the flesh is in the way.' He knew that she knew that he was playing the Behan Game. She was part of the conspiracy, a member of the cast.

Meaningless expletives were only part of the game. They had nothing to do with Brendan Behan the writer who, to use Coleridge's distinction, had an abundance of genius and very little talent. Talent is what puts the scaffolding up and the cement on the bricks. It's genius that conceives the building to send it soaring.

And Behan, as I flatter myself for having perceived so early, had genius as a writer. In 1953 I told an English class in the University of New York that an Irish writer they must look out for, as a genius, was Brendan Behan. If I were as lucky with horses I'd be a millionaire but then how many horses have been like him?

Amongst other things, he did two short stories for Radio Éireann that were full of the genius and of the newness and freshness of it, as close to the truth as pain to a wound, full of Dublin gurrier speech, transformed by feeling and rhythm and vision into poetry, and shaped with the roundness of the much told tale. I think they may be read in his book about Ireland. Maybe he had told and retold them. On paper they were alive. Over the microphone in his halting speech and strong accent, they were authentic with a life that had never been revealed before, except for a laugh. He could have been a great short-story writer, speaking for a Dublin Joyce knew only by nocturnal adventure or guesswork.

But the craft was too lonesome for him. From beginning to end it meant quietness, solitude, working alone to discipline without an audience. I'll never forget how lost and alone he looked one day when, on receiving the red-light signal in the studio, he failed to go ahead. When I went in to see what was wrong, he lifted his head, shaggy and jowled like the head of a battered Roman emperor and stammered, 'I'm not feeling too good. I can't let you down.' He was falling into a sort of mild coma. It was a warning of that disease which at last helped to carry him off. And remembering how it had carried off my own father as a young man, I nearly wept for him as for a doomed brother.

He was like a doomed brother a few weeks before he died when he came into Radio Éireann to see the Productions Director, Micheál Ó hAodha, and myself. Both of us felt that he was making his last rounds and that he was conscious it was the last. He sat in an old armchair and for nearly an hour told us a story about an adventure he had had in New York. In his good days he would have told that story in a few minutes, a gale of words, with mimicry, gestures, splurges of good-natured abuse and obscenity, but here at the last he took a slow hour, groping in long silences for the words, the memories, that seemed to elude him down ever-receding caverns. Several times we tried to help him by suggesting words to him and every time something of the old fire flashed up, the old volcano erupted. 'Don't be putting words into my mouth', he raged. 'Who's telling this story?'

He always told his story in his own way, precisely in his own way, and that was his genius. In his own way he wanted to give rather than to take. Did he die too young? Who can say? Perhaps he felt that he had given what he had been created to give.

*Beannacht Dé len a anam.*[1]

NOTES

Francis MacManus (1909–65), Irish writer and member of the Irish Academy of Letters; became Director of Talks and Features in Radio Éireann in 1947.
1. 'The blessing of God on his soul.'

# A Last Instalment*

## JOHN B. KEANE

When you meet the undertaker
Or the young man from the Pru,
Have a pint with what's left over –
Now I'll say goodbye to you.

Brendan Behan

The above four lines, better than any others, give a whole picture of the Dublin tenements where Brendan Behan first saw the light.

The 'young man from the Pru' was the collector for the Prudential

* *The World of Brendan Behan*, ed. Sean McCann (London: New English Library, 1965), pp. 201–5.

Insurance Society. He came around every week to collect the instalments on the policy which would bury the 'ould wan'. When the ould wan was dead, the insurance money rarely went to the undertaker. The ould wan was always 'buried dacent' with lashings of booze in case the family would be for ever disgraced in the eyes of their neighbours. The undertaker called weekly for his money after that and the young man from the Pru who was prudent enough to instigate a new policy came hot on his heels.

Behan first came to Listowel, where I live, when I was eighteen. I was in my first year of apprenticeship in a chemist's shop. My immediate superior was a man called Michael Quille who had been acquitted of a murder charge while he was in the IRA. He had spent a few years in jail with Behan and the bold Brendan called to pay his respects.

That was in 1949, Brendan's companion was an Irish sprint champion by the name of Tony McInerney. They were on their way to Dunquin in the Dingle Peninsula to spend a few days with Kruger Kavanagh. Both were armed with guns but neither, like myself, had any money.

Michael Quille gave a few pounds to Behan. I borrowed a few bob from my mother and we went to Alphonsus Sheehy's pub where I was to read my poems. I subsequently did and Behan, as Michael Quille reminded me on the night of the premiere of my first successful play, advised me to stop feckin' about with poetry and write dramas about the people I knew.

'Poetry is all right,' Behan said between songs that night, 'but it's all written.'

To give him his due, he read some of the poems in Dublin public houses afterwards, punctuating the phrases with expressions like 'Now there's a grand shaggin' line!' or 'Bejazus now, that's nicely put!'

There are a thousand stories about Behan and, no doubt, thousands more in the embryo stages. In his cups, or sober, he was chain lightning and the wit flowed from him like champagne but it didn't flow half as fast as his money. God only knows how much he subscribed to the upkeep of talented touchers, to down-and-outs, to old women and street urchins, to the needy mothers of large families and to friends who increased in relation to his fame. He never turned a deaf ear to a fellow soul in genuine plight.

Once, in a Dublin public house, he was touched for a fiver by a gentleman with a nose for suckers. Behan turned him down curtly.

'I remember a time, Behan,' said the toucher, 'when you hadn't an effin' farthing to your name!'

'That may be,' said Behan, 'but you don't remember it half as well as I do!'

A few years before he died, Behan attacked me in the *Irish Times* because of my attitude towards compulsory Irish. I like Irish and I speak Irish but I never approved of *compulsory* Irish and I still don't although Brendan and I frequently spoke in Irish. The *Times* letter was a scathing one and I replied as best I could, sorry that we should have to differ publicly.[1] A few weeks later the *Times* quoted me at length from an address delivered in Cahir, Co. Tipperary. In the address I defended melodrama and challenged anyone to define the difference between drama and melodrama. I suggested that critics had made melodrama the poor relation of the legitimate theatre, that they had derided it and held it up as something to be ashamed of. Yet all the great dramatists, with some exceptions of course, were indebted to melodrama for their immortality. I gave Behan's *The Hostage* as the perfect example.

An hour after the comments appeared, Behan was on the phone.

'Johnny, me darling,' he said, 'that was great this morning!'

'What was great?' I asked.

'Ah, don't be so shaggin' modest', he said. 'What you said in the *Times* of course.' He spoke for nearly an hour and it gave me all I could do to get a word in edgeways. We expanded on the theme of melodrama and the line sizzled when he opened up.

'Are you stewed?' I asked.

'Not a drop!' he exploded, 'as God is my judge.'

I reminded him of his attack in the *Times*.

'You're too thin-skinned,' he said. 'Sure if I took notice of my critics, I'd be in Grangegorman long ago.'

Not long after that we were both invited to take part in a debate on the Irish Theatre in the Shelbourne Hotel Ballroom in Dublin. The Abbey Theatre also sent along a spokesman in the shape of one of its finest actors, Ray McAnally. He spoke manfully in defence of the Abbey Theatre which he left shortly afterwards.

At one stage he said that the Abbey paid its authors 10 per cent royalties for capacity houses. I interrupted to remind him that all I got for *Sive* was 7½ per cent. 'It must have played to half-empty houses', he said, although he knew as well as I did that people were turned away every night. I reminded him of this and suddenly a woman jumped from her seat and berated me for interrupting while somebody else was speaking. She said she was a Kerry woman and was ashamed that any person from Kerry should behave in such a fashion. 'The oul' bitch!' said Brendan, under his breath, 'she doesn't like the truth!' She stood in the aisle and would not be silenced. When I asked her to come on the stage, she refused. 'Well then,' I asked, 'what do you want?'

'I'll tell you exactly', said Behan in a loud whisper; 'she badly wants a good screw – that's what she wants.'

Seamus Kelly, the *Irish Times* drama critic was chairman on that night but there were no more fireworks. It was no fault of the chairman. The truth was that Behan and I saw eye to eye on most things. There was a little short of £300 taken at the box office. This went to a Dublin charity and, as far as I can remember, Behan added substantially to this sum from his own pocket. We were later heckled by a number of students as we left the hotel.

'You know,' said Behan in a loud clear voice, 'it's getting harder and harder to distinguish between Teddy Boys and students.'

The last time I met Brendan alive was in the foyer of the Ormond Hotel in Ormond Quay, Dublin. It was on the morning of the Kerry v. Dublin Grounds Tournament football encounter. He looked terrible and he was almost drunk when he arrived. My son Billy was with me. Brendan took him by the hand and we headed for the lounge.

'I thought you were in hospital?' I said.

'I was,' he said, 'but I escaped.'

He sat down with Billy on his lap. He had a genuine fondness for all children.

When I called for a drink he demanded a glass of gin. It was no use remonstrating. I thought if we had a drink and a chat I might get him to go back to his bed. He drank the double gin neat and called for another. He drank that neat and, swiftly, called for another. By this time a number of Kerry supporters had gathered around to listen to the conversation. I objected to his having the third gin but he abused me roundly. He put his hand into his waistcoat pocket and gave Billy a pound. There were several other children in the lounge. He called them over to where he sat and presented them with the contents of his pockets.

'I never had any money when I was a child!' he said but he didn't say it as if he were sorry for himself; it was just a statement of fact.

Some admirers pressed more double gins on him, although I asked them not to. When I went to the toilet later, one of these told me to mind my own business; that they were taking Behan with them on a pub-crawl. He challenged me to fight so I hit him and left him there. He didn't show up again. When I returned upstairs to the lounge, Brendan was maudlin and incoherent but he still sat with Billy on his lap.

'Don't drink any more', Billy said.

'Whatever you say, Bill,' said Brendan, 'but I'll have one more just to wash down the last one!'

A large crowd was now gathered in the lounge. He insulted most of these but he spoke mildly and courteously to the old Kerry footballer who sat at his table. A noisy young man pushed his way through the crowds and pumped Brendan's hand, much against Brendan's will.

'We were in the same brigade in the IRA', the young man shouted to all and sundry.

Behan suddenly sobered and took a long, hard look at the newcomer.

'Go, 'long, you bowsie!' he quipped. 'The only brigade you ever saw was the Fire Brigade.'

A few weeks later he was dead.

The IRA, like characters out of his plays, marched at either side of his coffin. Two nuns, from his kindergarten days, followed close behind. The gurriers, the bowsies, the ould wans and the chisellers were all there.

Respected publicans, wealthy businessmen, law men and wanted men, all walked side by side in that last trip to Glasnevin. The Dublin pubs did a roaring trade. Television cameras whirred and a Frenchman spoke over his grave. He would have enjoyed it all but he would have preferred if the ould wans with the shawls and the down-and-outs with the caps on the sides of their heads were up in front where they belonged, because the Dublin poor were closest to his heart and he never forgot that he was one of them. Never were so many characters gathered together in one place.

It was a scene that only Brendan Behan could create.

## NOTES

John Keane, Irish dramatist.
  1. See 'The Language', *Irish Times* (Dublin), 17 Jan 1961, p. 5.

# Rite Words in Rote Order*

## GABRIEL FALLON

I imagine that most people had heard of Brendan Behan long before they met him. At all events that is how it was with me. An in-law who frequented an off-Grafton Street poets' pub[1] assured me that there was a regular in that place – a house-painter by trade – of whom Dublin was destined to hear more than somewhat.

A year or so later I had a dinner appointment at the Clarence Hotel with Robert Emmet Ginna (whom I had met a few years previously) and Gjon Mili, a distinguished New York photographer, both of whom had come to Dublin to prepare an article for *Life* magazine on Sean O'Casey.[2] For the purposes of this article they were anxious to meet a Dublin writer who might comparably be in the position that O'Casey was in when he submitted his first play to the Abbey Theatre. To this end they had invited Brendan to meet them. They were amazed when I told them I had never met the man.

Two hours overdue Brendan arrived, flanked on each side by a Clarence waiter. It at once occurred to me that this appearance under guard, so to speak, was due to the man's innate shyness, a quality which few in time would account to him for virtue. Even at that moment shyness seemed no part of his make-up for he opened the ball by saying, 'You're bloody

* *The World of Brendan Behan*, ed. Sean McCann (London: New English Library, 1965), pp. 163–8.

Americans, aren't you; you and you, but not you, Gabriel; you're a poor Dublin slob like myself. I'll have none of this effin coffee lark.' (And turning to his waiter escort) 'What are you going to have boys?' The 'boys' – somewhat hesitantly – named their particular poisons and Brendan clinched the situation saying, 'Doubles all round!'

His hosts were delighted with him and so was I, though I privately assured them that their guest had little in common with the puritanical tea-drinking Sean O'Casey. Brendan shortened the evening for us by singing in Irish, English and French, and by convincing us in between that whatever writing he was destined to lay before the world's eyes it would be filled from top to toe with what Henry James called the evidence of 'felt life'.

Late that night, or, rather, early next morning he and I walked Dublin streets under a soft misty rain. He gave me in outline some of what he was setting down with much greater detail in *Borstal Boy*. We left each other in the knowledge that apart from being Dubliners we had one great bond in common. He and I had received our primary education at the saintly hands of a very remarkable woman – Sister Monica of the French Sisters of Charity as they were then called. Brendan never removed himself too far from the protection of her white 'cornette'. She figures at least twice in his writings and his brother Dominic has given a vivid picture of her in his *Teems of Times and Happy Returns*.

Alas, the 'cornette' has gone down in what Brendan would call the 'latest ecclesiastical fashion lark' and no one misses those 'white wings that never grew weary' more than he would have missed them unless perhaps it happens to be myself. Such was my first meeting with Brendan. It was not to be my last.

Others have written of that memorable first night of *The Quare Fellow* at the Pike Theatre when I met Brendan for the second time. He gladly autographed in Irish a programme for an English friend of mine saying that he wouldn't hold his birthplace against him. I was convinced that given health with discipline Brendan had it in him to be another and possibly a greater O'Casey. In my review of the play[3] I said so and promptly received an annonymous letter – obviously from a literary source – telling me that I was talking through my hat. As Brendan's fame spread further afield he was to feel the whips and scorns of Dublin's notorious literary jealousy of which there was not a single iota in his own make-up.

What a different Brendan I was to meet a few months later in the dress-circle of the Abbey-in-Queen's Theatre when *The Quare Fellow* was given its second Dublin presentation.[4] Here was a posh, pomaded young man, smartly tuxedoed in black and white with a profile like the head on an old Roman coin, sitting proudly between his father and mother. He knew this theatre well. His uncle, the famous P. J. Bourke,[5] had been its lessee for a long period and had presented most of his own melodramas on its stage. In his curtain speech Brendan duly made reference to this fact.

I much preferred the Pike production to this Abbey one which, despite some excellent acting, was completely overcast by a photographic stone-by-stone decor of Mountjoy Prison. In addition, some of Warder Regan's best and most moving speeches had been cut on the grounds that they might give offence. Brendan didn't seem to mind. Whatever the circumstances he was incapable of prideful resentment or of bearing malice.

It is inevitable that with such an explosive character as Brendan's one's chronological sense is likely to be bent or twisted. I know that I had seen *The Hostage* during its Wyndham Theatre run and loved every moment of Joan Littlewood's presentation of it. I had heard that Brendan had offered it to the Abbey Theatre of which I was now a director, no less. Of one thing alone I am certain. When this incident occurred Brendan had just returned from a boisterous inspection of the USA and Canada. I met him at the corner of Hawkins Street five minutes after the Scotch House had, fortunately, closed for the 'Holy Hour'.

He was wearing a well-cut expensive sports jacket with equally expensive pants, was suitably barbered and bore no evidence of recent, riotous living. Having inquired after each other's health and expressed regret at the drawn shutters which prevented us from sitting with well filled glasses between us I asked him if he had 'anything on the stocks'. I...h-have', said he, with that slight impediment which invariably affected his speech when sober. 'I...I'm...workin' on a bloody play.' 'Jay, Ga...Gabriel,' he added 'if only a p...play consisted of *two* b...bloody acts. I suppose that e...even you'd be writin' one.'

'Too true, Brendan, I would. But listen to me now. I hope that when you have this new play finished you will give it to the Abbey.' 'Wh...Why should I?' he replied, 'after what Earnan [Ernest Blythe] said when I offered him *The Hostage*?' 'Why, what did he say, Brendan?' Then came this magnificent piece of bi-lingualism. 'He said, "Ta se too-effin-well ro laidir!"' [6] It is to Earnan's credit that when I told him he laughed even more heartily than I did.

Then there was that first-night at the Gate Theatre of Miss Eve Watkinson's presentation of *The Way of the World* during the intervals of which Brendan insisted in carrying on a five-seats-away conversation with me to the amusement of some but to the disgust of the bourgeois majority. He insisted first of all in pointing out Miss Watkinson's father whom I knew anyway. He was the head of the Dublin firm of Panton-Watkinson, painters and decorators, and the point was that Brendan had at one time worked for that firm.

'Met him outside', said Brendan, this time without impediment. 'Said "Good-evening, Behan"; very posh; Jay, Gabriel, I thought he was goin' to say "Look here, you; put another effin' coat on that radiator!" ' This, believe it or not, is evidence of an existential innocence. Look at Duncan Melvin's excellent photograph of Brendan on the dust-jacket of *The Quare Fellow* and you will see it peeping through.

He returned to his seat before the end of the final interval and shouted across to me, 'I suppose you and I are the only scholars who know how this effin' jag ends. D'ye know how I happen to know?' I signalled a negative. 'Believe it or not, Gabriel, they have a copy in the library up in the effin' Joy' [Mountjoy Jail].

There was the Dublin Theatre Festival symposium (on Dublin's corniest problem, 'What's Wrong with the Irish Theatre?') of which I was chairman at the Rupert Guinness Memorial Hall. Brendan, cheerfully sober, was one of the panel. Quite unexpectedly at least so far as I was concerned, Brendan was bitterly and unfairly attacked by a fellow dramatist who was also a member of the panel. It was obviously an outstanding instance of Dublin's now widely known jealousy. Who wrote Brendan's plays for him, this speaker wished to know and more to the same effect.

When the man had finished Brendan placed his cigar in the ash-tray, took a final mouthful from his glass of soda water, and indicated to me that he wished to speak. It was the only occasion on which I had seen Brendan moved to anger, a slow ice-cold anger, as he calmly tore apart Dublin's literary pretensions and demolished his opponent's statements in a recital of incontrovertible facts. It made one sorry for the original speaker. When it was finished Brendan became his old self again; he never needed the excitation of hard liquor to be jolly good company. The only remark he passed to me afterwards about his attacker was one imbued with all that charity demanded of us by St Paul. It was what I expected of him.

The last meeting of the long-standing and perhaps unfairly treated Technical Students' Debating Society was held in a top back-room on Parnell Square. The motion was, 'That Brendan Behan is not a worthwhile Irish writer.' As I had been a good friend to the Society in its time they asked me to preside at this their final meeting. Since the subject of the motion was in town it was thought that he might attend. Perhaps as well he didn't.

I had to listen as speaker after speaker gave vent to some of the greatest nationalistic-*cum*-pietistic bolony yet launched against Brendan, his works and pomps. Only one speaker against the motion approached anywhere near the truth. When it came to my turn to sum up I launched out so deeply in Brendan's praise that next morning an Irish Sunday newspaper thought fit to give its report a special heading 'ABBEY DIRECTOR EULOGISES BEHAN'.[7] About ten o'clock that morning the 'phone rang. It was Brendan. He told me the Editor had phoned him the night before, read my remarks to him, and asked for a comment. 'Well,' he said to the Editor, 'it's one thing when a lot of bloody ignorant yahoos praise you up to the skies; it is quite another thing when someone with a little intelligence says a few nice things about you.'

The Editor then read him the anti-Behan speeches, warning him beforehand that he had no intention of printing them. Brendan listened in silence. The Editor then asked him if he had any printable comment to make on the attitude of the speakers. 'I have,' said Brendan, 'if you'll print it.' 'What is it?' asked the Editor. 'Well, here it is in a sentence', said Brendan, 'but I don't believe you'll print it: "Crawthumpers of the world unite; you've nothing to lose except your effin' brains!"' And that was that.

That Brendan was a lovable character there is not the slightest doubt. It would be indeed true to say of him that 'he nothing common did or mean' except that he would strenuously object to being coupled with Andrew Marvell's tribute to King Charles I. He was generous beyond measure. Someone rightly said of him that he had a heart as big as the Isle of Man. There was a sense in which Brendan could say with Bernanos,[8] 'Je ne suis pas un écrivain',[9] and mean it. He had none of the artificial elements of composition so prized by the born writer. He loved life even more than he loved literature. I think he would have been content to be described in words taken from *Finnegans Wake*: 'The ring man in the wrong shop but the rite words in the rote order?' an epitaph, incidentally, that makes him perhaps an even greater writer than at the moment we take him to be.

He had much of the innocence of childhood about him, a rich sense of wonder and a great basic humility. He told millions of television viewers that he was a bad Catholic and he did so with all the earnestness of the publican in the parable. Many took advantage of him; he was more sinned against than sinning. Like most of us he was afraid of the finger of God. His greatest virtue was integrity. He was what he was, and absolutely. He carried good and evil, each in its place, as he himself might have put it 'so that God can see more quickly where he is on the day of judgement'. And he went from us in the faith of his own Warder Regan in *The Quare Fellow* with someone holding his hand and 'telling him to lean on God's mercy that was stronger than the power of men'.

## NOTES

Gabriel Fallon (1898–1980), Irish civil servant, actor, author, and Director of the Abbey Theatre.

1. McDaid's in Harry Street.
2. Gjon Mili, 'Tea and Memories and Songs at a Last Fond Visit', *Life*, LVII (9 Oct 1964) 92–3.

3. Gabriel Fallon, 'Behan's Play Should Not Be Missed', *Evening Press* (Dublin), 20 Nov 1954, p. 3.

4. *The Quare Fellow* was produced at the Abbey Theatre, Dublin, on 8 October 1956.

5. For a note on Patrick J. Bourke see p. 148.

6. 'It is too-effin-well strong.'

7. 'Abbey Director's Spirited Defence of Brendan Behan', *Sunday Independent*, 29 Jan 1961, p. 5.

8. Georges Bernanos (1888–1948), French novelist.

9. 'I am not a writer.'

# The Importance of Being Brendan*

## MICHEÁL MacLIAMMÓIR

I can never remember my first meeting with Brendan Behan. He was one of those men of powerful personality who yet – in my case at any rate – make no profound impression on the first brief encounter, and who, when one looks back over a period that has vanished forever, seem always to have been there.

It may be that fact, that odd feeling that one has always known him, that accounts for the only astonishing incident of my knowledge of him. For our meetings were seldom and invariably by chance. We never said to each other, 'Let us meet tomorrow at such and such a time and dine in such and such a place.' Probably he would not have turned up if we had done this. Anyway I never associated him with dinner, still less with luncheon – there is no attempt in that phrase to get a cheap laugh at the expense of his most expensive weakness – and I never really discovered how much we had or had not in common, how much we would have grown in friendship or in the reverse. We never sought each other out: on the other hand I think we never avoided each other. Certainly I never avoided him, and he always appeared glad when, through this chance or that, our paths crossed.

He bored me only when he was drunk for the beautifully simple reason that people who are drunk always bore me, and contrary to much popular belief he was by no means always drunk. Whether sober or drunk his manners were very beautiful in their way, and even in his Bacchanalian

* *The World of Brendan Behan*, ed. Sean McCann (London: New English Library, 1965) pp. 206–8.

moods he was always good-natured. I think that is what I liked most about Brendan: he was a big man in the sense that he had in his composition no spark or smouldering of *dranntail*, that sour, snarling, embittered, resentful, fang-baring grin for which there is no exact equivalent in the English language and that is so ominously familiar to all of us. He was as generous as he was on occasion violent and unreasonable; and that in itself should be enough to endear him to our hearts.

I suppose it was the Brendan the public chuckled over that I cared about less. I always felt that this side of him would disappear one day and that although, as I wrote at the time, the fact that the mere mention of his name calls forth chuckles and frowns from the more ascetic of theatrical circles as well as from those bar-flies who abound in Dublin as in other places and who have nothing whatsoever to do with the art of the theatre beyond their gaping pleasure in the easy notoriety it offers (with such frequently disastrous consequences) to its children, is no proof at all that Mr Behan is not a true native of the House of Harlequin. Indeed, his apparent drawbacks, his boisterous and assertive personality, his flair for notoriety (of a not entirely aesthetic pattern), his easy juggling with the most readily understood quips and cracks of his own town and of his own time, all go to prove that he is. And yet to the more analytical sense, his finer qualities – his warmth and generosity, his tenacity, his zest for life, the absence in him of that bitter begrudging spirit of denial that so often characterises what one might call his 'type' in many another Irish playwright – these things cause one to regret the other, at present more insistent, qualities through which he has been popularised. In other words, I seem to scent in Mr Behan the writer of a tragedy that will come straight from the depths of his being and in which the easy, the too-easy, laughter-getters of the Dublin playboy – the Old Stage Irishman of the Sea, as I think in his latest and most convincing yet still not quite real creation – will not be, perhaps, abandoned, but will take, as they took with the earlier O'Casey, their subordinate and rightful place.

I suppose I have made it clear that we were never bosom friends, and that makes my behaviour on a certain night in Australia all the more inexplicable. From the moment of arrival at the airport in Sydney where my tour of *The Importance of Being Oscar* and *I Must Be Talking to My Friends* began, I had been asked about him and once or twice had made some remark of a lightly snappish nature from the sheer monotony of hearing so many questions on the same subject. One evening, just before my opening performance, there was one of those radio or television interviews inseparable from an actor's life on tour, and for some reason unknown and unexplained I began to talk of Brendan as I had never done in my life. It was very curious. I heard my voice saying things that were perfectly sincere yet that came from a source of which I seemed to know nothing at all: it was as though I were listening to the voice and words of somebody else. When at last the interview was over my manager, Brian Tobin, said to me, 'I never realised before how much you liked and admired Brendan: anybody listening to you tonight would think he was your ideal writer as well as being your dearest friend. What in God's name came over you?'

I could not tell him. I did not understand myself. I still do not understand. All I know was that on the following day the news of Brendan's death was in the newspapers and on every radio in the country. We made careful calculations in the differences of time between Dublin and Sydney. Brendan had died at the moment I was pouring out my panegyric to the air.

## NOTE

Micheál MacLiammóir (1899–1977), Irish actor and dramatist; one of the founders of the Galway Gaelic Theatre, and in 1928 founded the Dublin Gate Theatre Company with the English actor Hilton Edwards.

# A Monstrous Egotist*

## DESMOND MacNAMARA

Brendan was, as he once boasted or confided to me, when scrambling down the slopes of Glencullen in the Dublin mountains, a monstrous egotist. By this, he seemed to mean that he suffered a compulsive need to talk, ask questions and tell funny anecdotes, preferably scandalous. He differed from egotists in that he was usually prepared to listen, and indeed, carefully question any cogent riposte. Although his words poured out like a waterfall, his company, certainly with one or two people, usually induced a sparkling dialogue. Knowing that I, in particular amongst his friends at that time (1947–60 maybe) had a particular taste for the utterly absurd, he used to file away examples of lunatic follies to retail when he met me, or during lazy symposiums in the small hours of the morning when the drink, or even the Turkish coffee, was finished. He did the same thing with racing tips for the poet Paddy Kavanagh, and similarly with other subjects for other people. I think it was this personalisation that made him at times a sympathetic and convivial raconteur. Latterly, when drink had corroded his soul, he became a dangerous bore, though even towards the end he would occasionally awaken you (his host) in the dawn hours and talk

* This is the first appearance in print.

brilliantly and with wit. Alas, the daylight usually brought on the thirst, and he would become a noisy bore again.

I leave it to those more domestically concerned to comment on his sometimes vicious and always uncharitable attitude towards members of his family (father, mother, Brian, Dominic – not the Furlongs). This was not a continuous feud, but it certainly erupted with scalding lava: often at acutely embarrassing times. This has to be seen in a context of intense family loyalty and occasional manifestations of affection. Undoubtedly, however, he often thought that 'they' collectively were trying to do him down and I was often abused for demurring.

The above is a very brief estimation of Brendan's impact on me from the time that I first met him carrying a banner in Dublin, at the age of sixteen, to a few months before he died. I last parted from him with some relief (and very good reason for relief), but when I read of his death, in Rome in a half-page headline in *La Stampa*, I nearly fell into the Barca fountain with shock. The Piazza di Spagna was floodlit and empty at 3.30 in the morning when I bought the paper from the kiosk, just taking in its early delivery: BRENDAN BEHAN, DEAD IN DUBLIN 8.30 hours (or something like that). A Roman friend, summoned by phone, took me on a dawn tour of the tombs on the Via Appia, with a bottle of grappa which helped to contain the cold vacuum within me. My wife Skylla and my ex-wife Beverlie were, I discovered later, doing exactly the same thing in London, except for the presumptuous vanity of the empty tombs.

## NOTE

Desmond MacNamara, Irish artist who did a bust of Behan's head. He also wrote three review articles on Behan in London periodicals: 'Saints and Ladders', *New Statesman*, LXX (5 Nov 1965) 705; 'Early and Late', *New Statesman*, LXXII (18 Nov 1966) 750; and 'The Biggest Heart in Ireland', *The Tablet*, 17 Dec 1977, pp. 1201–2.

# The Home and the Colonial Boy*

JOHN RYAN

Youth inflicts the mortal wound
which age comes too late to heal.

Arland Ussher

When somebody enters your life for the first time, the initial image is imprecise – blurred. It takes time for the details to achieve focus. After all, it has yet to be established whether, in fact, the object is coming or going. For all we know it might, like a star, be receding. For that reason it is easier to remember when you *last* saw your father than when you first saw him.

While I am hazy as to the exact time I first met Brendan Behan (though I am sure that it was sometime late in 1943), I have no doubt as to the location – it was Des MacNarmara's[1] flat on the top floor of the Monument Café at 39 Grafton Street. Mac ran a sort of non-stop, Fabian *salon* in these premises from 1944 to 1948. I say non-stop because the pad was open to all-comers, quite literally, morning, noon and night. Mac was a gifted sculptor whose speciality was *papier-maché*. His one-room-studio-*cum*-bed-sitter was shared with his wife Beverlie and some cats. Mac worked all day producing puppets, masks, stage props, window-models, even costume jewellery from his protean goo – indeed I still retain a door-knocker in the shape of Roger Casement's[2] head ('the ghost of Roger Casement in knocking on the door . . . ') which, though of paper, has the consistency of cast-iron. It has been much coveted.

Mac cherished the company of writers, musicians, poets, artists or, lacking these avocations, the bizarre, the unorthodox or the innocent visionary. He could (and did) hold lengthy conversations on every imaginable topic with an unending stream of visitors, comprising loafers, itinerants, even celebrities. I remember T. H. White, whose book *The Once and Future King* became the musical *Camelot*, as a frequent caller and Erwin Schroedinger, the refugee from Nazi Germany – to whom de Valera had

---

\* *Remembering How We Stood: Bohemian Dublin at the Mid-Century* (Dublin: Gill and Macmillan, 1975) pp. 61–79.

given sanctuary in the Institute for Advanced Studies. Schroedinger was a colleague of Einstein's who had expressed the theory of relativity for the first time in mathematical formulae, his hobby was weaving tapestry and he referred to himself as 'a naïve physicist'. E. J. Moeran, the Irish composer, was a frequent visitor.

Informal meals were eaten throughout the day and night, as a large black kettle always hung suspended over the turf fire in the corner. The Macs were true vegetarians – even excluding fish and eggs from their diet. One, therefore, would be likely to get a large, fresh hunk of vienna roll smothered in scallions, tomatoes and cheese, chased down with a mug of strong tea. The Macs were humane, as well as sophisticated, and knew that it would be unfair to extend their cult of vegetarianism to their room-mates of the feline category. To this end, meat, in the form of rib steak, was provided regularly for the cats.

It was after Brendan's Borstal and Curragh internment camp period but before the Walton Jail, Liverpool, days. I think he was actually on the run at the time, for he arrived and departed by night, although he sometimes slept there too – there was a spare bed of some description which he used.

He was about twenty years old. Good looking too, by any standards, especially with that shock of curly hair. He could have done with a few more inches in height, perhaps. Also his hands and feet were diminutive considering his overall bulk. But he had sparkling eyes and very fine, even teeth, of which he was inordinately proud. The only appendage that accompanied him *everywhere* was the toothbrush in his upper pocket. (Alas for the teeth – the butt of an automatic was to smash them out some years later in a brawl that was as ugly as it was futile; being neither founded on political conviction nor gainful crime.) He was reasonably trim but possessed of one of those bodies that seem to yearn for weight.

Dionysian in his appetites even at this early age, his meals were orgiastic affairs of uninhibited recklessness, where pints and porter-house steaks would be lowered away to a band playing. Indeed, in the Behan household in Kildare Road, it was not unusual to find a galvanised bathtub, such as were once used for bathing children, full of simmering mass of Irish stew in which it was likely an entire chicken might be found floating – or a sheep's head! With his father and four of the sons all out working as house-painters, good money was coming in at last and all was possible. The fame of *Chez* Behan spread and even Patrick Kavanagh made a pilgrimage there to partake of the fabulous fare about which he had heard so much.

Predictably, the all-vegetarian MacNamara menu was not really his dish, though he discreetly kept his dislike of this 'rabbit food' (as he called it) to himself, even reasoning that it was 'intellectual' fodder and, as such, likely to be good for the brain.

One night when the MacNamaras were out visiting, they left Brendan to hold the fort against their return but, more importantly, to feed the cats. I was pottering about my own studio, which was next door, when my attention was distracted by an attractive smell of cooking coming from the Macs' residence. Deciding to investigate, I entered the room only to find 'your man' frying a large juicy steak for the cats. He was turning it when I came in and, as it sizzled afresh, great wafts of unbearably succulent aromas filled the room. The cats arched their backs and purred...

'Christ,' gasped Brendan, 'God forgive me, I can't help it.' With that he did his best to push the entire steak into his mouth. Loud and prolonged screams issued from the demented tabbies.

'God's teeth,' I cried, 'what are they going to say when they come back and find you've eaten the cats' meat?'

'They won't know', he mumbled between half masticated mouthfuls, 'c-cats c-can't t-t-talk' (he was using the Behan stutter I was to get to know so well).

'They *will* know, because these cats cry when they're not fed. In fact, they set up an infernal din', I argued.

'—— it, you're right', he mumbled apprehensively. 'Jaysus, do you think we could stuff radishes or scallions into them?'

'Not a chance', I said, 'they're true carnivora.'

'What's that when it's at home?'

'Flesh-eating mammals', I replied. Just then we heard the Mac-Namaras clambering up the stairs.

'Don't say a word', he pleaded. He had obviously had an inspiration, for without further ado he caught hold of the cats and, in turn, pressed each protesting muzzle into the melted dripping in the pan.

'What's the matter, little dears?' asked Bev, confronted with the sight of the three cats and the sound of their lamentations – a woeful threnody.

'Did you feed them at all, Brendan?' she asked suspiciously.

'Jaysus,' said he, 'can't you see the bastards lickin' their chops?' and so they were. His stratagem had worked, for no matter how they complained, the irrefutable fact was there for all to see; they were plastered with fat and dripping!

'Good gracious,' said Bev, 'there was a good pound of meat in that.'

'Yerrah,' complained Brendan piously, between burps, 'there's no plasin' some bastards.'

Hitler and Behan were both unfulfilled house-painters. Destiny had bigger plans for them – though, as events were to show, not necessarily better. Brendan, like all his brothers and his father, learnt the trade of painter, which included a spell at the 'Tech'. The daddy, Stephen, was President of the Irish Painters' and Decorators' Union, which, of course, was a help when it came to getting jobs. I remember an occasion when Brendan was painting the Gaiety Theatre. I was strolling down South King Street when he came bounding out through the swing doors in his white overalls which were, like Joseph's coat, of divers colours. Something was amusing him vastly. 'For Jaysus' sake come here till I tell you, he chortled while at the same time more or less aiming me into McArdle's pub across the way. It seems that there was a rehearsal of Terence Rattigan's *The Winslow Boy* in progress and that he was up in the flies – supposedly painting. The infant prodigy playing the title role was behaving as child stars are expected to behave and therefore giving everybody concerned a very hard time. Brendan from his lofty eyrie manoeuvred himself into a handy position directly above the prodigy and was able to allow the contents of a gallon tin of white primer to descend and envelop the head of the insufferable child. I am aware that he varies the telling of this story in *Confessions of an Irish Rebel* but this is how I remember getting it from him at the time, immediately after the event.

Again I recall that my brother Paddy asked him to paint the name his firm (Ryan and Co.) on the door of his office. Brendan painted it in Roman capitals with gold leaf and shadow. All was middling-good except the N which was upside down. The technical name in the trade for this work was 'writing' (hence 'sign-writing'). One day I met an old crony and fellow committee man of Stephen's in the Painters' and Decorators', called Pa O'Toole. I asked him did he know the Behan boys. He thought he did. He wasn't sure about Brendan because he had spent so much time in the nick that he wasn't all that well known in the trade. To make it easier to distinguish him and because he had already had some small pieces in Irish published, I referred to him as 'Brendan, you know, the writer.' 'The writer?' he queried in surprise. 'There's only one writer in that family and that's the father, Stephen. Did you ever see the sign for Guinness he done up there on the gable over Slattery's in Phibsboro? Them letters is seven foot high. And the pint he drew beside it, with the shine down the side and the big foamy head? Now that's writing. No...Stephen was the only one ever wrut in that family.'

Once Freddie May, the composer, gave both of us complimentary tickets to a performance of the opera *Pelléas et Mélisande*. We were, perhaps, too young fully to enjoy its exquisite felicities, for presently Brendan grew restive. He leaned back on his plush seat the better to peer into the recesses of the rococo ceiling. At last he found what he was seeking. 'Look,' he whispered urgently, stabbing chubby fingers upwards, 'between them fat, flying babies up there – that patch on Orpheus' arse – I was supposed to have washed that down. Ha! Ha! Jaysus...' Sure enough a rectangle of darker hue showed through the flights of the *putti* and the cavorting gods. A dismounted horse-Protestant just in front of him, not sharing his enthusiasm for unwashed ceiling allegories, pinned him to his seat with her opera glasses and silenced him with a vice-regal 'ssshhhhhh...'.

Brendan brought me his first short story when I was Editor of *Envoy*. It was called 'A Woman of No Standing'.[3] As a piece of writing it is as good as anything else he ever wrote; some think it his best individual piece. It has freshness, compassion and humour. My office, which was under Mac's old studio, which he had relinquished, had now become the casual meeting place for the Grafton Street boulevardiers and the MacDaidian intelligentsia. Brendan would come in for a fag or the 'lend of a loan' of a half note, or any other reason why. But this was his first professional appearance as you might say. The full span of his creative career only bridged the years 1950–60, just ten years. It is not all that surprising that this, his first piece, should be as good as his later work. *Borstal Boy*, his acknowledged *chef d' oeuvre*, was itself partly finished at that time because he actually offered me a whole wad of it – though it was too late for publication, the last number of *Envoy* had gone to press. He wasn't sure what to call it but had provisionally dubbed it *Another Twisting of the Rope*. I suggested *Bridewell Revisited*, a title which he was quite enthusiastic about. However, when it did see the light of the publishing day, it was under the bland and uninventive title of *Borstal Boy*, a title which, no doubt, the pass BA 'reader' who read it for his publisher, bearing in mind the possibilities of a *News of the World* readership, had thought terribly swinging.

In 1965 while searching through the old archives of *Envoy*, Anthony Cronin[4] and myself found the manuscript. Cronin was the first to spot it, recognising it from the actual physical shape it had assumed after months of close proximity (in the inside pocket) with the Behan anatomy, when he had hawked it from pillar to post. Written on it in his own hand was 'A bit I'm not ashamed of; the title supplied by John Ryan for whom my affection is tenacious, invincible and reckless.'

Sometime in 1952, a friend of mine who was then working as a photographer on the long vanished but then ever-so-trendy *Picture Post* and who wished to be rid of at least some of the austerities of post-war London (the puritan Chancellor, Sir Stafford Cripps – better known to his victims as Sir Stifford Crapps – had decided that the nation go into sackcloth and ashes for at least a decade to atone for winning the war) if it were only for a week, asked me if there was anything stirring in Dublin in the way of a story that would furnish him with the necessary excuse to come over for a paid holiday.

I told him that it was not a time of momentous happenings in Ireland. However, I eventually came up with a story which I thought might just do. There was a bizarre young man of Rabelaisian proclivities who had spent, intermittently, the years since he was sixteen in various prisons for the cause of the Republic. I had recently published his first short story. Amongst other things, I had seen him float down the River Seine with a bottle of champagne which he was, at the same time, consuming with considerable expertise. Dan Farson (for he was the friend) took photographs and I wrote the article. A new editor of *Picture Post* (the editorial casualty rate at the time was about one a week) turned down the whole thing on the grounds that Behan was unknown and of no interest anyway. As we had been commissioned we were paid. The article and pictures subsequently appeared in a New Zealand illustrated magazine. That was the first time that Brendan appeared in the full glare of the public stage. It was not to be the last time. I often wonder what that same editor thought in the subsequent ten years as the Behan legend blazed out across the globe igniting a thousand headlines.

Like myself, he was born under the sign of Aquarius. No wonder then that he was so well suited to the liquid world. He could surround a bottle of whiskey more happily than any man I knew. Like François Rabelais[5] (to whom he bore more than a superficial resemblance) he might as truly have said 'I drink for the thirst to come.' Equally he liked to submerge himself in the fluid element. We used to go to the Forty Foot bathing place and it was there that Farson took some of his most memorable photographs of Behan delightedly wallowing in the sea, true as a turtle, or recumbent on the shore, like a basking shark. One morning, as he was dressing there, he remarked to a priest, who was a daily swimmer, 'You know, Father, after this early dip I really believe I've earned my breakfus.' 'But of course', the priest replied. 'Aye,' said Brendan, rubbing his hands in anticipation, 'a large brandy and a plateful of benzedrine.'

When I had the yacht *Southern Cross*, Beatrice and he used to come out sailing in Dublin Bay. His pleasure was to sit in the stern (usually blocking all approaches to the tiller) and spin for mackerel. Usually the boat, even in light airs, was too fast, a characteristic which was the subject of much fluent cursing on his part. 'The only thing you can catch from this feckin' thing', he would say, 'is a feckin' submarine.' Despite this, we always had a bottle or two of red wine below decks so that all our voyages had auspicious endings.

After the publication of Ulick O'Connor's biography of Brendan[6] there was much righteous indignation, rending of garments and general foaming at the mouth because of the suggestion that he had been somewhat homosexually inclined. The then Chief of Staff of the IRA, Cathal Goulding, had written a bellicose 'review' of the book in *Hibernia* which was little short of a declaration of war on the book's author.[7] Some of the tension was taken out of the situation by a heading in one of the Sunday papers which brought the thing back to its comic-opera proportions. It ran, 'Quare Fella – Queer? Query'. As one who knew him well (but not *all that well*, I hasten to add!) I can only relate that he made no great bones about the matter to his friends. His was a voracious sexual appetite and in Dublin vernacular of the time 'would get up on the back of the Drimnagh bus!'

I think that even apart from the years of enforced confinement with other men, he might have considered homosexuality as simply another tasty morsel or savoury on the *smörgasbord* of the Bohemian running buffet. But only as 'afters' so to speak, following the main course. Booze, as always, took precedence over all; this was the one subject about which he was neither lighthearted nor irreverent. The definition of an Irish 'queer' is supposed to be 'a man that prefers women to drink'. He certainly did not come into that category. He was openly ribald on the subject, just as he was derisive and blasphemous about most of the things that ignorance wraps in a cocoon of modesty and piety. He was vastly ahead of his comrades in intellectual stature, being, in the main, free of hypocrisy and humbug. After the publication of O'Connor's book, they wanted to give the impression of loyal friends rushing, posthumously, to the defence of their calumniated pal. All they succeeded in doing was to spell out their own distinctively bourgeois *mores* as they struggled to drag him down to their suburban level. He had faults, but intellectual dishonesty was not one of them.

It was I who introduced Brendan to Eddie Chapman. We met accidentally at Dublin Airport, casually introducing ourselves over a drink in the bar – we were travelling by air and so had time to spare. I cannot imagine such a meeting in the soulless enormity of the present complex but in those days it was quite an intimate place with nothing but the comings and goings of a few DC3s to bother the management and a daily passenger turnover that the belly of a jumbo airliner could now swallow without any sign of indigestion.

It turned out that this Eddie Chapman was a famous safe-cracking expert who in pre-war years had specialised in 'doing' Odeon cinemas. He had worked his way through every one of the multitudinous branches of this organisation in the United Kingdom from the Mull of Kintyre to the Channel Islands. He was aided in his scheme in that they had all been designed by the same architect who, being no Mies van der Rohe, was content to let the same plan serve for all. Eddie could walk in with a blindfold on him and reach out and infallibly touch the safe – useful when working in the pitch dark.

Nemesis caught up with him on the Channel Islands, however, just when there were no more Odeons left to lay his burglarious hands on, and there he was sentenced to many years in prison. But hope in the shape of the Wehrmacht lay just beyond the horizon. When the Germans invaded Alderney in the summer of 1940 they did a little deal with Eddie, whereby he was 'sprung' on condition that he teamed up with the Nazi spy organisation.

He was trained by them in Berlin mainly in the complex art of sabotage. In time he was parachuted into England with a radio transmitter, a quantity of gelignite and a very large sum in genuine Bank of England notes. The bulk of these he buried beneath a tree 'somewhere in England' to await the outbreak of peace and his own happy return. He then gave himself up to the nearest police. British Intelligence immediately grasped the importance of his potential so he agreed to continue acting as a German agent while being in fact one of their own on condition that the rest of his sentence be struck from the rolls.

During the war he made several trips to and from England to the continent, departing by German submarine, and returning by parachute (with British MI5 shepherding him like a broody hen, her chick all the

332    BRENDAN BEHAN: INTERVIEWS AND RECOLLECTIONS

time) and staging acts of 'sabotage' that he was supposed to have pulled off. One of his best deceptions was to radio back to Germany false information regarding the location of V1 and V2 bombs when they struck, which is the main reason why so many fell on the garden suburbs and not the port or industrial sector of London.

Eventually the Germans did get wise to him and he was awaiting the end in a concentration camp when once more an army came to the rescue – this time the liberating American one. The Germans had given him the Iron Cross first class but all he got from the Imperial Majesty (not counting the free pardon of course) was a hundred pound fine for contravening the Official Secrets Act *after the war*, by publishing a brief memoir in the magazine *Lilliput*.

By the time I introduced them (*circa* 1948) Eddie had acquired a small freighter, the *Sir James*, a vessel of some 400 tons which was then plying the trade routes of the Irish Sea. What cargoes she carried or from whence and to whom I never did discover. Eddie had a manner about him which discouraged such enquiries. When he smiled, gold wisdom teeth flashed on either side of his mouth but his eyes never smiled. There are some questions best left unasked.

At my instigation he was kind enough to sign Brendan on as (the Lord forgive me) an 'able-bodied' seaman. For about six months they roamed the seas on many divers mercantile enterprises, and strange things befell them. They even managed to find a brothel in the sea port of Drogheda which they had reckoned to be as unlikely as finding one in Vatican City. It was of the stay-at-home and do-it-yourself variety being managed and staffed by a mother and her five daughters.

One day Eddie asked Brendan to paint the masts, reasoning that he must have some expertise at least in this field. Brendan proceeded to paint the mast upwards from the base to the top, or to be more nautical about it, from the heel to the truck. This ensured that when he made any of his frequent descents during the operations (be it for jar or pee) he must do so by slithering down a greasy pole which liberally plastered him with marine paint of the consistency of raspberry jam. Eddie pointed out that the correct procedure was to have yourself hoisted aloft on a bosun's chair to the truck and to paint as you lowered yourself down. His answer was to tell Eddie not to teach his grandmother how to suck eggs and to stick to navigating the leaky old hooker even though he knew —— all about that too.

By the middle fifties Brendan Behan had become almost as infamous as the other B.B. of the mid-century – Brigitte Bardot. And as big a bore, not a few would impiously add. It was hard to say which part of the fame that accreted to him was of his own manufacture, and which was simply mud from the Fleet Street ditch that had clung. He seemed to be wired up to the media; his umbilical – the telephone wire. He only had to drop his pants in Grafton Street, Dublin, for the teleprinters to cackle in Galveston, Texas, or Osaka, Japan.

When the box-office receipts flagged in the West End, he would quite seriously wonder whether the time had not arrived to awake the lethargic Albions once again. Without further ado, having established this, he would take a plane to London, get into a brawl or two, have himself barred from the theatre which was showing his own play, having rushed onto the stage and made a drunken speech.

The parallel of the sorcerer's apprentice irresistibly presents itself here. For the more he, the journalist's friend, provided free copy, particularly for the 'splutter' press, the more it wanted and the more he was expected to perform. The trouble about this kind of ballyhoo is that the recipient begins to believe it himself. He began to act earnestly the role of drunk-in-ordinary to the British and American public – he could have added 'by Royal appointment' after Princess Margaret had come to see *The Hostage* and all but fallen out of her seat at the joke about 'Vat 69' being the pope's telephone number; a joke I myself heard at Kilashee, a preparatory school for Clongowes Wood, very nearly kicking out the tailboard of the cot I was sleeping in at the time.

The sad thing was that he was, without needing to lay on anything thick, a genuine wit and wag. There was an abundance of 'copy' in what he said, more than enough to satisfy the needs of the most avaricious of journalists. You don't come across a man who can engage Groucho Marx, effortlessly, in repartee, every day of the week. Once in an elevator in a New York hotel, Groucho commenced some anecdote by saying, 'I was making *A Night at the Opera* when . . . .' Brendan at once intervened with: 'That's like Michelangelo saying, "I was doing the murals in the Sistine Chapel at the time . . . ." '

Another incident – the real comedy of which the press missed – being as usual, in pursuit of sensation rather than wit – was when he was flying by Air France from Paris to London. Shortly after departure, the 'plane was struck by lightning. Brendan, who was in the jigs anyhow, reacted in fear-shaken fashion. Apprehensive of any further consequences, the pilot decided to return to Orly for the purposes of unloading Brendan. At the airport he made a speech from the ramp to the inevitable assembly of press; in his quite good French: 'Je suis préparé à mourir pour la France, si c'est nécessaire, mais certainement pas pour l'Air France!' ('I am prepared to die, if necessary for France – but not for Air France!')

This was taken to be an insult to the 'honour and dignity' of France and, as a result, he was lodged in the 'cage', that ubiquitous article of the French penal code that can be found in all police stations. There he spent the night with some Algerian nationalists. Brendan entertained the company during the night with songs and ballads. At one point, a member of the *gendarmerie*, who had been trying to sleep, rattled the bars of the cage with his sub-machine-gun, making the ominous comment, ' Regardez la mitrailleuse' ('See the machine-gun') – to which Brendan replied, 'Je le vois: dommage que tu ne l'avais pas à la Ligne Maginôt.' ('I see it. It's pity you didn't have it on the Maginot line.') He told me the whole story on our way to the Air

France office in Westmoreland Street in Dublin to collect the money owed
to him for his unused ticket. The papers simply proclaimed the fact that he
had been drunk and disorderly.

As the illness grew, the drinking increased; he was stupefied from both. I
had dinner in Jim Downey's Steak House on Eighth Avenue, New York,
with Beatrice and himself one evening in April 1963. 'You've come a long
way from Mac's studio in Grafton Street where you ate the cats' dinner', I
observed. But he was too sick and tired even to smile. He just sat there like a
mound of blubber – or Orson Welles in the last reels of *Citizen Kane*.

A myth that might well be exploded is the one that got a universal airing
immediately after his death, which is typical of the kind of smaltz[8] that
infests the more yellow journalism on such melancholy occasions: that was
the one that seemed to imply that it was the inconsiderateness of his friends
that had hastened his death. Nothing could be further from the truth. A
few things should be remembered: Behan, though generous in many ways
(particularly to the really down-and-out), was notoriously tight-fisted
when it came to buying a round in the company of his coevals – 'slow on the
draw' as they used to say in the vernacular. His taste ran to treble brandies
in these latter years. This exotic preference, coupled with his unwillingness
to return the compliments, didn't greatly endear him to the Irish, who are
very down-to-earth when it comes to the mechanics of drinking, however
elevated they may become as a result of its consumption. At this time, be it
also remembered, he was also quite an appalling messer. One would have
to rifle the annals of Bacchus to find a more determined nuisance in drink.
If he wasn't falling on you and spilling drinks over you, he was mauling
your wife or girlfriend to the accompaniment of an unbroken dirge of truly
'foul' language. He would punch and claw you if he felt you weren't giving
him 100 per cent attention – not the easiest thing to mime when you were
hearing some story you had heard a million times before. One day, when
he was not all that much advanced in alcoholicity, he felt the need to
expose his genitals to a pub half-full of indifferent boozers. It was a
depressing, though poignant, illustration of what Paul Valéry[9] meant
when he wrote, 'When one no longer knows what to do in order to astonish
and survive, one offers one's pudenda[10] to the public gaze.'

Once, in the Bailey,[11] he vomited straight out onto the floor in mid-
sentence, but completed it, nevertheless. He would empty a pub in about
two minutes flat. I should know. I worked for one of the few from which he
was not barred. Old friends fled when they saw him coming. Even the
needy who depended on him for the odd drink began to dread him. One of
the last of his 'minders', Eddie Whelan, a married man with children who
was a paid drinking companion, told me how he would be dragged from
bed at any old hour of the night, by Brendan, who would arrive in a taxi, to
commence the day's marathon of drinking. 'People think I do well out of
this,' he confided, ' but I was making better money as a bricklayer. Pity to
God I ever gave it up.'

Brendan and I dined once more that year. This time back in Dublin at the Bailey. It was a quiet afternoon and we were the only ones in the restaurant at the time. Anthony Cronin joined us. One of the waiters, Roy, had a transistor which was emitting signals that only he was able to interpret. Presently he volunteered the information that the sounds seemed to suggest that President Kennedy had been shot and killed in Dallas, Texas. Brendan started crying, 'He invited me to the reviewing stand for the inauguration', he mumbled. Then he called for a taxi. It was years afterwards that I heard that he had been driven straight to the American Embassy where he was one of the first to sign his name on the Book of Remembrance. Behan, the showman, was never slow in following up an event potentially favourable for publicity, however befuddled he was by alcohol.

His drinking, which was entirely self-inspired and self-motivated, had taken on epic proportions. He had passed from drinkard to drunkard to alcoholic and, finally, to dipsomaniac. One day, on an impulse, he had withdrawn £500 from the bank, picked up an acquaintance, Philip Corley, with whom he had been out on the tiles the previous night, and with him, took a plane from Dublin Airport bound for America. Finding that there was no bar service on the Dublin–Shannon stage of the flight and noting that Corley had, in a hold-all, packed a bottle of after-shave lotion, he grabbed it, unscrewed the top, and swallowed the contents in one almighty draught. They refused to take him any further than Shannon.

I saw him from time to time during those last months. He would lope into the Bailey, more dead than alive. Sometimes he would simply stare. A photograph which was taken in an automatic 'photo booth' at Amiens Street station a month or so before his death will give an idea of the terrible condition that had so rapidly overwhelmed him.

Oddly, he is least remembered for what he did for his country. As a young member of the Irish Resistance, he had freely sacrificed his youth for the ideal of a free and, he hoped, socialist, non-sectarian Ireland. While his contemporaries had their fling, he languished in British jails and Irish internment camps. Even as a boy, he had tried to enlist in the International Brigade in the Spanish Civil War. He came very close to the firing-squad after the shooting incident at the 1916 Commemoration march to Glasnevin in 1943. He was not wanting in courage. Of all the writers, poets or painters of his generation, he was the only one who took up arms, literally, for the freedom of his country. If he was selfish and egotistical in other things – he was a completely committed patriot. What he did with utter unselfishness cannot be taken from him. The value of his literary estate may be argued, but not this. When he died, the IRA gave him a burial with all they could provide by way of full military honours – a guard of honour, an oration and, after the mourners had departed, a furtive firing-party at the grave.

An uncommonly mild day it was, that nineteenth day of March in the year of 1964. A surgical theatre in Dublin's Meath Hospital. The patient is unconscious and breathing heavily. A tube enters his throat (a tracheotomy) beneath the ample, rounded chin; another, presumably for intravenous feeding, is connected to some part of the abdomen. A hand lies authoritatively across a generous chest – it is the pose that a politician might take after delivering a ponderous, post-prandial cliché, anticipating a round of applause.

There is a Roman quality to the massive young head and the great mane of brown hair that tumbles rebelliously over the edge of the operating table. A large, well-proportioned frame, not unduly corpulent, covered in a soft unwrinkled skin that could have been a girl's (it is almost downy), which has now taken into its natural pigmentation a curious, lemon-coloured tinge.

The theatre is silent save for the barely audible scratchings of a pen as a worried-looking nurse makes notes in the day-book. A coloured house-surgeon – Pakistani perhaps – is darkly silhouetted against the window, a stethoscope non-chalantly swinging, pendulum-wise, between his knees. Muted, faraway city murmurings only emphasise the prevailing afternoon stillness. James Clarence Mangan, another poet, had died in this same hospital, young and destitute, a hundred years earlier. There is a sense of restfulness about the place, as though the outcome of some great struggle had been decided. Time itself seems to be dying and this, in turn, induces a torpid drowsiness. I feel like a swimmer effortlessly floating on the water of Lethe.

The breathing sound persists, relentlessly, like a metronome, while the stethoscope involuntarily keeps time. The only urgency is in that sound, the sound of the body's motor, itself part of an abandoned vehicle running out, on the last of its fuel. What signals the body's own computer must be sending forth now that the surgeons have thrown in their hand? Futile signals calling up spent reserves, urging exhausted components. Betrayed, the body lingers on death's threshold; more reluctant than the spirit to enter...

As a gesture of farewell, I touch the hair of his head. My hand lingers, it is warm.

'Ave atque vale',[12] I think. (It is difficult, in grief not to be rhetorical – even with oneself).

We leave the room and descend the stairs, Kathleen, Stephen and myself. Earlier they had called on me at the Bailey[13] and asked me to take them to the hospital. This I did, thinking no more than that was required. Both, however, insisted that I accompany them all the way. I knew that Brendan's condition was terminal, that he was grossly cirrhosed and I was loath on that account to appear as an idle spectator. I was relieved when I heard the hospital receptionist say that only members of the family could be allowed to see him, until they countered this by telling her that I was

Rory Furlong – Kathleen's son by an earlier marriage and Brendan's own half-brother! Like it or not I now had to enact the role of her surrogate offspring. Later in the day the *real* Rory had trouble getting in himself, due to this earlier deception.

I remarked, limply, that Brendan looked rather well, apart from that yellow hue. He did, in fact. Death evidently takes a great weight off the mind, for what I saw in him, I have seen in others – the mocking erasure of the years, life's final prank, death's first joke – he looked positively young.

'He won't live beyond this afternoon, John, dear', his mother said quietly.

We made our way back to the Bailey. The clans had begun to gather and the drink to flow. A period of great conviviality, never long separated from death among the Irish, was now imminent. Only the final confirmation was required for the balloon to ascend in earnest. At six o'clock a 'phone call came from the Meath. Yes, all was well now. Brendan Behan had died peacefully. He had just turned forty. Kathleen was right.

Next morning, Muscovites, reaching for the samovar, read the news in *Pravda*. Less surprised, Brooklyn taxi-drivers learnt all about it in the *Daily News*; the private, deadly struggle in the Meath Hospital was done and the thin-spun life slit, irrevocably. In the moment of consummation, the intimacy and the urgency were both lost. This, terrible silent event now balloons grotesquely into the banalities of the front page... But time will take up the theme from here, will tone it down into history and, later, lovingly embroider it as legend.

## NOTES

John Ryan, former Editor of *Envoy*.
1. For a note on Desmond MacNamara see p. 324.
2. Roger Casement (1864–1916), British consular agent and Irish rebel.
3. 'A Woman of No Standng ' was published in *Envoy* in 1950.
4. For a note on Anthony Cronin see p. 29.
5. François Rabelais (? 1494–1553), French humorist and satirist.
6. Ulick O'Connor, *Brendan Behan* (London: Hamish Hamilton, 1970).
7. Cathal Goulding, 'From the Reverential to the Scurrilous', *Hibernia* (Dublin), 7 Aug 1970, p. 11. For a note on Cathal Goulding and his recollections of Behan see p. 282.
8. Smaltz or Schmalz (slang) = overly sweet sentimentalism.
9. Paul Valéry (1871–1945), French poet and essayist.
10. Privy parts.
11. See references to the Bailey, pp. 236, 239 and 272.
12. 'Hail and farewell.'
13. John Ryan was the owner of the Bailey at the time.

# Additional Bibliography

The references in this list – arranged alphabetically – comprise secondary material, which may be of use in additional fields of biographical inquiry.

Adams, Cindy, 'Brendan Behan: Ireland's Stormiest Writer', *Pittsburgh Press*, 3 Nov 1963, p. 24. (Interview with Behan.)

Allsop, Kenneth, 'Beneath the Froth', *New York Times Book Review*, 12 May 1968, pp. 10–12. (Recollections of Behan.)

American Academy of Dramatic Arts, 'Interview with Brendan Behan', WNTA-TV, 17 Nov 1960.

Andrews, Eamonn, *This Is Your Life*, BBC interview, 1962. (On Stephen Behan.)

Belser, Lee, 'Life Never Boring for Wife of Behan', *Los Angeles Mirror*, 29 May 1961, p. 2. (Interview with Beatrice Behan.)

Bestic, Alan, 'Broke – But He Gave a Coin to My Child', *Today* (London), 25 Apr 1964, pp. 24–5. (Recollections of Behan.)

Binzen, Peter H., 'Teacups Tinkle for Author: Irish Playwright Behan Switches to Tea in Visit Here', *Evening Bulletin* (Philadelphia), 12 Nov 1960, p. 3. (Interview with Behan.)

'Blanking Success', *Time*, LXXII (8 Dec 1958) pp. 78–80. (Interview with Behan.)

Brady, Seamus, 'The Behan They Don't Know', *Daily Express* (London), 12 June 1963, p. 5. (Recollections of Behan.)

——, 'The Love Match of Brendan and Beatrice', *Irish Digest*, LXXVIII, no. 2 (Aug 1963) pp. 75–8. (Interview with Beatrice Behan.)

Braithwaite, Dennis, 'A Curse on Canada, Behan Says', *Globe and Mail* (Toronto), 10 Apr 1961, p. 11. (Interview with Behan.)

'Brendan Behan Visits Hub', *Boston American*, 2 Sep 1960. (Interview with Behan.)

'Brendan Intensely Religious', *Evening Press* (Dublin), 30 Mar 1964, p. 3. (Recollections of Behan by C. A. Joyce, the former Governor of Hollesley Bay Borstal.)

Buckwald, Art, 'Ireland's *Enfant Terrible*', *New York Herald Tribune*, 23 Mar 1959, International Edition, p. 5. (Interview with Behan.)

Coughlan, Anthony, 'With Brendan Behan to Traynor's Funeral', *Irish Democrat* (London), no. 229 (Jan 1964) pp. 6, 9. (Interview with Behan.)

Court, Monty, 'Behan Comes Back a Far, Far Quieter Fellow, But Still Talking', *Daily Mail* (London), 15 Oct 1959, p. 7. (Interview with Behan.)

de Burca, Seamus, 'Profile of Brendan Behan: The Quare Fellow', *Irish Digest*, LVII, no. 4 (Oct 1956) pp. 13–14. (Biographical sketch.)

——, 'In Search of Stephen Behan', *Irish Digest*, LXXVII,no. 9 (Mar 1963) pp. 43–6. (The story of *This Is Your Life* BBC programme on Stephen Behan.)

——, 'The Background of Brendan Behan', *Waterfront* (Dublin), III, no. 7 (Aug 1963) pp. 10–11. (Recollections of Behan.)

——, 'The Essential Brendan Behan', *Modern Drama*, VIII, no. 4 (Spring 1966) pp. 374–81. (Recollections of Behan.)

Delargy, Hugh, 'Behan', *Sunday Citizen*, 22 Mar 1964, p. 6. (Recollections of Behan.)

Delehanty, James, 'Six Hours with Brendan', *Kilkenny Magazine*, no. 2 (Autumn 1960) pp. 41–4. (Interview with Behan.)

Donleavy, J. P., *The Ginger Man* (New York: Delacorte Press, 1965) *passim*.

'Don't Like This Dying Lark at All', *Irish Times*, 21 Mar 1964, p. 9. (Recollections of Behan by two former teachers.)

Ellison, Bob, 'Brendan Behan', *Rogue* (Evanston, Ill.), VI (May 1961) pp. 51–2, 66. (Interview with Behan.)

Elmes, Judith, 'Ten Years after His Death', *Sunday World* (Dublin), 10 Feb 1974, p. 10. (Interview with Beatrice Behan.)

Fallon, Gabriel, 'Brendan's Genius', *Evening Press* (Dublin), 27 Mar 1964, p. 9. (Tribute to, and recollections of, Behan.)

Faulkner, Joe P., 'Behan "the Milkman" Here for a Dry Run', *New York Journal-American*, 2 Sep 1960, p. 3. (Interview with Behan.)

Fitzgerald, Maurice, 'Half an Evening with Behan', *Canadian Forum*, XXXIX (Oct 1959) pp. 147–8. (Recollections of Behan.)

Foley, Donal, *Three Villages: An Autobiography* (Dublin: Egotist Press, 1977) pp. 79–80. (Recollections of Behan.)

Freeman, Donald, 'Brendan Behan on a Dry Day', *San Diego Union*, 2 Dec 1960, p. A26. (Interview with Behan.)

Greene, Sheila, 'Dublin's Own Brendan Behan', *Irish Digest*, LXII, no. 4 (June 1958) pp. 20–2. (Recollections of Behan.)

Hand, Michael, 'My Life Without Brendan', *Sunday Press* (Dublin), 20 Dec 1964, p. 9. (Interview with Beatrice Behan.)

Hawkins, Peter, 'The Genius Who Can't Stop Drinking', *Sunday Pictorial* (London), 12 July 1959, pp. 12–13. (Behan needs proper treatment.)

'Irish Playwright Finds Catskills a Haven', *Catskill Mountain News* (Margaretville, NY), 4 Aug 1961, p. 1. (Interview with Behan.)

Jordan, John, 'Behan', *Hibernia*, Apr 1964, p. 13. (Tribute to, and recollections of, Behan.)

Kelly, Seamus, 'Behan Was Dublin's Own – the Essence of a Joycean Character', *Irish Times*, 21 Mar 1964, p. 9. (Tribute to Behan.)

King, Jim, 'Brendan Behan Goes on the Wagon', *Today* (London), I, no. 24 (6 Aug 1960) pp. 25–6. (Interview with Behan.)

'Like Sitting on a Tornado', *RTE Guide* (Dublin), 8 Feb 1974, p. 7. (Recollections of Behan.)

Littlewood, Joan, 'Behan's Unbodied Soul', *Irish Press* (Dublin), 14 July 1977, p. 6. (Recollections of Behan.)

Lynch, Brendan, 'The Other Side of Brendan Behan', *Irish Socialist*, no. 36 (May 1964) pp. 2, 4. (Obituary and recollections.)

Lyons, Leonard, 'The Lyons Den', *New York Post Magazine*, 11 Dec 1960, p. 7. (Recollections of Behan.)

MacColl, René, 'A Brain Hit by a Bottle', *Daily Express* (London), 21 Mar 1964, p. 5. (Recollections of Behan.)

MacCormack, Joseph, 'When Behan, of Emerald Isle, Visited Staten', *Staten Island Sunday Advance*, 7 Mar 1965, p. 9. (Recollections of Behan.)

McKnight, Gerald, 'How I Stay Married to Mr Mitchum', *Sunday Mirror* (London), 26 Jan 1964, pp. 22–3. (Interview with Beatrice Behan.)

McNamara, Helen, 'I'm the Fella Who Interrupts', *The Telegram* (Toronto), 20 Mar 1961, p. 32. (Behan as conferencier at *Impulse!* at the O'Keefe Centre, Toronto.)

Moseley, Virginia, 'A Week in Dublin', *Modern Drama*, IV, no. 2 (Sep 1961) pp. 164–71. (Discussion on the Irish theatre by Behan and others.)

'The Night Behan Was Not Himself', *Daily Herald* (London), 15 Oct 1958, p. 2. (Recollections of Behan.)

O'Farrell, Mairin, 'A Dublin Literary Pub', *Hibernia* (Dublin), July–Aug 1964, pp. 12–13. (Recollections of Behan and others by Paddy O'Brien, head barman of McDaid's.)

Ó hAodha, Micheál, 'Behan the Ballader', *Irish Times*, 22 Mar 1974, p. 10. (Recollections of Behan.)

O'Kelly, Seamus G., 'The Brendan Behan I Knew', *Evening Herald* (Dublin), 31 Mar 1964, p. 9. (Recollections of Behan.)

——, 'Brendan as I Knew Him', *Evening Herald* (Dublin), 1 Apr 1964, p. 4. (Recollections of Behan.)

——, 'Brendan', *Evening Herald* (Dublin), 2 Apr 1964, p. 6. (Recollections of Behan.)

O'Neill, John Drew, 'Brendan Go Bragh!', *Michigan Quarterly Review*, IV (Winter 1965) pp. 19–22. (Recollections of Behan.)

O'Sullivan, Terry, 'Brendan Behan Drank Here', *Irish Digest* (Dublin), LXXXVI, no. 1 (Mar 1966) pp. 11–14. (Interview with Behan.)

Pearson, Greg, 'Irish Playwright Avoids "Gargle": Brendan Behan Captivates Tijuana Gathering', *San Diego Union*, 11 June 1961, p. 31. (Interview with Behan.)

Pitman, Robert, 'Mr Behan of Dublin makes the Potted Plants Shake', *Sunday Express* (London), 12 Oct 1958, p. 6. (Interview with Behan.)

——, 'The Genteel Muse Who Keeps Mr Behan Working', *Sunday Express* (London), 5 Jan 1964, p. 6. (Interview with Rae Jeffs, who edited Behan's later works.)

Preger, Janie, 'Brendan', *Guardian*, 6 Mar 1965, p. 5. (Recollections of Behan.)

Robbins, Jean and June, 'Beatrice and Brendan Behan: Love Remembered', *Redbook Magazine*, CXXVI (Mar 1966) pp. 60, 103–10. (Interview with Beatrice Behan.)

Robinson, Liam, 'The Behan I Knew Was a Man of Three Faces', *Sunday Express* (London), 22 Mar 1964, p. 8. (Recollections of Behan.)

Robinson, Robert, 'You Deserve To Be Hung', *Sunday Graphic* (London), 15 July 1956, p. 13. (Interview with Behan.)

Ross, Don, 'Brendan Behan Here for His Play', *New York Herald Tribune*, 3 Sep 1960, pp. 1, 7. (Interview with Behan.)

Russell, Arnold, 'CTV Brendan Was a Two-Pint Man', *Reynolds News* (London), 22 July 1956, p. 1. (Behan interviewed by Clifford Davis for *Show Talk*.)

Russell, Francis, 'Dublin in the Doldrums', *National Review* (New York), XVI (July 1964) pp. 612–17. (Recollections of Behan.)

Stuart, Francis, 'A New Spirit', *Irish Press*, 4 Apr 1964, p. 6. (Tribute to, and recollections of, Behan.)

Sylvester, Max, 'I Can Stop Brendan Drinking', *Irish Digest*, LXXVIII, no. 2 (Aug 1963) p. 76. (Recollections of Behan.)

Tanfield, Paul, 'A Man and His Habits', *Daily Mail* (London), 12 Sep 1958, p. 12. (Interview with Behan.)

Thomas, Leslie, 'She Drove Brendan to Drink...Milk', *Evening News and Star* (London), 6 May 1965, p. 4C. (Recollections of Behan.)

'To Hell with Everybody', *Books and Bookmen* (London), IV (Nov 1958) p. 13. (Interview with Behan.)

Van Vliet, James, 'Outspoken Irishman Ends Montreal Visit', *Montreal Star*, 14 Dec 1960, p. 3. (Interview with Behan.)

Watson, John, 'Seein' Behan Is Believin' ', *New York Journal-American*, 13 Nov 1960, p. 43. (Interview with Behan.)

Webster, Hugh, *At Home with the Behans*, interview with Behan and his family, broadcast by the Canadian Broadcasting Corporation on 4 Nov 1962.

'We Can't Turn Out a Yeats Every Week', *Evening Press* (Dublin), 6 May 1959, p. 6. (Interview with Behan.)

# Index

Works by Behan are listed under Behan, Brendan.